THE
PROMISE
OF ISRAEL

Also by Daniel Gordis

God Was Not in the Fire:
The Search for a Spiritual Judaism

Does the World Need the Jews?
Rethinking Chosenness and American Jewish Identity

Becoming a Jewish Parent:
How to Explore Spirituality and Tradition with Your Children

If a Place Can Make You Cry:
Dispatches from an Anxious State

Home to Stay:
One American Family's Chronicle
of Miracles and Struggles in Contemporary Israel

Coming Together, Coming Apart:
A Memoir of Heartbreak and Promise in Israel

Saving Israel:
How the Jewish People Can Win a War
That May Never End

Pledges of Jewish Allegiance:
Conversion, Law, and Policy-Making
in Nineteenth- and Twentieth-Century Orthodox Responsa
(coauthored with David Ellenson)

THE PROMISE OF ISRAEL

Why Its Seemingly Greatest
Weakness Is Actually
Its Greatest Strength

DANIEL GORDIS

WILEY
John Wiley & Sons, Inc.

Cover design: Erica Halivni

Published by John Wiley & Sons, Inc., Hoboken, New Jersey
Published simultaneously in Canada

For general information about our other products and services, please contact our Customer Care Department within the United States at (800) 762-2974, outside the United States at (317) 572-3993 or fax (317) 572-4002.

Wiley also publishes its books in a variety of electronic formats and by print-on-demand. Some content that appears in standard print versions of this book may not be available in other formats. For more information about Wiley products, visit us at www.wiley.com.

Library of Congress Cataloging-in-Publication Data:

Gordis, Daniel.
    The promise of Israel : why its seemingly greatest weakness is actually its greatest strength / by Daniel Gordis.
      p. cm.
    Includes bibliographical references and index.
    ISBN 978-1-118-00375-6 (cloth); ISBN 978-1-118-22177-8 (ebk);
    ISBN 978-1-118-23547-8 (ebk); ISBN 978-1-118-26028-9 (ebk)
      1. Israel—Politics and government—21st century.   2. National characteristics, Israeli.   3. Zionism.   4. Arab-Israeli conflict—1993—Influence.   I. Title.
DS128.2.G66   2012
956.94—dc23

2011053472

Printed in the United States of America
10 9 8 7 6 5 4 3 2 1

For
Ada and Menahem Ben Sasson
and the children we share,
Talia and Avishay Ben Sasson-Gordis

וכל בעלי אומניות שבירושלים
עומדים לפניהם ושואלין בשלומם
אחינו אנשי המקום פלוני באתם לשלום

[ע״יפ] משנה מסכת ביכורים פרק ג

Breathes there the man with soul so dead
Who never to himself hath said:
"This is my own, my native Land"?
Whose heart hath ne'er within him burned
As home his footsteps he hath turned, . . .
From wandering on a foreign strand?

Walter Scott
The Lay of the Last Minstrel
August 1804

עוד לא אבדה תקוותנו
להיות עם חפשי בארצנו

We have not yet lost our hope
Of being a free people, in our land

"Hatikva," 1878

Contents

Introduction

ASLEEP UNDER FIRE

For I dipt into the future, far as human eye could see
Saw the Vision of the world, and all the wonders that would be;
Till the war-drum throbb'd no longer and the battle flags were furl'd
In the Parliament of man, the Federation of the world.
—Alfred Lord Tennyson, "Locksley Hall," 1837[1]

What struck me most about California when I started to visit it was its newness. Nothing seemed old. The cars all appeared new; the people dressed young and acted younger. To a young East Coast kid just starting a career, California seemed all about the future, almost devoid of a past.

But all of us have pasts. All of us come from someplace, and even in the shiny new West, it often takes very little for people to start talking about their lives, their deepest regrets, and their senses of how they have, or have not, honored the legacies from which they were born. It's amazing, actually, what people tell a clergyperson, no matter how young he or she may be. When I first headed out to Los Angeles after finishing rabbinical school, I had no real conception of what awaited me. Some of what I hazily imagined actually came to be. Much did not. But one of the things that I remember most clearly is the stories that people, especially elderly people, told me, even though they barely knew me.

There was one story that I heard several times, in one form or another, always from people around the age of my grandparents. These people told me how their siblings who had arrived in America before them would meet them at the New York harbor. The new arrivals came off the boat with almost nothing to their names, but they had, in addition to their meager belongings, Jewish objects like candlesticks for the Sabbath or tefillin that they had transported with great care. The sibling (usually a brother) who had arrived in the United States a few years earlier would take the bundle with these Jewish religious objects, nonchalantly drop it into the water lapping at the edge of the pier, and say, "You're in America now. Those were for the old country."

The men and women who told me these stories were much, much older than I was, and the events they were describing had unfolded more than half a century earlier. When I was younger and first heard them, what horrified me was the mere notion of throwing those ritual objects into the ocean as if they were yesterday's garbage. As I grew older, I was struck by the fact that these elderly people still remembered that moment and that it troubled them enough for them to recount the story to a young person like me, so many years later.

Later still, I began to understand the deep pain and mourning implicit in those stories. There was a sense of having betrayed the world from which they had come. There was a sense of the cruelty of their brothers' cavalier discarding of the bundles; it might have been well intentioned, but it was callous and mean, and half a century later, it still evoked such pain that they sought to talk about it.

Before we judge these siblings at the pier, we should acknowledge that both sides were right. Both the elderly Jews who told me their stories and the brothers who had tossed their possessions into the oily, filthy water reflected a profound truth. The brothers were right that there *is* a price of entry to the United States and that it is a steep one. In large measure, many immigrants have done as well as they have in the United States precisely because they were willing to drop bundles of memory, ethnicity, and religious observance into the harbor. And the people who told me these stories were right that the pain and the anger that they felt about that price were real, abiding, and deeply scarring. They had given up something of themselves when they came to the United States, and the scars never fully healed. Being forced to pretend that they had paid no price at all only made matters worse.

Jewish, Muslim, Buddhist, Hutu, Pashtun, or Christian—it makes no difference. All of us can imagine and even feel the visceral horror of being told to take our past and figuratively toss it into the harbor. Those immigrants were told that they were welcome, as long as they dispensed with the heritage with which they had come to their new "home." But the story of demanding such sacrifice for acceptance is hardly over. It continues for some immigrants to the United States today, and it occurs in the international arena as well.

Sad to say, it is that same attitude that the United States (like much of the West) now exhibits toward Israel. You are welcome to join us, the West essentially says, as long as you drop your ethnic heritage in the ocean forever. We welcome you to the family of nations, but with a price: we want you to be precisely like us. Be different, and our patience will soon run out.

Later portions of this book will explain why preserving ethnic heritage is such an important human endeavor. For now, though, we ought to acknowledge how troubled we should be by saying to anyone—anywhere and at any time—that he or she must abandon a precious heritage and not transmit it. Those elderly immigrants who told me their stories had no choice when they arrived at the shores of New York. Often penniless and usually frightened, they had nowhere else to go. When their siblings took the parcels and dropped them in the water, there was little the new immigrants could do but stifle their cries and hold back their tears.

Israel, however, is not in that position. Israelis are independent, and the Jewish state rightly resists the demand that it become just like all those other states that are not based on a particular ethnic identity. Even though we rarely think of matters in these terms, the sad fact is that it is Israel's very unwillingness to be a state like all other states in this regard, its resistance to erasing its uniqueness, that now has Israel locked in conflict with much of the West.

This book makes an audacious and seemingly odd claim. It suggests that what now divides Israel and the international community is an idea: the ethnic nation-state—a country created around a shared cultural heritage. This is what has the West so put out with Israel. Israel has lost its once-charmed status in the international arena, I argue, because of a conflict over this very idea. It is true that the Israelis and the Palestinians are still tragically locked in an intractable and painful conflict; the issues of borders, refugees, and Palestinian statehood still await resolution. But those matters, as urgent as they are, are not the primary reason for Israel's unprecedented fall from international grace.

Israel is marginalized and reviled because of a battle over the idea of the nation-state. (The dictionary defines *nation-state* as "a form of political organization under which a relatively homogeneous people inhabits a sovereign state . . . a state containing one as opposed to several nationalities," so I use *nation-state* and *ethnic nation-state* interchangeably in this book.) Israel, the quintessential modern example of the ethnic nation-state, came on the scene just as most of the Western world had decided that it was time to be rid of the nation-state. Today, Europe's elites wish to move in one direction, whereas Israel suggests that humanity should be doing precisely the opposite. The now young countries that emerged from what was once the Soviet Union and the former Yugoslavia are mostly nation-states; their creation—and the demise of the larger conglomerates that once included them—attests to the widespread and deep-seated human desire to live in a manner that cultivates the cultures that we have inherited from our ancestors. But many of Europe's intellectual elites prefer to pretend that we have no lessons to learn about human difference and cultural heterogeneity from the demise of the USSR and Yugoslavia.

Israel suggests that they are wrong. The conflict *in* the Middle East is about borders and statehood, but the conflict *about* the Middle East is over universalism versus particularism, over competing conceptions of how human beings ought to organize themselves.

The purpose of this book is to explain the ancient origins of this conflict, how this tug-of-war about an idea has developed, how Israel got caught in it, and, most important, how a world bereft of the idea that Israel represents would be an impoverished world. Instead of being so commonly maligned, Israel ought to be seen as a beacon among nations, a remarkably successful nation that has persevered despite wars fought on its borders and that has brought prosperity to its people despite a shared history of misfortune. Israel has secured significant rights for all of its citizens, including even those who reject the very idea of Israel's existence. All of this has been accomplished because of Israel's commitment to the future success of the Jewish people, not in spite of it.

What is at stake in the current battle over Israel's legitimacy is not merely the idea on which Israel is based, but, quite possibly, human freedom as we know it. The idea that human freedom might be at risk in today's battles over Israel might seem far-fetched or hyperbolic. This book will argue that it is not, and that human beings everywhere thus have a great stake in what the world ultimately does with the Jewish state.

Imagine a world in which instead of maligning Israel, the international community encouraged emerging ethnic nations to emulate Israel. Egyptians, for example, may have demonstrated for regime change and for democracy, but they did not gather to demonstrate against Islam or their Arab identity. They have no plans to become the "America" of Africa, secular and heterogeneous. They wish (or so the most Western of them claim) both to celebrate their Muslim heritage and thousands of years of Egyptian history and to join the family of modern democratic nations. As they do so, to whom can they look for a model of a stable, prosperous, and open state based on a shared religion and heritage? There is no denying that Egypt, Syria, Pakistan, and many other Muslim countries would benefit from being more like Israel instead of hoping for its destruction.

Yet it is not only Middle Eastern and Muslim nations that should be looking harder at the Israeli experiment. The whole world would benefit from thinking in terms of the questions Israel raises. The United States, Sweden, Brazil—it makes no difference. All citizens of every nation would benefit from asking themselves, explicitly, what values they hope their nation will inculcate in its citizens, what culture they are committed to preserving and nourishing. Such conversations would change the way Israel is seen in the world, but they would also change how everyone else sees his or her own country—and how people come to think about the reasons that countries actually exist.

The idea of a state for a particular ethnicity strikes many people as problematic, immoral, and contrary to the progress that humanity has made in recent decades. The idea of a state meant to promote the flourishing of one particular people, with one particular religion at its core—a state created with the specific goal of Jewish revival and flourishing—strikes many people as worse than an antiquated idea. It sounds racist, bigoted, or oppressive of minorities.

When the United Nations voted to create a Jewish state in 1947, the fires of the Second World War had barely been extinguished. Dispossessed Jews were still wandering across Europe by the thousands. The enormity of the genocidal horror that the world had allowed the Nazis to perpetrate was still sinking in. One of the many effects of that horrific period of history was that despite opposition from many quarters, creating a state for the Jews seemed like the right and expedient thing to do.

But times have changed. Memories of the Shoah are fading.* Jews are no longer dispossessed refugees; in most of the world, they are settled and prospering, and today it is the Palestinians who are stateless. Postwar Europe has decided that it was unfettered nationalism that led to the horrors of the two world wars; therefore, much of Europe's intellectual elite now believes that the nation-state is a nineteenth-century paradigm that should be relegated to the dustheap of history,

---

*Holocaust means "burnt offering" or "sacrifice to God." I thus avoid it when discussing the Nazi genocide of the Jews. Europe's Jews were not sacrificed; they were tortured, murdered, and annihilated. There is a profound difference. This book uses the word Shoah, which means "utter destruction" (see Zephaniah 1:15 and Proverbs 3:25), to honor that distinction.

just like those bundles that were dropped into the harbor to sink out of sight.

In several important respects, Jews drew the opposite conclusion from the horrific century they had just endured and barely survived. Battered by Europe and by history, the Jews emerged from the Shoah with a sense that more than anything, they needed a state of their own. Just as some of the world thought that it might move beyond nations, the Jews (who had dreamed of a restored Zion for two millennia) now intuited that nothing could be more urgent than finally re-creating their state. Zionism and postwar Europe were thus destined for conflict.

Zionism was not a matter of mere refuge; it was a matter of breathing new life into the Jewish people (the subject of my book *Saving Israel: How the Jewish People Can Win a War That May Never End*), of reimagining Judaism for a world after destruction, and, ironically, of insisting on the importance of the very difference that the Nazis had focused on as they perpetrated the horrors of the Shoah. What was at stake was much more than differing views about the nation-state; it was a battle over fundamental worldviews. For it was not only the nation-state on which Europe and postwar Jews differed. At issue was also the whole question of human differentness. To much of the world, the racially motivated genocide of twentieth-century Europe suggested that human difference ought to be transcended.

At our core, it therefore became popular to assert, human beings are largely the same. Our faces may have different shapes and our skin colors may differ, but those are simply superficial variations. We may speak different languages, but our aspirations are very similar. We may cherish different memories, but the future we create can be a shared one. Because human beings are essentially similar, this argument goes, the countries that separate peoples and cast a spotlight on their differences should now be dissolved, too. John Lennon put this idea to music in his song "Imagine": "Imagine there's no countries / It isn't hard to do / Nothing to kill or die for / And no religion too."

We might well have expected the Jews to embrace this vision. After all, since it was their difference that had condemned them to the horrific fate of the Shoah, we might have thought that the Jews would enthusiastically join the quest for a world without difference. In a world without difference, the Jews might finally be safe. But here too the Jews disagreed.

The Jews disagreed because whether or not they could articulate it, they intuited that they and their tradition have been focused on differentness from the very outset. The image of Abraham as the world's first monotheist says it all: Jews have long been countercultural. And they have celebrated difference in many ways. The Talmud itself notes that it is differentness that is the very essence of humanity: "If a man strikes many coins from one mold, they all resemble each other," it asserts. "But the Supreme King of Kings . . . created every man in the stamp of the first, and yet not one of them resembles his fellow."[2] Difference matters, Judaism has long said, not just for individuals, but for peoples, too. Later in this book, we will see how this commitment to differentness became so central to Jewish life and thought.

But this commitment to difference, to celebrating the uniqueness of the Jewish people, was never meant to foster rejection of those who are not Jewish. Indeed, at its best, Jewish celebration of difference is also about the celebration of the other. The horrific excesses of human history have certainly led many to see in difference a frightening and terrible idea; too often the distinction between "us and them" was drawn to make it seem okay for "us" to kill "them" and for "them" to kill "us."

Israel, however, with all of its imperfections, has for decades been drawing lines and then reaching across them. Israelis do not pretend that being a global citizen is either sufficient or terribly meaningful, yet they willingly send medical teams to Japan or Haiti in a crisis. The Jewish state is a country that could very soon be annihilated without a moment's notice by Islamic extremists in Iran and that has been at war with Arab countries since even before its independence, but its national government has more democratically elected Muslim officials than all the other non-Muslim states combined—more, even, than the United States.

The Jewish tradition is replete with references to the differences between the Jews and other nations. From the very outset, Jews saw part of their purpose as being different, as having something to say that the rest of the world ought to hear. In a world without difference, the very point of Jewishness would be lost. Whether or not they could articulate it, Jews understood that being just like everyone else, even if that might somehow make them physically safer, was not at all what thousands of years of Jewish tradition and survival had been about.

Even after the horrors of what they had just experienced because of their difference, most Jews emerged from the Shoah determined to preserve their collective inheritance. Some enthusiastically embraced international movements like socialism or communism. But many more sought to celebrate their difference, to breathe new life into the unique way of living that had been theirs for thousands of years, to gather up the fragments of their texts from a century in which both their books and their bodies had been burned indiscriminately, and to fashion anew their libraries, memories, holidays, and long-dormant language. To do that, they realized, they would need a state. They had prayed for one for two thousand years, but now, after the Shoah, that age-old prayer took on newfound urgency.

Increasingly, however, the rest of the world has decided that it does not agree. The United Nations and much of the international community are notoriously complicit in the push to rob Israel of its status as standard-bearer for the nation-state idea. As long as a country that is openly rooted in a religious or cultural tradition prospers, as long as its democracy serves its citizens well, as long as it defies the predictions of secular scholars and pundits who believe that religion and ethnicity are the handmaidens of imperialism and fascism, it must be reviled.

Otherwise, it could prove the intellectual elites of western Europe and North America, who believe that an experiment like Israel cannot work, wrong. What was once a well-meaning, liberal academic orientation to religion, ethnicity, and statehood has morphed into an international diplomatic witch hunt that smacks once again of intolerance for the Jew and the Jewish state, that is filled with the sense that in any conflict in which Israel finds itself, the Jewish state must be wrong. Sides are being chosen daily, and Israel's fate is being decided, often by people who do not realize what is really being disputed. My simplest goal in writing this book, beyond advocating one side or the other, is just to make clear to people what the two sides are and what is really at stake in this battle of ideas.

Israel's real problem, this book demonstrates, is that the state of Israel was founded to move the Jews to precisely the condition that the rest of the Western world was trying to avoid. For that reason, too, the Jewish state was almost bound to be in conflict with the West. That is why many in the ostensibly forward-thinking international community have now decided, consciously or not, that it is time to bring the Jewish state to an end. They propose to do so without armies and without violence. They will bring Israel to its knees with words, with philosophical and principled arguments, and with appeals to the loftiest moral standards. After all, they note, both apartheid South Africa and the Soviet Union were felled in large measure by a widely shared international view that they were illegitimate, founded on ideas that were simply indefensible.

Given this new tactic, those who believe in the ongoing importance of a Jewish state need to ask themselves the right questions and provide principled answers. Can an argument really be made for a state that seems so out of sync with the direction of modern progress? In the twenty-first century, is there really a place for a country that defines itself as Jewish (or committed to any other ethnicity, for that matter); that does not see all its citizens as equally central to its mission; and that unabashedly declares that one religion, one people, one ethnicity, and one heritage will be more essential to its national life than any others? How could Israel's supporters possibly defend such a country?

Such a state seems anathema to everything that many of us have been taught to believe.

Many of Israel's supporters have no idea what to say in response to such attacks on Zionism and its legitimacy, and Israel has paid a terrible price for the silence of today's Zionists on these issues. Its international status has plummeted with scarcely a countervailing word being said about why the Jewish state matters. The campaign to defend Israel has been sporadic, reactive, defensive, almost entirely devoid of theoretical argument, and focused almost exclusively on the conflict with the Palestinians. Zionists' failure to make a case for their particular sort of state creates the impression that they *know* they cannot really justify Israel's existence; it feeds a suspicion that they have decided that it would be best to stay under the radar, because when push comes to shove, what Israel is cannot be thoughtfully defended.

But in today's world, Zionists can no longer afford the luxury of staying below the radar. The questions are too powerful, the focus on Israel too intense. No longer can the case for Israel be made simply by hoping that no one raises the question of whether the *idea* of a Jewish state is defensible. Those who believe in the importance and the legitimacy of the state of Israel need to be able to explain why a country founded for a particular people, ethnicity, tradition, and religion has a place—indeed, a noble one—in the twenty-first century.

Therefore, Israel's response to these challenges has to be equally thoughtful and no less compelling. Israel's defense must also be based on moral claims. In a nutshell, what needs to be said is this: What is at issue between Israel and the international community is whether ethnic and national diversity ought to be encouraged and promoted. Israel has something to say about the importance of human difference that is at odds with the prevailing attitudes in the world today. It is a country that insists that people thrive and flourish most when they live in societies in which *their* language, *their* culture, *their* history, and *their* sense of purpose are situated at the very center of public life.

Let's address one common objection right at the outset. Contrary to what many naysayers will claim, a country does not have to be entirely homogeneous to accomplish this. As even PBS (which is often very critical of Israel) once noted, "As a Jewish state, [Israel] is both homogenous and multiethnic."[3] As strange as it may sound, countries can have a predominant ethnic character and be deeply tolerant of minorities at the same time. Every nation-state has minorities, and part of the challenge to the majority is not only to accommodate the minority but also, even more, to help those citizens flourish.

Indeed, flourishing is the key issue. Israel is a country based on a belief that human beings live richer and more meaningful lives when those lives are deeply rooted in a culture that they have inherited and that they can bequeath. Human life flourishes most when a society's public square is committed to conversations rooted in that people's literature, language, history, narrative, and even religion. There is the possibility of a more fully integrated life in the nation-state in which all these spheres of human life overlap to much greater extents than other countries make possible. Ultimately, human diversity will be protected most by an amalgam of countries, each of which exists for the flourishing of a particular people, culture, way of life, and history *and*, at the same time, engages in an open and ongoing dialogue with other cultures and civilizations.

The world celebrated the Arab Spring in 2011, but that story is not yet fully written. Will it bring democracy? Rights for women? Tolerance for gays and lesbians? It would be foolish and naive to expect that we'll see any such progress soon. Still, there's no reason that Egypt couldn't develop an engagement with modernity while staying committed to the dignity of its past. There's no reason that Libya, finally freed of Muammar Gaddafi, couldn't in theory develop both intellectual openness and a freedom of the press, since both could actually strengthen the nation's understanding of Islam. Syrians too could someday live richer and more meaningful lives if those lives were deeply rooted in a unique Syrian culture coupled with freedom of choice at the voting booth. Even Iran could discover that Iranians flourish most when the public square is committed to open conversations rooted in Persian literature, language, history, and narratives, in constant and vigorous dialogue with the West and other civilizations that have very different takes on core human values.

But does the West really want to see those countries develop in that way? If Egypt remained deeply and profoundly Egyptian, and Iranian culture and history defined the Iranian public square, would the West approve, or would the West say that as long as those countries insist on maintaining those ancient attachments, they are not fully liberated? Would the West not still tell them they are doing it wrong? Perhaps. But the West would be wrong; difference and uniqueness do not mire people in the past but rather give them guidance and meaning as they build a better future.

This is now the challenge for Zionists. Precisely because Israel stands for a conviction not held by most of the enlightened world today, the time has come to defend Israel by boldly addressing the conversation that is at the heart of this book. It is time for Zionists not only to discuss borders, settlements, security, and Palestinian statehood but also to proclaim that what is at stake is not just the Jewish state, not just the future of the Jews, but a profound vision for how humanity can most compellingly chart its future. No other country in the developed world calls into question today's assumption that eradicating differentness is the best path toward human flourishing. That is precisely what makes Israel so countercultural, so divisive, and often so maligned. And that is what makes Israel so vitally important.

Today's infatuation with the notion that human difference ought to be papered over is not the first time that the world has embraced a dangerous and dead-end philosophical fad. In the past century alone, humanity has lived through infatuations with unfettered socialism, then with communism, and even with the belief in the nobility of imperialism. But Israel is a reminder to the world that there are moments when someone—be it a prophet in biblical times or a nation-state in today's international community—has to speak truth to power and insist on what is right and true, regardless of how unpopular the idea is. Israel represents the argument that the nation-state is not a fad, but rather an ancient and still compelling vision for humanity.

Like the ancient Hebrew prophets Isaiah, Amos, and Hosea, who were highly unpopular in their own time but whose visions for humanity are still cited thousands of years later, the state of Israel is meant to be a clarion call to all of humanity. If Israel can survive (and that is by no means certain), history may one day come to thank the Jewish state for its role in reminding humanity what it stood to lose when it began to pretend that our differences were unimportant.

Chapter One

THE ISRAEL MODEL

O mankind! Lo!
We have created you male and female,
and have made you nations and tribes
that ye may learn from one another.

—Koran 49:13

The Palestinian people have a momentous decision to make. Eventually, they will have their own state, but statehood is not an end in itself. States are the settings in which peoples determine what it is that they have to say to the world. Ideally, states ought to be the locus of a spirited and challenging dialogue between a people's own values and traditions, on the one hand, and the perspectives of the rest of the nations of the world, on the other hand. States should be the places where our cultures develop, improve, and become more moral and nuanced, ever enriched by insights that we glean from other cultures and other traditions, communicated by other peoples through *their* states.

The Jews have used Israel for precisely this purpose. As we will see in the pages that follow, the values and laws at the heart of Israeli society are deeply Jewish, but they are not *only* Jewish. They are faithful in many ways to the insights and commitments of the Jewish tradition, but they have expanded the freedoms that Judaism prescribes by injecting into Israeli society much of what Western civilization has had to teach.

Will the Palestinians do the same with a sovereign Palestine? As the world debates the Middle East, as Israel is disparaged for what many think is its role in delaying Palestinian statehood, the international community would do well to ask this question: What will the Palestinians do with a state? Will they turn the bitterness of the difficult century they have endured into a thirst for vengeance, or will they, like the Israelis, sanctify the memory of their losses by energetically building for the future?

Palestinians must now decide how they will balance a commemoration of the losses of the past with a drive to create a radically different future, and they must choose between the worlds of the Ottoman Turks and the British, between the models of Jordan and Israel. Will they use sovereignty to create a Palestinian version of what Egypt, Jordan, Syria, Lebanon, Saudi Arabia, and many other Arab states already are, or will they embrace Israel's model of cultural, moral, and intellectual dialogue with the West? Will they replicate the closed Arab countries that already exist, or will they create a state that might transform the Arab world?

These are the questions about Palestinian statehood that truly matter but that few dare to ask. The international community is quite right to care about the plight of the Palestinians, to pity the condition in which they find themselves. Many Israelis share those concerns as well. But what freedom- and justice-loving people everywhere ought to be asking the Palestinians is this: When you get your state, what will it be about? What is your plan for creating not just a refuge but a successful nation, one that can help create a better future not only for you, but for Muslims everywhere?

The Palestinians would be enriched by being pressured to answer these questions. Survival alone is not a purpose; neither is sovereignty. Instead of solely focusing on their suffering as refugees, the homes they lost, or a way of life that can no longer be recovered, the Palestinians should be preparing to articulate a positive, content-filled message that would add depth and richness to the world we all share.

Is the world willing to pressure them to do that? We do not yet know, but the world's record thus far gives us little cause for optimism.

We do know that if the Palestinians are told that the choice is between a secular democracy based on the model of the United States or a religious dictatorship, they're not likely to choose the former. If I could achieve only one goal with this book, it would be to expand the conversation to include a third option: an open and free democratic government running a country in which a particular people's heritage and religious traditions are accorded profound importance but are also asked to be in dialogue with the West. What I have in mind is what is called the *nation-state* or *ethnic nation-state*: a state that combines liberalism (individual rights, free speech, freedom of the press, and the like) and representative democracy in a setting in which one people (such as the French, the Tibetans, or the Jews) largely defines that society.[1]

What kind of society do the Palestinians wish to foster? Will they have the courage to embrace minorities and to welcome dissent? Will they create a public square in which the values of Islam and the commitments of the West struggle for the hearts and souls of everyday citizens, in which both Islam and the West learn from each other? Will they guarantee the freedoms of those who would dare to challenge even Islam's most sacred commitments? If they can do this, then Palestinian statehood will enrich not just Palestinians but also the one and a half billion Muslims throughout the world. If they cannot or will not, then sovereignty and the end of living under Israeli occupation will not have made them any freer.

There is nothing simple about this challenge that the Palestinians must face. The tension between promoting a core set of social beliefs and affording freedom to those who challenge those tenets is not easy for any society. Europe struggles with a massive influx of Muslims, France under Nicolas Sarkozy brazenly evicted more than a thousand Roma (often called Gypsies) in 2010, and the United States continues to squelch the cultures of Native Americans. Few among even the most educated Americans can say anything sophisticated about those cultures, and most know very little about either the current conditions of the hundreds of Native American tribal groups across the United States or about their traditional cultures. That ignorance is the result not of accident but of intentional policy. Minorities are a challenge for any country, particularly when they challenge the story that country tells about itself.

Ethnic nation-states, many people therefore believe, will inevitably make such matters worse, for if a state is explicitly committed to the flourishing of one particular people or culture, then those who are of a different background will almost certainly be marginalized. But Israel's experience suggests otherwise. Strange as it may sound, Israel is more than simply the Jewish state; it is also a model of what Palestinians ought to consider creating with their own sovereignty. Israel, not current Arab nation-states, is the model that Palestinians should choose to emulate.

Consider the radical difference between the ways that Israel and the Arab nation-states approach the challenge of minorities. Despite the fact that Israel was specifically established to be a Jewish state and has been at war with the Arab world since before its formal independence, it continues to guarantee freedom of religion and the rights of minorities, including Arabs, both Muslim and Christian. The Jewish state's Declaration of Independence affirms that Israel

> will foster the development of the country for the benefit of all its inhabitants; it will be based on freedom, justice and peace as envisaged by the prophets of Israel; it will ensure complete equality of social and political rights to all its inhabitants irrespective of religion, race or sex; it will guarantee freedom of religion, conscience, language, education and culture; it will safeguard the Holy Places of all religions; and it will be faithful to the principles of the Charter of the United Nations.[2]

Minorities in Israel, including the members of the Arab minority that makes up about 20 percent of the population, are full legal members of society. They are entitled to vote, to hold public office, and, by and large, to live wherever they choose.[3] Arabic is one of Israel's official languages, and there are laws that secure the Arab population's right to receive information in Arabic.[4] Arabs, including Muslims, Druze, and Bedouins, are elected to the Knesset in every election.

The first non-Druze Arab Israeli government minister, Raleb Majadele, was appointed in 2007, and Arab Israelis have served as ambassadors and consuls abroad. An Israeli Arab, Salim Joubran, was appointed to the Supreme Court (and is still serving), and the Israel Defense Forces (IDF) counts among its leadership several high-ranking Druze and Bedouin officers, including major generals.[5] The only Israeli political party that has ever been prevented from participating in the political fracas was Rabbi Meir Kahane's Kach Party, which Israel's courts held was racist. No Arab party has ever been shut down by the courts.

If anything, ironically, some of the most urgent claims of religious inequality come from non-Orthodox Jews, who cite countless examples of discrimination against Conservative and Reform Judaism by the Orthodox establishment.

Obviously, none of this ought to blind us to the undeniable reality that real discrimination does exist in Israeli society. Mixed Arab-Jewish neighborhoods are still relatively rare in Israel.[6] In addition, because army service is not required of Israeli Arabs, they find themselves too often excluded from the entrepreneurial and social networks that frequently form among those who have served together in the military.

There is also a wide gap between the economic statuses of Jews and of Arabs. The Arab community has a lower level of education than the Jewish population; despite the fact that Arabs make up approximately 20 percent of the citizenry, according to the Israeli Central Bureau of Statistics, Arab students made up only "12% of all first undergraduate students, 6% of masters degree students and 4% of doctoral students."[7] The Or Commission found that

> government handling of the Arab sector has been primar-
> ily neglectful and discriminatory. The establishment did

not . . . take enough action in order to allocate state resources in an equal manner. The state did not do enough or try hard enough to create equality for its Arab citizens or to uproot discriminatory or unjust phenomena. Meanwhile, not enough was done to enforce the law in the Arab sector, and the illegal and undesirable phenomena that took root there.[8]

But even Amnon Rubinstein, an Israeli professor of law and a well-known secularist and liberal, has asserted that matters are indeed getting better. In a 2010 journal article, he pointed to the presence of an Arab judge on the Supreme Court and an Arab minister of science and noted that the economic gap was growing smaller:

Whatever discrimination may exist is diminishing fast. The gap between the financial support allocated to the Jewish and Arab sectors has of late been reduced dramatically. For example, the disparity in education subsidies has in recent years substantially decreased: When I was appointed minister of education in 1993, the subsidy ratio was 1.7 to 1; today, the ratio is 1.1 to 1.[9]

In a fascinating note, Rubinstein pointed to some ways in which Israeli Arab *Christians* actually do better than the Jewish majority, and he drew an important conclusion:

In addition, we must remember that discrepancies between the sectors are not always the result of discrimination. Perhaps the best evidence of this is the Christian Arab minority (comprising only 9 percent of the Israeli Arab population). Although they are identical in ethnicity, language, and nationality to Muslim Arabs, the Christians boast remarkable achievements: Their child mortality rate is comparable to that of Denmark, *and the percentage of students accepted into university is higher than that of the Jewish population.* Hence, the state cannot be held entirely responsible for the privations of its Muslim Arab

minority. Ideological differences and lifestyle choices must also
be taken into account.[10]

Rubinstein's point is clear. There is still inequality between Jews and
Arabs in Israel (although the gap is shrinking), and while some of the
responsibility clearly lies at the feet of the state, much of it lies with
Israel's Arabs themselves. Israel's most vociferous critics would do
well to think about that.

The Palestinians will not only need to choose which example to follow in the treatment of minorities—Israel's or that of the Arab world
(which will be described below)—they will also have to make a similar choice regarding freedom of the press and of expression. Freedom
of expression is a critical means of judging the openness and intellectual self-confidence of a society, and there is reason to wonder whether
the Palestinians will foster a society that has the confidence to allow
expression of all sorts, no matter how challenging to the ruling elite.
Here too they would be wise to study Israel's model; in Israel, despite
the conflict in which the Jewish state has been embroiled since its
re-creation, the cacophony that is the public square is well reflected
in the press, on the airwaves, and virtually everywhere that one turns.

In fact, Zionists have seemed to relish their lack of consensus. The
title of Arthur Hertzberg's classic book, *The Zionist Idea*, is actually an
intentional misnomer, for there has never been just one Zionist idea.
Zionism is an amalgam of competing ideas, and the conflicts have been
passionate (and even nasty) for more than a century. There were Zionists
who sought a state, but others who thought that the Jews would be better off with only a spiritual center in Palestine. There are secular Zionists
and religious Zionists, committed socialists and proponents of unfettered
capitalism. There are Zionists who believe that the Arab world is intent
on destroying Israel and who therefore argue that no land should be
ceded in an attempted settlement of the conflict, and there are those who
believe that land for peace is still possible. There are those who favor a
country that is strongly colored by Jewish religious life and values, and
there are others who would like Israel to approximate something like a
Hebrew-speaking, secular European country.

But one thing that Zionism has never sought to do, whether before statehood or during, is to squelch the debate among all these views. To this day, each of these viewpoints has its own newspaper and regularly gets a hearing on radio and television. All those views have been represented in the Knesset and in the public square at large.

In essence, Israeli society is a vigorous and bustling marketplace of ideas. The Zionist experiment has been a project of melding the ancient and the modern, of re-creating a Jewish nation from groups that had been scattered across the globe, and of much more. It has been a matter of cherishing the Jewish roots of the Jewish state and at the same time forcing them to participate in a free market of ideas with competing notions from the Western world. It has been about giving Jewish tradition a privileged place in the public square while preserving the rights of those who do not wish to observe Jewish law. For instance, intercity buses do not run on the Sabbath and holidays, the food in the army is kosher, and bread cannot be legally displayed for sale during the week of Passover. But local Tel Aviv buses *do* run on the Sabbath, nonkosher restaurants can be found all over the country, and bread is still obtainable during Passover if one wants it.

The mélange of views that is Zionism simply states unabashedly that Israel is a country, to paraphrase Abraham Lincoln, "by the Jews, of the Jews, and for the Jews" that also works to guarantee the rights of non-Jews in its society.[11] Israel offers Jews a refuge because it is committed to the flourishing of the Jewish people while also struggling to decide who else should be granted refuge within its borders.

Choices such as these are not simple: if Israel offers a safe harbor to all those who seek to enter, it will cease to be a Jewish state. However, if it ignores the plight of all those who arrive at its borders, it betrays its obligation to remember that it was created in the aftermath of genocide and that Jews know what it is not to have anywhere else to go. That is why the debates continue without being settled. No one, however, has sought to silence any of the sides in the debate.

The closer you look at Israeli society, the harder it is to believe that this debate is a problem with Israel (as many in the West suggest) and not one of its greatest strengths.

Israeli society may not always be gentle, and it can sometimes be tough and occasionally even ugly. But it takes the free exchange of ideas very seriously. This is, in many ways, a long-standing Jewish tradition. The Babylonian Talmud is, for all intents and purposes, a twenty-volume argument in which even the losing positions are preserved and studied for the insights they have to offer. Modern Israeli society has inherited that ethic.

Israelis do nothing to silence even their own most vociferous critics; those critics come and go as they please, even retaining their academic positions if they care to do so. Shlomo Sand, a professor at Tel Aviv University, wrote a much discussed book, *The Invention of the Jewish People*, in which he argued that the very idea of a Jewish people is a fiction; Jewish peoplehood, he insisted, was a creation of nineteenth-century Jewish intellectuals. If Zionism was about reviving the Jewish people, he intimated, then Zionism was faulty at its core. The book, which sold well, was widely dismissed as shoddy scholarship.[12] Yet Sand remains on the faculty of Tel Aviv University and even enjoys quasi–folk hero status among some elements of Israeli society.

Ilan Pappe, an Israeli-born historian who is deeply critical of Israel's conduct of its wars and its treatment of Arabs, has argued the rather radical view that Israel engaged in intentional ethnic cleansing of the Palestinians in its earliest years.[13] Long after he had begun to espouse this argument, he participated in the highest levels of Israeli discourse and even ran for the Knesset; he has since moved away from Israel, but he visits often and faces no problems traveling freely to the country he has excoriated.

Niv Gordon, of Ben-Gurion University, stayed with Yassir Arafat at his compound in 2002 when it was under attack by Israel and actually encouraged the international academic boycott of Israel.[14] (Anthony Julius, in his magisterial history of anti-Semitism in England, *Trials of the Diaspora*, notes with intended irony that "while most Jewish anti-Zionists are realists about Israel, they tend to be idealists about the Palestinians."[15]) Nonetheless, Gordon continues to teach at Ben-Gurion University and regularly appears in the press.

These men are controversial, and their views are reviled by many, both inside and outside Israel, but the notion that they might be harmed or even dismissed from their university posts as a result of their opinions is completely foreign to Israeli culture.

Israel's tolerance of dissenting views extends far beyond the academy. It protects even the ultra-Orthodox, who for the most part do not serve in the army; many of them live off the dole of the state and do not work, and some, most egregiously, actually believe the state to be illegitimate (because of its secularism and because it was created before the arrival of the messiah). But no matter. These ultra-Orthodox (and occasionally anti-Zionist) citizens can vote, they are elected to the Knesset (where they direct millions of state budget dollars annually to their own yeshivot), and most do participate, willy-nilly, in the exchange of ideas that is the state of Israel.

Powerful opponents of the government's policies persist in other fields, too. Amos Oz, Israel's best-known novelist and a short-list contender for the Nobel Prize on several occasions, regularly espouses deeply critical views of Israel, of the rabbinate, and of Israel's failure to make peace. But he teaches at Ben-Gurion University and appears all over Israel with virtually rock-star status.

David Grossman, another of Israel's stellar novelists, is equally derisive of the state. In 2006, after his son was killed in the Second Lebanon War, Grossman become a radical critic of the government. He decried "Israel's quick descent into the heartless, essentially brutal treatment of its poor and suffering" and railed against the "equanimity of the State of Israel in the face of human trafficking" as well as "the appalling employment conditions of our foreign workers, which border on slavery" and "the deeply ingrained institutionalized racism against the Arab minority."[16] On another occasion, he refused to shake Prime Minister Ehud Olmert's hand at a formal public ceremony— but Israel guarantees people the right to insult the prime minister that way.[17] Grossman too works and travels without interference and is considered by many an important Israeli moral and intellectual voice.

Not for nothing did Freedom House's 2010 survey of freedom in the world note that Israel is the *only* country in the Middle East and North Africa region that qualifies as free.[18] Nor is it any surprise that the *Economist*'s democracy index similarly ranked Israel as the most democratic country in the Middle East.[19]

Some may argue that this phenomenon is simply the result of importing a European populace into the Middle East, but that is not true; something much more dramatic is unfolding in Israel. Had Europe of the 1930s and 1940s been as tolerant of diversity as Israel is today, history would have unfolded very differently; there might have been no international consensus on the need for a state of Israel in the first place. Israel has actually created something new and special in the international arena. Its energetic disagreements about how to run a country alongside its vigorous debate about how to preserve a cultural heritage and religious tradition cannot be found anywhere else.

A successful process of nation creating does not mean that all of the country's founding elites have to agree. Joseph Ellis, the extraordinary and lyrical historian of the early United States, writes, "With the American revolution, as with all revolutions, different factions came together in common cause to overthrow the reigning regime, then discovered in the aftermath of their triumph that they had fundamentally different and politically incompatible notions of what they intended."[20] Ellis's conception of revolutionary countries holds true for Israel as well. Like the U.S. Founding Fathers, those involved in bringing about Israel's independence did uncover "fundamentally different and politically incompatible notions" of what they were seeking to create.

The miracle of Israel, like that of the United States, is that it has worked. Although Israel has been at war since before its re-creation, internal political violence has been, with very few tragic exceptions, almost nonexistent.[21] As Ellis notes, "In . . . the French, Russian and Chinese revolutions, as well as the multiple movements for national independence in Africa, Asia, and Latin America—the leadership class of the successful revolution proceeded to decimate itself in bloody reprisals that frequently assumed genocidal proportions."[22] But that did not happen with the United States, and it did not occur in Israel, either. Israel's revolution against the British did not unleash the bloodletting of most other revolutions.

What will happen as Palestine moves forward?

Chapter Two

WHERE A TRADITION MEETS THE WORLD

If someone tells you there is wisdom among the nations, believe him.

If he tells you that there is Torah among the nations, do not believe him.

—*Lamentations Rabbah* 2:13

One of the most memorable moments in *Fiddler on the Roof* is the scene in which Leibisch, the young scholar, asks the venerated rabbi if there is a proper blessing for the czar. "Of course," the rabbi tells him. "May God bless and keep the czar—far away from us!" Everyone laughs, but few people fully appreciate the joke.

The dig is aimed not only at the czar but also at the Jews. For Jews, it seems, do have a blessing for nearly everything; that is part of what the joke pokes fun at. There is in fact a real blessing to be recited upon seeing a king: "Blessed are You, Lord our God, Who has given of His glory to flesh and blood." The second dimension to the joke in *Fiddler on the Roof* is how the rabbi alters *that* blessing and substitutes one that asks that the czar be kept far from the Jews.

There's another, lesser known Jewish blessing, to be recited when one encounters a non-Jewish scholar: "Blessed are You, Lord our God, Who has given of His wisdom to flesh and blood."[1] It might seem like an innocuous utterance, but it actually signifies something very important: Judaism has long recognized that there is profound wisdom to be gleaned from the gentile world. The second part of the rabbinic source quoted at the opening of this chapter indicates that Jewish tradition *does* insist that there is learning and sanctity in Judaism (the Torah) that cannot be found elsewhere. But the notion that nothing can therefore be learned from the rest of the world is completely foreign to the Jewish tradition; thus the first part of the quote.

Part of what accounts for Israel's extraordinary success is that it has internalized this worldview. Israel is a unique experiment: Jewish tradition is given primacy in many areas, but there is simultaneously a constant recognition of the wisdom to be gleaned from an ongoing interaction with the world. As we've mentioned before, the Jewish state has served as the arena in which the Jewish tradition (on which the state is founded) is forced to accommodate itself to moral and intellectual insights from the West.

Given the ways in which the idea of the ethnic nation-state is disparaged among intellectual elites in Europe and the United States, one might well expect that Israel would be a backward, intolerant state. In fact, in numerous measurable ways, Israel is more open than every other similar state.

If a Palestinian state is to do for the Palestinians what Israel has done for the Jews, Palestine is going to have to foster a variety of Islam that is equally open. Can it?

The status of women in Israel is a case in point. Israel is a deeply traditional and religious country in many ways; significantly, it has no separation of "church" and state, and most of traditional Judaism is hardly liberal about the role of women. Even though Judaism in antiquity far surpassed other cultures in its concern for women's welfare (insisting, for example, that when a man divorced a woman, he could not simply dispose of her but had to provide for her economic sustenance), women were undeniably still second-class citizens. Even today, women in traditional Jewish communities do not have the same freedom and opportunities for learning and leadership that are available to men. Given that background, it might seem that there was little chance that a Jewish state would accord women equal status with men.

In reality, however, there is simply no resemblance between the status that women had in traditional Jewish communities and what they have achieved in Israel. According to the World Economic Forum's *Global Gender Gap Report 2009*, a report that tracks and indexes the magnitude and scope of national gender-based disparities according to economic, political, educational, and health-based criteria, Israel places in the top fifty countries in the world with regard to sexual equality, ahead of almost half of all European Union member states.[2] In fact, Israel had moved up eleven places since 2008, as a result of

> significant improvement in the economic participation and opportunity afforded to women, the proportion of women among legislator, senior official and managerial positions, and gains in the perceived wage equality for similar work. Israel also gains ground on the political empowerment sub-index because of an increase in the percentage of women in parliament [Knesset], from 14% to 18%.[3]

In how many other countries, for example, has there been a female head of state (Golda Meir), or a period in which women served as both head of the opposition party in parliament and president of the Supreme Court (Tzipi Livni and Dorit Beinisch, respectively, from 2008 to 2012)?

A similar accommodation of Judaism's religious strictures to the freedom of the West can be seen in Israel's treatment of gays and lesbians. The Hebrew Bible is open to multiple interpretations on many subjects, but homosexuality is not one of them. The Bible's condemnation of male homosexuality is unambiguous; social liberals thus rail against what they see as the Bible's intolerance, while many social conservatives argue that contemporary society has strayed too far from the Bible's teachings in its accommodation of gays and lesbians. But on one issue liberals and conservatives agree: the Bible's position is not in the least bit unclear.

Nothing much changed in the centuries that followed biblical times. The rabbinic tradition evinced no toleration of homosexuality, male or female, and that attitude persisted into the Middle Ages and Judaism's great legal codes. Even today, in most traditional Jewish communities, gays and lesbians are still far from accepted; most have to lead very closeted lives. What, then, was the likelihood that a Jewish state, with a distinctly conservative Jewish orientation and a hyper-conservative chief rabbinate, would be tolerant of homosexuality?

As it turns out, a religious-ethnic tradition in dialogue with the West has made Israel one of the freest societies for gays and lesbians to be found anywhere. *Out* magazine, one of the most widely circulated magazines serving the gay community in the United States, named Tel Aviv the gay capital of the Middle East.[4] Israel has openly gay Knesset members (a scenario one can scarcely imagine in any other Middle Eastern country's parliament), and it regularly hosts gay pride parades, both in liberal, cosmopolitan Tel Aviv and in the far more conservative and religious Jerusalem.[5] In fact, the rights afforded to members of the LGBT (lesbian, gay, bisexual, and transgender) community in Israel eclipse those in many Western nations as well, including the United States. Israel's army never had a "don't ask, don't tell" policy, and openly gay men have served in combat units for years.

The Jewish state is also a signatory of the U.N. Declaration on Sexual Orientation and Gender Identity, distributed in the U.N. General Assembly in December 2008.[6] Whereas Israel signed the document without much fanfare, the declaration was opposed not only by the Vatican (for obvious religious reasons) but also by every Arab country. The Arab bloc endorsed an alternative statement that had been advocated at the General Assembly by the Syrian representative; it insisted that supporting the original declaration could "lead to the social normalization, and possibly the legitimization, of many deplorable acts including pedophilia."[7] Even the United States, it should be noted, refused to sign the declaration during the George W. Bush administration; it did so later under President Barack Obama.[8]

As may be expected, some religious elements in Israel reject this openness. There are members of the ultra-Orthodox (Haredi) community who, using the Bible's language, have called homosexuality an abomination, and in one noteworthy case, a leader of the hard-line religious community stated emphatically (though somewhat less than scientifically) that homosexuality is "the reason why there are earthquakes in the world."[9] The Haredi community protests, sometimes in significant numbers, at gay pride parades, particularly in Jerusalem. But what is different in Israel from other countries in the Middle East is that when the police show up in force at such events, it is to provide protection to the gay community, not to attack it.

The pressures of the religious Right notwithstanding, freedom of sexual choice is legally protected in Israel, and in general, opposition to gay rights is nowhere near as vociferous as it is in other places. In Tel Aviv, for instance, one can live an openly gay life, just as one can in New York or San Francisco. Israel manages to be an ethnic nation-state committed to a profound Jewish consciousness at the very center of its discourse and behavior without imagining that the Jewish tradition has a monopoly on wisdom or insight. It is a country that combines profound Jewish sensibilities and commitments with an epistemological humility that makes most of its citizens open to insights from other societies, cultures, and states.

That is not always an easy balance to maintain, and Israel often stumbles along the way. There remains much that Israel has to do to improve. But this much is clear: Israel's experience proves that the ethnic nation-state, even when it is based on an ancient heritage with deeply traditional values, does not have to be repressive or locked in the past. Israel is the very model of a nation struggling to be faithful to the call of its roots while embracing a sometimes uncomfortable dialogue with the West. The freedom that can result is often surprising.

In 2004, Abdolkarim Soroush, an Iranian intellectual who once worked with Ayatollah Khomeini, wrote an open letter to Iran's minister of Islamic guidance, Mohammad Khatami, and railed against what that Islamic nation-state was doing to free thought. "The present generation as well as generations to come must never forget this ominous message of religious despotism," he wrote, "that in Iran today, the best newspaper is the one that is closed, the best pen is the one that is broken, and the best thinker is the one that is nonexistent."[10]

Throughout the Arab world as well, many intellectuals know that their own heritage is stifling them. They understand and admit that the Arab world has protected its power structures by not allowing the same kind of divisive yet enriching debate that is a hallmark of Israeli life. The Arab world suppresses debate when it should be fostering it. The types of freedom that Israelis take for granted, even as they lambast their government for one failure or another, are nowhere to be found in the Arab world. In the Reporters without Borders "Press Freedom Index 2010," Israel was ranked number 86 in the world (and improving). Israel's standing was significantly hurt by the fact that it still has a military censor and that it is one of the countries in which journalists were killed in 2010. Yet even so, and despite a ranking that many Israelis thought should have been higher, Reporters without Borders noted that "its press still enjoys latitude that is unequaled in the region."[11]

In contrast, Israel's Arab neighbors and Iran all languish toward the bottom of the list. Of the 178 countries rated, Jordan did best among Israel's neighbors, at 120. Egypt came in at 127, Iraq at 130, Saudi Arabia at 157, Sudan at 172, Syria at 173, and Iran at 175.[12] It is disappointing that even after Egypt's Arab Spring revolution of 2011, the freedom that many thought would come did not materialize. Indeed, one of the first acts that the Egyptian army took was to begin arresting bloggers and others who were critical of its post-Mubarak policies.[13]

This is the larger context in which the Israeli experiment should be judged. How many other countries this new, with incessant wars on all fronts, or surrounded by political instability, can boast similar freedoms? But while Israel is unusual (and, in the Middle East, unique), it need not be. There's no reason that Egypt, for example, couldn't build a new state that blends freedom and debate with a respect for Egyptian culture and Islamic teachings.

When the Palestinians get their own state, they could alter the future of not only the Palestinian people but also, quite possibly, the entire Arab world if they adopt and then model this kind of country. After all, they know it well from their close interaction with Israel. But will they? The signs are not entirely positive.

Even in the allegedly more tolerant Palestinian West Bank (relative to the Hamas-dominated Gaza Strip), small infractions on the part of the press can lead to horrific punishment. In one absurdly Kafkaesque example, Mamdouh Hamamreh, a Palestinian reporter working for Al-Quds TV, which is sympathetic to Hamas, said he was held for more than fifty days in Palestinian lockup after he was tagged in a Facebook image that mocked Palestinian president Mahmoud Abbas.[14] He denied having anything to do with posting the image, but still, even prior to his hearing, he admitted that he'd learned his lesson. "I censor myself now," he said. "I'm careful of what I say." That, of course, was precisely what the authorities wanted. The free exchange of ideas is sorely lacking in the Palestinian Authority. So too is the freedom to be tagged by someone else on Facebook.

A similar intolerance is evident throughout the Arab world regarding the treatment of minorities and political dissenters. Saddam Hussein's wholesale murder of the Kurds in Iraq is now well documented. So too was Gaddafi's brutal suppression of the Libyan uprising in 2011 and Syrian president Bashar al-Assad's massacre of thousands of largely peaceful protesters the same year. Egypt has abused Coptic Christians for decades simply for the crime of being different. Even the supposedly enlightened Hosni Mubarak opened fire on unarmed protesters during the 2011 revolution in Egypt, a crime for which he was subsequently brought to trial.

Consider too how Arab countries have treated their Jewish minorities, compared with Israel's treatment of its Arab population, discussed in chapter 1. When the state of Israel was re-created, most Arab countries expelled their Jewish populations; today, their Jews are all but gone. In 1948, Morocco had a Jewish population of approximately 265,000. Today, 3,500 Jews remain there.[15] Yemen had 55,000 Jews; today, there are about 200.[16] Egypt had about 75,000 Jews, but today only 100 remain.[17] Algeria had 140,000 Jews; now not a single Jew remains.[18]

One might be tempted to suggest that those expulsion orders were horrible decisions made in the heat of the moment or in an era long since over (which one might well say about those Palestinians who were forced out of Israel in the 1948 War of Independence).[19] However, it is worth remembering that Palestinian officials continue to insist that no Jews will be permitted to live in Palestine.[20] The fear of the mere presence of Jews is so deep that the Arab countries threw them out, Abbas insisted in 2010 that a future Palestine would be Jew-free, and the *Economist* reported in 2011 that "the Palestinian Authority under President Mahmoud Abbas has repeatedly sought to block joint projects between Jewish settlements and neighbouring Arab villages for fear that co-operation would make the settlers feel more at home." This policy clearly demonstrates a willingness to hurt Palestinian interests for the sole purpose of precluding Jews from remaining where they now live should the West Bank become a Palestinian state.[21]

Why do the Palestinians insist on becoming one of the world's few countries without a minority? Is it that they are so deeply afraid of the intellectual and moral discourse that might result? And why is the Western world so fearful of challenging them on this close-minded and foolish orientation? When will the Palestinians realize that they're better off following Israel's model, not Libya's?

This utter lack of openness bodes quite poorly for the status of women in Palestine, as long as the Palestinians create their state according to the model of the Arab states that already exist. For the status of women in Arab countries is simply abysmal. According to the *Global Gender Gap Report 2009*, Kuwait ranked second highest in the region (behind Israel, which was ranked at 45) in the treatment of women, yet it did not even make it into the global top 100 (it placed at 105). It was followed by Tunisia (109), the United Arab Emirates (112), Jordan (113), Bahrain (116), Algeria (117), Syria (121), Oman (123), Morocco (124), Qatar (125), Egypt (126), Saudi Arabia (130), and Yemen (134).[22] There are only 134 countries in the ranking, so regarding women's rights, Arab countries are essentially at rock-bottom.

In its 2005 report on women's rights in the Middle East and North Africa, Freedom House stated that women in Arab countries typically do not have independent legal identities and do not have recourse in cases of domestic violence and other forms of abuse. The participation of women in political life is the lowest in the world.[23] It is commonly known that Saudi women are not permitted to drive and, perhaps more heinous, can be lashed for having premarital sex.

In fact, in some parts of the Arab world, the attitude to women is so reprehensible that it causes death. In a 2002 blaze in Mecca, for example, fifteen schoolgirls died when they were prevented by the religious police from leaving a burning building because they were not wearing the correct Islamic dress.[24] Honor killings are another horrific part of women's reality in the Arab world (and in some other Muslim countries, such as Iran and Pakistan). These are cases in which women and girls are murdered by a father, a brother, or a husband for behavior that is considered to blemish the honor of the family; this can range from meeting a boy without the family's permission to having premarital or extramarital sex or even being raped (in which case the rapist often goes unpunished). According to Amnesty International, honor killings are still widely reported throughout the region.[25]

The Palestinians too have a long way to go regarding women's rights. Today, women in the West Bank and Gaza are afforded an appallingly low level of protection. As of this writing (2011), there are no laws that protect women from domestic violence. According to surveys conducted by the Palestinians themselves, more than 60 percent of women who have ever been married report having been psychologically abused by their husbands.[26] Almost 25 percent of Palestinian women who have ever been married report having been beaten by their husbands at some point. Will the Palestinians continue in this direction, or will they create a society open enough for Western views to affect the way that women are perceived and to gradually turn violence against women into the anathema it certainly ought to be?

It comes as no surprise that the situation is no better for homosexuals in Arab (and other Muslim) countries. In contrast to their treatment in Israel, homosexuals are legally and socially persecuted almost uniformly throughout the rest of the Middle East and often have no rights whatsoever. In August 2009, Human Rights Watch published a report documenting a nationwide campaign of extrajudicial executions, kidnappings, and torture of gay men in Iraq.[27] Gay men in Gaza face up to ten years in prison.[28] Transvestites are imprisoned and lashed in Saudi Arabia.[29] Algeria, Egypt, Jordan, Lebanon, and Morocco all ban homosexuality under secular law, and it is punishable with fines and prison terms.[30]

There are five countries in the world that actually execute homosexuals: Iran, Mauritania, Saudi Arabia, Sudan, and Yemen (as well as some parts of Nigeria and Somalia).[31] Iran even executes gay teenagers.[32] But when questioned about these policies, Iran's president, Mahmoud Ahmadinejad, responded that it was not really an issue, since "in Iran we don't have homosexuals like in your country."[33]

Compare this to Israel's rating as one of the world's freest societies for gays and lesbians. Again, the Palestinian people must answer some critical questions: What will they do with the opportunity that statehood affords them? Which model will they pursue?

Who pays the price for this narrowness in the Arab world? It is not just journalists, women, dissidents, or gays and lesbians. The price is paid by every citizen of these countries, for the narrowness that xenophobia fosters yields societies that simply cannot engage with or compete in the modern world. When the Palestinians choose between the model that Israel offers and the model of the current Arab states, they will not simply be choosing between an open society and a closed one, or a free society and a repressive one. They will, in effect, be choosing between a sustainable nation-state and a country doomed to failure. The fear of the other that now has Arab societies locked in its grip and the insistence on suppressing dissent at every turn are worse than repressive. Ultimately, they create countries in which ideas are simply not welcome, and where social repression and economic doom are inevitable.

The real difference between Israel and its neighbors is an openness to the world, a willingness to allow for a marketplace of ideas that lets people wonder and dream, express themselves, and live fully. It's hard to measure results such as these, but we can still point to some highly instructive indicators.

Consider illiteracy among women, for example. In Egypt, 45 percent of women are illiterate; in Israel the figure is about 4 percent.[34] In the matter of universities, the differences are astounding. Israel, a tiny country with a tight budget, ranks far beyond all Arab and other Muslim countries, including the Gulf Arab states like Saudi Arabia that have virtually limitless assets. In a 2009 ranking of the world's top universities, Hebrew University ranked number 102 (shortly later, it climbed to number 57 on the strength of an award received by a professor of mathematics), Tel Aviv University was number 114, and the Technion (Israel's equivalent of MIT) ranked 132.[35] In contrast, there was not a single university from a Muslim country that ranked in the top 250. King Fahd University of Petroleum and Minerals in Saudi Arabia ranked highest among them at 266, and it was followed by the National University of Sciences and Technology in Pakistan, at 350. Others ranked far lower.

The success of Israel's academic community is nothing less than astonishing, given the country's age and circumstances; by the same token, the failure of the rest of the Arab and Muslim countries is an unnecessary tragedy.

Fouad Ajami, a Johns Hopkins University expert on Arab affairs, has lamented the fact that Egypt, which was once the center of a vital Arab and intellectual culture, is now emblematic of what is wrong throughout the Arab world. Egypt, he noted in 1995, published only 375 books per year, while Israel produced 4,000 books that year.[36] *And Egypt has a population ten times that of Israel.* The numbers remain similarly skewed. Bernard Lewis, an eminent Princeton University scholar, similarly notes the following:

> Book sales present an even more dismal picture. . . . A report on the Arab Human Development in 2002, prepared by a committee of Arab intellectuals and published under the auspices of the United Nations, again reveals some striking contrasts. "The Arab world translates about 330 books annually, one-fifth of the number that Greece translates. The cumulative total of translated books since the Caliph Maa'moun's [sic] time [the ninth century] is about 100,000, almost the average that Spain translates in one year."[37]

These are more than idle statistics. The tragedy of the Muslim world is that the glorious intellectual openness that characterized

Muslim Spain and Turkey centuries ago has long since disappeared. Fareed Zakaria, an author and a CNN commentator on international affairs, understands that something has gone fundamentally wrong with the Arab world in particular. In the last fifty years, Zakaria writes, "the West progressed and parts of the non-Western world also began modernizing. . . . [But] the Arab world stayed stuck in primitive political and social arrangements. Arab politics is not culturally unique; it is just stuck in a time warp."[38] As Bernard Lewis argues, the explanation that this backwardness is the result of Western imperialism is no longer convincing:

> Many regions have undergone the impact of the West, and suffered a similar loss of economic self-sufficiency, of cultural authenticity, and in some parts also of political independence. But some time has passed since Western domination ended in all these regions, including the Middle East. In some of them, notably in East and South Asia, the resurgent peoples of the region have begun to meet and beat the West on its own terms—in commerce and industry, in the projection of political and even military power, and, in many ways most remarkable of all, in the acceptance and internalization of Western achievement, notably in science. The Middle East still lags behind.[39]

Indeed, something has gone terribly wrong. Why should Israel have won three times more Nobel Prizes than Egypt when its population is just a tiny fraction of Egypt's? Why has a citizen of Iraq, Jordan, Lebanon, or Saudi Arabia (to name just a few) never been awarded a Nobel Prize?

It is a painful thing to say, but the Palestinians ignore this fact at their own peril: tragically, the Arab world simply does not contribute to the world's progress in any meaningful way. Arab societies produce virtually nothing other than oil. The Arab Spring grew out of a desperate demand for basic economic subsistence on the part of young people who had gotten educations but who were trapped in countries that produced nothing and therefore could not offer them a brighter future.

What has happened to the culture that was once at the very cutting edge of science and philosophy, many centuries ago? What grand idea, powerful insight, great invention, or life-enhancing movement has emerged from the Arab world in almost a millennium? Tragically, examples are rare indeed, for Islam's intellectually rich tradition has been completely derailed.

This is not an argument about the worth of Arab culture or the potential role of Islam in the governing of the state. It is about poor governance and societies that are unfortunately in the grip of fear. There's no reason to think that Islam couldn't once again be fully compatible with intellectual advancement. All it would take to be more like Israel in results is to become more like Israel in process.

If the Palestinians were to set aside the animosity created by a century of conflict and to acknowledge that it is Israel's model that offers them and their state a way out of this cultural, intellectual, religious, and economic dead end, Palestine could alter the future of the entire Arab, and perhaps Muslim, world. But for that to happen, the Palestinians will have to acknowledge that the very country that they had once hoped to destroy is the country that they should be emulating.

None of this should be taken to suggest that Israel is a perfect nation-state, for it is not. As discussed above, Israel is deeply flawed in many ways, and significant challenges still lie ahead. The groups in Israeli society that are least exposed to the West or that hail from nondemocratic traditions still pose a threat to Israel's openness and decency. There are occasional assaults on Israel's democracy from the ultra-Orthodox population, just as there are from a few Russian-born politicians. Israel has not treated even all Jews well at all times, and it has certainly not always treated either its Arab citizens or the Palestinians now under its control equally or kindly. Even Israel's most ardent supporters would be foolish to deny that.

But what Israel does illustrate is that nation-states, even those locked in the grip of a never-ending war, can be remarkably tolerant and even transcend some of the limitations of their own traditions.

When democracy, the rule of law, an embrace of liberal Western values, and a robust tradition of debate in the public square all coexist, extraordinary things can happen even in the most unlikely circumstances. Freedom of ideas can persist, even in the Middle East. Societies must simply decide to take freedom seriously, because only in genuinely free-thinking societies can people achieve the heights of spirit that make life worth living. That is precisely what Israel has done.

In some ways, the Palestinians have already recognized that they want an Israel. When Israel was created, there *was* no Palestinian national movement. Palestinian Arabs had long thought of themselves as Southern Syrians, and the term *Palestinian* was actually used to refer to the Jews of Palestine. The birth of Palestinian Arab nationalism was a slow process, and it derived largely from the Arab residents of Palestine witnessing the revitalization of the Jewish people in Palestine and then in the newly created state of Israel. The great irony of the Jewish revival in the state of Israel is that it has spawned not only a Jewish renewal but a Palestinian yearning for statehood as well. The Palestinians have seen the new sense of self and the fresh confidence that statehood has granted the Jews; having watched the Jewish cultural flourishing that Israel has made possible, the Palestinians have decided to seek the same.

The choice that the Palestinian nation makes as it begins to build its state may well determine the very future of the Palestinian people. Jews too once had to chart the future of their own country. Even with all the missteps, Israel has transformed the Jews. One can only hope that the Palestinians might one day do the same, bridging East and West, the traditions of Jordan and the culture of Israel, enriching us all, wherever we live and whatever we believe.

Chapter Three

DIFFERENCE MATTERS

The very idea of a "Jewish state" . . . is rooted in another time
and place.
Israel, in short, is an anachronism.
                                    —Tony Judt, "Israel: The Alternative"[1]

In January 1982, my wife and I were in Moscow. We had signed up
to visit Soviet Jewish refusenik families waiting for permission to
emigrate to Israel. Although we were hardly professional spies, we
had been pretty well prepared by our contact. We were told to expect
to be followed, which refuseniks would be harder to find or reach,
what kinds of things I should teach if we could get a study group
together, and what to bring for the bitter Moscow winter. We were kids,
really, and more than a bit scared, but we never really thought twice
about whether to go. Nor did we imagine the effect it would have on us.

On one of our first nights there, we met a Muscovite family on our
list. We huddled in their tiny, freezing apartment and tried to encourage the couple and bolster their morale. That, after all, was the purpose of our trip. But the conversation, which was mostly in Hebrew
because their self-taught and broken Hebrew was infinitely better
than our nonexistent Russian, soon took an unexpected turn.

"When are you going to leave America and go to live in Israel?" they asked.

It would have been easy to lie and say something like "in two more years, when we finish school," but somehow, lying to people in their condition—out of work, hungry, spied on, and harassed, all because they had applied to leave the Soviet Union—seemed out of the question. But a mild fib didn't work much better.

"We're still thinking about it."

"Thinking about what?"

"About whether we're going to move to Israel." It was a bald-faced lie, and they knew that immediately. Moving to Israel wasn't anywhere on our radar screen, and they could tell. They said very little, but it wasn't hard to divine what they were thinking: "You, you who have the option to go at any minute, just don't want to? What does that mean? How could you not want to be there?"

Thirty years later, I still recall the discomfort I felt at that moment. I remember my desperate desire to be back in the freezing, snowy Moscow winter air—anywhere but in that cramped apartment, facing people whose courage I couldn't hope to match. The successful and secure Israel I've described was already in place. There was a place where *my* people were at the center, where *my* way of life was celebrated and encouraged. Why didn't I, as a committed Jew, even think about moving there? Even though I did not understand this then, I've since come to believe that I had internalized many of the same misunderstandings that keep much of the world blind to Israel's accomplishments and importance.

In the frigid Moscow winter, I suddenly felt like a fake. Although we had been sent to offer *them* support, it had taken only minutes for them to teach *us* what mattered.

With time, although it took years for me to fully appreciate this, I came to understand that what had motivated them to apply for permission to leave the Soviet Union was precisely what had led us to get on a plane and go to Moscow. They had infinitely more courage than we did, of course, but what we all shared was a deep sense that our journeys in life were animated by something more powerful than any of the standard measures of personal success, such as graduate school or jobs.

What motivated them to take on the Soviet behemoth was the sense that they were part of something particular and unique, not universal. They were part of a distinct people, and *living* as part of that people mattered to them more than anything else. My new wife and I, living in New York and just beginning graduate school, had "better" things to do than go to Moscow in the dead of winter. But we too sensed that there was something about our identities that was not exhausted by getting another academic degree, by being married, or by starting out on the road to adulthood together.

Now, some thirty years later, I wonder whether that simple and innocent question, "When are you going to leave America and go to live in Israel?", is what ultimately got us to move to Israel many years later. There was something extraordinarily stark about the contrast between their desperation and our privilege, their courage and our passivity, their clarity and our pretense. Thanks in large measure to them, I began to wonder: What would it take for me to be able to look back on my life and feel that I had lived in the way that most honored and contributed to the unique story of which I was a part?

Part of the central premise of this book is that there was nothing terribly unusual about that Soviet refusenik couple or that young American couple crowded into a freezing Moscow apartment. Indeed, I believe that the powerful feeling of belonging that tugged at both couples is actually a deep-seated human need that almost all people share. At our cores, most of us want to belong to something. We want to inherit a narrative and a history, a way of life and something in which to believe—and we want to pass it on.

As strange as it may seem, it is in that context that we have to understand the international community's current distaste for Israel. Part of what the world cannot abide about Israel is that it has become the place where one small people, the Jews, brought back from the precipice of extinction after the horrors of the twentieth century, has begun to thrive again. Yes, Israel is a refuge for Jews who have nowhere else to go, but it is much more than that.

Israel is not just a Hebrew-speaking, falafel-eating version of the United States, in which the goal is "life, liberty, and the pursuit of happiness." Israel is a country, as we noted earlier, "by the Jews, of the Jews, for the Jews." It was created for a distinct purpose: Jewish healing and, ultimately, Jewish flourishing. It is a country in which a Jewish take on history, a distinctly Jewish way of preserving memory and the Jewish language, color the public square. It is the country in which Jewish holidays, and not Christian or Muslim holidays, create the rhythm of the calendar year. It is a country in which Jewish history is coupled with geography in ways that simply cannot happen anywhere else. The particularism at the heart of Israel, the belief in the importance of preserving distinct ethnicities as a means of preserving human dignity and freedom, is so core to Israel that it extends to the other peoples who live there as well.

But the notion that the differences among peoples, ethnicities, and cultures are a positive thing that ought to be consciously preserved is a very embattled notion in the world we inhabit. (American "multiculturalism" is more lip-service to this notion than a genuine interest in the differences between ethnic groups; *multiculturalism* is de facto a code word for tolerance of different origins, but does not reflect a real celebration of difference.) That is why today's battles over the Jewish state are battles over ideas. Certainly they are also battles over land, security, and the rights of the Palestinians. But at its core, the battle that rages in the Middle East is really about ideas, and in the realm of ideas about belonging and human difference, Israelis and Europeans (along with many others, including academics across the globe) find themselves on opposite sides of the divide.

What has happened? Why have so many thoughtful people who once considered Israel a good idea now begun to say that the Jewish state was a mistake and that it should cease to exist? A few different factors contribute to this phenomenon.

The first has to do with the plight of the underdog. The international community sees an Israel with a thriving economy and a powerful army arrayed against a people without a country, with a sputtering economy, and with only rudimentary weapons (relative to Israel's cutting-edge arsenal), so it decides that the imbalance of power has to be rectified. Most of the negative parallels used against Israel fall into this category; whereas Israel was once the underdog, the mere fact of its success now makes it the imperial power, precisely the sort of occupying force that history has continually overthrown.

The Palestinians are right to want independence; most Israelis understand that. What is ironic and painful for Israelis is the fact that the world's focus on the Palestinians' condition stems in large measure from Israel's unparalleled policy of permitting the international media freedom of movement, yet the reporting avoids almost all discussion of how the occupation began or what the Palestinians have and have not been willing to do to bring it to a peaceful end. Now that it is no longer the underdog, it often seems that Israel can do no right, especially when defending itself.

The second commonly mentioned factor is refugees. The international community is understandably anxious to resolve refugee problems wherever they exist. Approximately seven hundred thousand Palestinians fled their homes and villages during Israel's War of Independence, and their descendants now number in the millions.[2] But because Lebanon, Syria, and Jordan (the primary countries to which they fled) have not made most of them citizens, they are essentially landless and thus refugees. Israel continues to insist that it cannot possibly absorb the millions of people who now call themselves Palestinian refugees and still remain Jewish and democratic; thus, many people see Israel as the cause of a humanitarian problem.

The third factor in the change of attitude toward Israel is the uncomfortable but obvious fact that Israel is sometimes unjust, immoral, or injurious—though significantly less than is commonly claimed. Innocent Palestinian civilians *do* die in the conflict; such is the horrific nature of war, especially when it is conducted in densely populated civilian areas. Israel's army has an infinitely better record of moral behavior than most armies, but the present situation is still incendiary. Checkpoints are undeniably demeaning; the presence of Israeli soldiers in Palestinian villages sows fear and resentment.

Israeli soldiers are human and fallible. There are occasional beatings and sometimes unjustified shootings. These are rare, but they happen. When Israeli soldiers do engage in behavior that is simply wrong, they sully Israel's image even further and become a cause célèbre in the international press, which has had access to the conflict for years far beyond what it is permitted, for example, in Iraq or Afghanistan.

The fourth and final factor, even though it is denied by many, is anti-Semitism. It would be wrong to dismiss every criticism of Israel as anti-Semitic, but there is, unfortunately, no doubt that *some* of the rhetoric claiming that Israel ought not to exist at all is fueled by distaste for the Jews and for the revival of Jewish life that Israel has made possible. Anti-Semitism is a highly adaptive virus; it has taken on theological, racial, and economic forms in the past. Today we see much less race-based animus toward the Jews, but instead of attacking the "Jewish race," anti-Semites direct their venom at the Jewish state.

All of these issues are real, but none would require the elimination of the Jewish state for them to be overcome. (Even anti-Semitism would not be silenced by the disappearance of Israel; history has shown that it would simply adapt and take another form.) Yet eliminating Israel is a much discussed goal for some and Israel is the only country on the planet whose right to exist is questioned. Why is that? Even allowing for the complexity of the situation and Israel's role in it, there is something perverse in how Israel is viewed that cannot be explained simply by the litany of complaints against it.

Europeans now rank Israel and North Korea as the two countries most dangerous to world peace.[3] Is Israel really the same sort of threat to world peace as a nuclear North Korea? Is it more dangerous than Pakistan, which possesses nuclear weapons and harbored Osama bin Laden, or than Iran, which seeks nuclear capabilities, has threatened to wipe Israel off the map, and heaps venom on the West? Is it more repugnant than the entire mass of Arab countries in which there is no free press, few rights for women, no tolerance for gays and lesbians, and usually no democracy? Is Israel really more problematic than all of those countries?

It obviously isn't. So something else must be at play, and those who are most opposed to the continued existence of Israel are fearful precisely because that "something" might spread.

Israel is by far the most watched nation-state in the world. It is also the most criticized. Although criticism of any country, including Israel, is legitimate and necessary (for no country improves without internal and external critique), something ugly and unfair has arisen with regard to the Jewish state. In 2007, Amnesty International condemned Israel more than it condemned Syria, Saudi Arabia, Libya, Lebanon, and Algeria. (Most amazing, when Richard Goldstone repudiated his own 2009 report on the 2008–2009 Gaza War, writing that "if I had known then what I know now, the Goldstone report would have been a different document," Amnesty International still held Israel as guilty as it had before, arguing that "recent Israeli government calls for the United Nations to retract the 2009 report" constituted "a cynical attempt to avoid accountability for war crimes."[4]) Amnesty International also published more items condemning Israel than it did condemning the Palestinian Authority, Hamas, and Hezbollah combined.[5]

Two years later, Robert Bernstein, the founding chairman of Human Rights Watch, went public in the *New York Times*, acknowledging with great sadness that his organization's focus on Israel's human rights record had clearly taken on political and anti-Israel dimensions, all under the guise of human rights work:

> The Arab and Iranian regimes rule over some 350 million people, and most remain brutal, closed and autocratic, permitting little or no internal dissent. The plight of their citizens who would most benefit from the kind of attention a large and well-financed international human rights organization can provide is being ignored as Human Rights Watch's Middle East division prepares report after report on Israel.[6]

Why this hyperattentiveness to Israel? The causes are many, but the one that may be the most important is too often overlooked. That critical reason is the fact that debates about the Jewish state are closely linked to debates about the idea of the nation-state. In many ways, today's discourse about Israel is often nothing more or less than a camouflaged conversation about the nation-state. As the West debates the benefits and (more commonly) the ills of the nation-state—a country in which a relatively homogeneous group of people (such as Jews, Kurds, or Chechnyans) inhabits and guides a sovereign state—it is the Jewish state to which they point when they seek to prove that the nation-state is an idea that has run its course.

A prime example of this linkage was the much discussed article in a 2003 issue of the *New York Review of Books* by the historian Tony Judt. Entitled "Israel: The Alternative," Judt's argument against the Jewish state was based primarily on his claim that the very idea of the nation-state was a bad one. Because the nation-state was an idea long since debunked, he insisted, Israel ought to go as well. Judt didn't mince words:

> The problem with Israel, in short, is not—as is sometimes suggested—that it is a European "enclave" in the Arab world; but rather that it arrived too late. It has imported a character-istically late-nineteenth-century separatist project into a world that has moved on, a world of individual rights, open frontiers, and international law. The very idea of a "Jewish state"—a state in which Jews and the Jewish religion have exclusive privileges from which non-Jewish citizens are forever excluded—is rooted in another time and place. Israel, in short, is an anachronism.[7]

Judt deserves credit for one major element of his argument: unlike other attacks on Israel's sovereignty, his is at least not unprincipled. It's true that his article focuses a great deal on the Israelis and the Palestinians, but his claim ran deeper than the common exaspera-tion with the conflict. Judt's argument that Israel is an anachronism stemmed from his belief that the very notion of the nation-state was outmoded. Israel, according to Judt, was a bad idea in both practice and theory. Of course, Judt did not suggest that other nation-states were also anachronisms. Nor did he suggest that the Palestinians' desire for a state of their own should be stopped in its tracks because it would be folly to found yet another nation-state. Judt singled out just one state, Israel, for a fundamental ideological reason: the notion that the theories behind Israel's founding no longer merit a place in modern discourse.

Judt's aversion to the idea of the nation-state is not unique to him; it is largely consistent with the views of other European intellectuals and political leaders who believed in the creation of a more unified whole: the European Union. In 1992, thirteen European countries signed the Maastricht Treaty, thus establishing a unified governmen-tal and economic body to oversee the affairs of its member states.

The purposes of the new union were explicit, and the wording of the treaty left little to the imagination: "Recalling the historic importance of the ending of the division of the European continent and the need to create firm bases for the construction of the future Europe," the thirteen original signatories "resolved to establish a citizenship common to nationals of their countries."[8]

In his book *Postwar: A History of Europe since 1945*—perhaps the definitive history of the period—Judt articulately describes this movement of the European continent away from individualized nation-states:

> At the beginning of the twenty-first century, the dilemma facing Europeans was not Socialism or Capitalism, Left versus Right, or the Third Way. It was not even "Europe" versus "America," since that choice had now been effectively resolved in most people's minds in favour of Europe. It was, rather, a question—*the* question—which history had placed upon the agenda in 1945 and which had quietly but insistently dislodged or outlived all other claims upon Europeans' attention. What future was there for the separate European nation-states? Did they *have* a future?
>
> There could be no going back to the world of the autonomous, free-standing nation-state, sharing nothing with its neighbor but a common border. Poles, Italians, Slovenes, Danes—even the British—were now Europeans. So, too, were millions of Sikhs, Bengalis, Turks, Arabs, Indians, Senegalese and others besides.[9]

Across the globe, many people began to believe that there was no future for the nation-state. In 1945, the English author Emery Reves published *The Anatomy of Peace*, which became a best-selling nonfiction book of that period. A friend of Winston Churchill's, Reves included with his book "An Open Letter to the American People," in which he urged that nations as they were then known should become a thing of the past. "We must aim at a federal constitution of the world, a working world-wide legal order, if we hope to prevent an atomic World War."[10] His proposal was endorsed by several U.S. senators and by no less a figure than Albert Einstein.

Similarly, as late as the 1990s, Strobe Talbott, a former U.S. deputy secretary of state and president of the Brookings Institution, wrote his own manifesto, "The Birth of the Global Nation." In it, he foresaw and advocated the end of the nation-state. "I'll bet that within the next hundred years . . . nationhood as we know it will be obsolete; all states will recognize a single global authority. A phrase briefly fashionable in the mid-20th century—a 'citizen of the world'—will have assumed real meaning by the end of the 21st century," he predicted.[11]

Talbott rightly saw this idea (which he believed would result in a universal peace) emanating from a transnational body as part of the legacy of Immanuel Kant. Kant thought that human nature made one international government both unlikely and dangerous, so he settled for the proposal of a federation of free states that would decide matters of war and peace while leaving daily governing issues to local populations. In his essay "Perpetual Peace: A Philosophical Sketch," Kant wrote that:

> There is only one rational way in which states co-existing with other states can emerge from the lawless condition of pure warfare. . . . They must renounce their savage and lawless freedom, adapt themselves to public coercive laws, and thus form an international state, which would necessarily continue to grow until it embraced all the people of the earth.[12]

Kant's notion that states should renounce their freedom and bequeath it to some international state was unrealistic, but it is an idea that has taken root everywhere from Reves to Einstein to Talbott to John Lennon. It has, in essence, captured contemporary popular imagination.

Judt's point is clear, and he is not incorrect: after World War II, Europe developed a strong antipathy toward the very idea of a nation-state. Consequently, Europe, along with much of the world, has developed a deep distaste for Israel, a country that has predicated its very existence on maintaining a distinct national, ethnic, and religious identity. Of course, other peoples and ethnicities, like those of the former Yugoslavia and the former Soviet Union, have now created their own nation-states, for that is a deeply embedded human desire. For Europe's elites, however, this is a move in the wrong direction; and Israel has become the proverbial lightning rod for the resentment that nationalism's refusal to die has aroused among Europe's universalist intellectuals.

Not everyone has the courage of Judt's convictions or his clarity of thought. Many others who are equally opposed to the nation-state also heap opprobrium on Israel. Instead of acknowledging that they are opposed to the idea of the nation-state and then engaging in a serious discussion of the idea, however, they express their quasi-philosophical commitments by focusing only on Israel, and usually on Israel's misdeeds. Then they ask whether the Jewish state—but only the Jewish state—has a right to exist.

Everywhere one turns, doubts about the nation-state are all summarily dumped at Israel's doorstep. There is no other country anywhere on the planet whose right to exist is debated in intellectual circles. China oppresses the Tibetans and severely limits civil liberties within its borders, but no one asks whether China has a right to exist. North Korea built a nuclear weapon in defiance of the West and literally starves its citizens to death.[13] But no one asks whether North Korea has a right to exist. The United States invaded Iraq with the intention of toppling its ruler but never suggested even for a moment that Iraq had no right to exist. Only with regard to Israel do people debate whether an entire country has a right to exist.

As José Maria Aznar, the prime minister of Spain from 1996 to 2004 and a non-Jew with no particular ax to grind in the conflict, noted in 2010, there *is* something different about the way that Israel is treated. Fair observers, he said, can no longer ignore it:

Uniquely in the West, [Israel] is the only democracy whose very existence has been questioned since its inception. In the first instance, it was attacked by its neighbors using the conventional weapons of war. Then it faced terrorism culminating in wave after wave of suicide attacks. Now, at the behest of radical Islamists and their sympathizers, it faces a campaign of delegitimation through international law and diplomacy.[14]

This ganging up on Israel has a reason, as we have said. It has unfolded because Israel has in large measure become a veritable code word for the nation-state, and the nation-state stands in direct defiance of the world's newfound infatuation with globalization.

We live, quite obviously, in an increasingly globalized world. As the Internet becomes more of a world-altering force, English becomes the de facto international language. With the global spread of retail chains, the stores found on Fifth Avenue are now very similar to those found in downtown London and on the Champs-Elysées in Paris. Teenagers in Budapest download the same songs from iTunes that young people in Boston, Buenos Aires, and Beersheba listen to, and McDonald's and Starbucks ensure that almost no matter where in the world Americans travel, they can have their burgers or coffee exactly as they do at home. Our music, our clothes, our food, and our language no longer say very much about where we come from or the culture of which we are the heirs.

Globalization has accelerated the conscious move toward homogeneity in the Western world. Our world is moving beyond difference. Consider the issue of language, for example. It is not only that the Internet is homogenizing languages; many languages are disappearing with alarming speed. The *New York Times* reported the following:

> Of the estimated 7,000 languages spoken in the world today, linguists say, nearly half are in danger of extinction and are likely to disappear in this century. In fact, they are now falling out of use at a rate of about one every two weeks. Some endangered languages vanish in an instant, at the death of the sole surviving speaker. Others are lost gradually in bilingual cultures, as indigenous tongues are overwhelmed by the dominant language at school, in the marketplace and on television.[15]

But Zionism did precisely the opposite for Hebrew, and Israelis see a miracle in the rebirth of their language. Not for nothing is Eliezer Ben Yehuda, the man credited with the revival of Hebrew as a modern language, considered a hero by Zionists and Israelis, with major streets named after him in several Israeli cities. (We will discuss him further in the next chapter.)

Similarly, although many people deny the importance of ethnic groups, Israelis take great pride in the ingathering of Jews from around the world and the re-creation of a Jewish nation. The academy may argue that the idea of the nation-state has run its course, but many Jews believe that the Jewish nation-state has literally saved the Jewish people, re-creating one people from fragments scattered around the globe.

In a world in which borders seem to matter less and less and could even be erased within an entity like the European Union, Israel insists that borders are critical and that different peoples ought to reside (for the most part) on different sides of those boundaries. In a world in which heritage and culture are ever more fleeting, Israel has demonstrated the power of building a society on a foundation of a shared way of life, powerful memory, and a common historical narrative. In an era in which Europe and the United States are buffeted by transformative waves of migration and immigration, Israel continues to insist that millions of Palestinians (the original refugees and their descendants) cannot be relocated to the Jewish state, because the Jewish state must remain exactly that: a home for the Jewish people. And as a result, the world is moving away from Israel.

There are, without question, dangers inherent in what Israel is seeking to accomplish, just as there are great strengths. But what matters most is the fact that for many, the quintessential example of the ethnic commonwealth, or the nation-state—a model that many believe has run its course—is the Jewish state.

Although Judt's article on Israel may have been a turning point in the conversation, he has had plenty of company over the years. Perhaps most dubious is the movement among academics to boycott Israel.

The left-leaning inclinations of the academy are well known.[16] To its great credit, it was the academy in the United States that contributed substantially to bringing the Vietnam War to a close, and the academy in other parts of the world has been on the cutting edge of many important human rights fronts, including women's rights and gay rights. But that academy is also principally opposed to the nation-state. And for that reason, among others, the academy has trouble with the idea of a Jewish state.

That much is fine. What is not fine, or fair, is the way in which academic boycotts of Israel are couched in humanitarian terms when these academics are actually simply opposed to the *Jews* having a nation-state. After all, many of those who are opposed to the Jewish nation-state believe that a Palestinian one should be created as soon as possible.

In 2002, for example, an open letter in the British daily the *Guardian* called for a moratorium on all cultural and research links with Israel until its government would be prepared to "[open] serious peace negotiations with the Palestinians along the lines proposed in many peace plans, including most recently that sponsored by the Saudis and the Arab League."[17] Initially, 123 academics signed the petition, including 90 British as well as (interesting to note) 10 Israeli academics.[18] Later, the number of signatories rose to more than 700.[19] This initiative ultimately proved the beginning of what would become a mass movement of many more boycotts to follow.

No matter what they claim, however, the true purpose of academic boycotts is not to change Israel's policy toward the Palestinians but to weaken the very state itself. Israeli academics, like those in many countries, are among the most left-leaning elements of Israeli society. There are few groups that are more critical of Israel's policies toward the Palestinians than university faculty. If the goal of the boycotts had been to change Israel's policies, these academics ought to have been supported and encouraged, lauded for their willingness to stand up to their government.

Yet Hebrew University was boycotted because of accusations that it had stolen land from an Arab family, even though Israeli courts ruled consistently that the university had acted appropriately and the matter was later settled through direct negotiations. Haifa University was boycotted for allegedly threatening the academic position of Ilan Pappe, a well-known Israeli leftist, even though the university publicly insisted that Pappe's position was wholly secure. Even the fact that Haifa University has a very significant Arab population in its student body did not lead to its being spared.

British academics in particular seemed to be searching for causes over which to boycott Israeli academics. But why would anyone boycott the very people in another society with whom one actually agrees, unless the problem was not their views but their existence?

The boycotts are not intended only to change Israeli behavior or Israeli policies. The usually unstated objection in much of academia is to Israel's mission. Many scholars would claim that this mission might be well meaning but that it is ultimately impossible or delusional. Few will say it so clearly, but for many, their preferred outcome is the destruction of the Jewish state.[20]

Unfair though they are, academic boycotts are enormously effective because they take aim at one of the most successful dimensions of Israeli life. If a nation-state's claim to success rests partly on its dynamic intellectual life, a particularly good way to undermine the argument for the nation-state is to undermine that intellectual life. An academic who is faced with the choice of staying in Israel and enduring a boycott or having a thriving career elsewhere might well choose to make a life in a different country.

Indeed, in a recent study of the problem of Israel's brain drain, two leading researchers concluded that "Israel is number one in terms of losing her educated citizens to the benefit of the U.S."[21] The added pressure of academic boycotts threatens to further the problem, robbing Israel of some of its best and brightest and pressuring some of Israel's most valuable citizens to make their contributions to a different country.

What is most disingenuous about these boycotts is the fact that academics are supposed to be able to discern the nuances of a complex situation, to see the gray in a discussion that people who are less trained might perceive as black and white. But these academics, by and large, have shown no penchant for nuance or balance. British academics have stubbornly refused to hear any pleas that Israel's point of view be heard. Nor have they been honest enough to acknowledge that what genuinely irks them is not Israel's treatment of the Palestinians but Israel's very existence. Their objection is part of a wider objection in the academic community to the very idea of the nation-state, but even those who are conscious of this hardly ever admit it.

Academics should surely know something about the history of boycotts in European anti-Semitism. Historian Anthony Julius offers numerous examples of instances in which boycotts were simply the first step on the road to something infinitely more pernicious. Some of the earliest boycotts of Jews, he notes, originated in France, and they were poorly camouflaged plans of a different sort. The French socialist P. J. Proudhon, Julius notes, first advocated boycotts of the Jews, insisting on their exclusion from all sorts of businesses and advocating the closure of their synagogues. But it wasn't long before Proudhon went further. "In the end, it will be necessary," Proudhon claimed, "to send this race back to Asia or exterminate it."[22] The Nazis also began with boycotts of Jewish businesses and professionals.

Julius articulates beautifully what boycotts really mean:

> What happens when people are boycotted? The ordinary courtesies of life are no longer extended to them. . . . The boycott is an act of violence, though of a paradoxical kind—one of recoil and exclusion rather than assault. . . . It is a denial, amongst other things, of the boycotted person's freedom of expression. . . . The boycott thus announces a certain moral distaste; it is always self-congratulatory.

And he continues:

> The academic boycott . . . was inconsistent with the general academic and political principles the boycotters professed to espouse; it punished indiscriminately—Israeli nationality was the only criterion; Jews would suffer disproportionately; it was not directed towards the achieving of any specific, achievable goals. The campaign was, in a word, irrational . . . and it was continuous with historical anti-Semitic discourse and practice.[23]

Julius is not the only British observer to have seen through the ruse. Howard Jacobson, a British novelist, pointed with irony to the boycotts' hypocrisy. The protagonist of his Booker Prize–winning novel *The Finkler Question* is Sam Finkler, a self-hating, anti-Zionist Jew. But Finkler is also an academic of sorts himself and therefore still harbors some commitment to freedom of intellectual exchange. He thus finds the academic boycotts as abhorrent as he does the Jewish state itself:

> Finkler had poured scorn on the idea, firstly because he thought it feeble—"What will we have next," he asked, "the Philatelic Association of Great Britain banning the licking of stamps in Israel?"—and secondly because it closed down conversation where conversation was most likely to bear fruit. "I am in principle against anything which denies dialogue or trade," he had said, "but to bar communication between intellectuals, who are always our best hope of peace, is particularly self-defeating and inane. It declares, inter alia, that we have a) made up our minds about what we think, b) closed our minds to what others think, and c) chosen to go on hearing nothing with which we happen to disagree."[24]

Throughout the novel, Finkler bashes Israel at every turn and at every opportunity. But the boycotts are too much even for him. For Finkler, the Zionist-bashing Jew, academic boycotts are the height not of intellectual purity but of cowardice and intellectual laziness at their very worst. It is unfortunate that Finkler is but a figment of Jacobson's creative imagination and not a real participant voicing the reason that this debate so desperately needs.

If only someone in the academic community who actually exists could make Finkler's point, noting that if what was at stake was Israel's morality, many other countries would also be the object of British boycotts. But no one makes that case as effectively as the fictional Finkler does. Israel has been selected for unique and unfair treatment.

The intellectual criticisms of nation-states, especially those with a religion at their core, is what leads to a commonly puzzled-over paradox. Many scholars criticize Iran for repressive belligerence while simultaneously criticizing Iran's favorite target, Israel. One might ask the following: How can you so stridently oppose the policies of two such very different countries that are actually in conflict with each other? Easily, it turns out—if you believe that both represent an outmoded reason for a country to exist.

That also explains why these critics spend so much more time attacking Israel: for it is infinitely more likely that Israel can be pressured into forgoing its role as the national home of the Jews than that Iran would give up being the national home of the Persians.

It is indeed quite possible that Israel can be more readily pressured than Iran or many other countries. It may even be possible to pressure Israel into nonexistence. But that does not make this unique pressure on Israel fair or smart. This is what Israel's intellectual foes should be asking themselves: What would make humanity better off, Israel becoming more like Iran, or Iran deciding that it wishes to emulate what Israel has become?

Chapter Four

UNIVERSALISM'S BETRAYAL

I was brought up as an idealist; I was taught that all people
were brothers, while outside in the street at every step I felt
that there were no people, only Russians, Poles, Germans, Jews
and so on . . . so I often said to myself that when I grew up
I would certainly destroy this evil.
                    —Ludwig Zamenhof, letter to Nikolai Borovko, ca. 1895[1]

In the late 1880s, two Russian men—young scholars who had been
born less than two years apart and scarcely a few hundred miles
away from each other—embarked on startling projects. They had
never met, and they never would. In fact, the two never exchanged as
much as a single letter.[2] Their careers and interests, however, proved to
be remarkably similar. Both had been raised as Jews and had received
substantive Jewish educations, but both were also enthralled with
secular European culture, which was now accessible to Jews in ways it
had never been before. Incredibly, each chose as his life's work a seemingly impossible undertaking: the creation of a language.

Their names were Ludwig Zamenhof and Eliezer Perlman.

Zamenhof decided to create an original language, whereas
Perlman chose to breathe new life into a long-unspoken one. With so

many professional and cultural options available to them in a recently emancipated Europe, what on earth could have motivated them to take on such seemingly thankless projects? Why did each undertake this strange journey of language creation, a project so ambitious that it was almost certainly destined for failure?

In order to understand Zamenhof and Perlman and the meaning of their respective ambitions, it's important to recall the context in which European Jews found themselves at that time. Not long before this, it had seemed that the social and legal emancipation of the Jews in western Europe would afford them a new opportunity to move out of the secluded and segregated communities in which they had lived for hundreds of years. Suddenly, Europe promised, Jews could leave the shtetl and become part of mainstream European society. Authors Jehuda Reinharz and Yaakov Shavit note the following:

> From the modern Jewish perspective, the nineteenth century opened with soaring hopes and expectations. David Frankel, one of the founding editors of the first Jewish periodical in German, *Shulamit*, expressed those hopes as follows: the "people of Abraham" were attempting, despite all the difficulties placed in their path, to attain recognition as equals in humanity, and *Kultur* (Culture) would enable them to embrace Europe. According to this optimistic view of the future, it was not Europe that would embrace the Jews who lived within its borders, but the Jews who would embrace Europe.[3]

The Jews would embrace Europe, accommodating themselves to the cultural and intellectual demands of the era. And why not, many asked. In this brave new world, Jews were being given legal rights and civil liberties for the first time. It would have been foolish to turn their backs on this great opportunity. Increasingly, they could join the intellectual world of Europe's great academies and enter professions previously off-limits to them. Jews not only saw themselves as beneficiaries of this trend, they even imagined that their ancestral faith would be given credit for what was unfolding across Europe.

"Jews described Judaism as a central partner in the historic creation of Europe and, moreover, described themselves as bearing a responsibility for Europe's destiny and future—and holding the keys to its salvation in their hands," Reinharz and Shavit explain.[4]

Dramatic change was afoot for Europe itself as well. Nationalism was all the rage. In 1848, the Swiss adopted a constitution, the Hungarians launched a revolution, and the move for German unification began. In the 1870s, both Bulgaria and Romania declared independence from the Ottoman Empire. Throughout the last decades of the century, people were organizing, building countries, defining borders, and celebrating cultures. An exciting world of unprecedented possibilities beckoned.

Might all of this change come together in a crescendo of new toleration? Could this be the moment that Jews would finally be accepted into France and Germany as French and German citizens? Would Jews be permitted to be genuine partners in these emerging nation-states, or would the new Europe simply invent new ways of marginalizing them?

The sad answer is that universalism has betrayed the Jews, time and again. It did so in the nineteenth century, and it does so today.

The ostensibly transformed Europe of the late 1800s brought mostly disappointment. The rich future for Jews that European intellectual openness had promised disappeared almost as quickly as it had arrived, leaving Jews angry, frustrated, and feeling betrayed.

Signs of this betrayal were everywhere. Russian intellectuals rabidly supported the vicious Russian pogroms that were a landmark of the early 1880s. In 1882, the First International Anti-Jewish Congress was held in Dresden, Germany, with the purpose of urging European governments "to make an effort to free themselves, their states, and their populations from the dictatorship of Jewish financial powers and thus from the political influence of Jewry." Karl Lueger, running on a viciously anti-Semitic platform, was elected mayor of Vienna in 1895. (His election was blocked at first by Emperor Franz Joseph, but the personal intervention of Pope Leo XIII allowed Lueger to assume his position in 1897.) Most notorious was the infamous Dreyfus affair of 1894 in France, leading many Jews to conclude that "enlightened" Europe had changed much less than they had previously hoped.[5]

Jews were concerned but also deeply divided. Some still held out hope that they might gain acceptance in Europe, whereas others were more despairing. Some continued to dream of a world united that might someday transcend states. That was in large measure the reason that so many Jews were attracted to socialism and other purportedly universalist movements. But other Jews began to place their hope in the nation-states just emerging. After the Dreyfus affair, even some radically secularized Jews like Theodor Herzl reached the conclusion that the only possible solution to the "Jewish problem" was a Jewish state, the title he eventually gave to his pioneering book.

Which would be better, a state for the Jews or a world without states? It was that often vitriolic debate that led Perlman and Zamenhof to set out on their respective language projects. Eliezer Perlman later changed his name to Eliezer Ben Yehuda ("Eliezer, son of Judah"). He became deeply attracted to Zionism; he believed that the future of the Jews should be charted in the land that had historically been theirs, where they could create a state along the lines of the states that were emerging in Europe. In order to do so, however, they would need to revive their ancient language. Ben Yehuda is recognized today as the father of modern Hebrew.

Zamenhof, in contrast, flirted with Zionism but left the movement soon after joining it. The solution to the Jewish problem, he believed, lay not in the creation of a Jewish state but in the forging of a universal society of the sort that Immanuel Kant, Emery Reves, and Strobe Talbott dreamed of (see chapter 3). Toward that very end, he sought to invent a new, universal language. He created Esperanto.

Ben Yehuda raised his children in Jerusalem and spoke to his son, Ben-Zion ("son of Zion"), only in Hebrew, effectively making the boy the first native Hebrew speaker in several thousand years. His project flourished: millions of people, his own descendants included, now speak Hebrew as their native language. Zamenhof stayed in Europe to pursue his universalist project, but it ultimately failed. He died in Warsaw, and all of his children were murdered by the Nazis.

Ben Yehuda and Zamenhof are long gone, but their implicit debate continues. It persists in the world at large between those who assert that the nation-state is the key to human flourishing and those who see the nation-state as a source of great evil, unmitigated violence, and terrible human suffering. More often than not, as we've noted, this debate focuses on the Jewish state.

Israel is plagued by enormous challenges and imperfections. The conflict with the Palestinians is ugly and has persisted for many more decades than it should have. The politics are rough-and-tumble, too often characterized by fraud and corruption. There are deep fissures in Israeli society between religious and secular, rich and poor, Ashkenazi and Sephardi. Driving in Israel can be appallingly dangerous, and even though the soldiers are, for the most part, thoroughly moral and decent, there are periodic cases of terrible misdeeds. All of that is the Israel one sees in the international media.

But there is another Israel, too, an Israel that makes possible the exploration of identity, culture, and diversity in ways that are not possible virtually anywhere else. It is an Israel in which ethnic sovereignty has afforded a people an opportunity to explore what it means to be committed to itself and to others. It is an Israel in which the very question of what it means to be a Jew is still being actively explored. It is an Israel that illustrates how profound life can be in the ethnic nation-state and how much would be lost were the nation-state to give way to universalism.

Why is this Israel so seldom described? Why does the international community show virtually no interest in this Israel?

No one has answered this question more pithily and incisively than Mark Lilla, a well-known Columbia University scholar of the humanities and political thought. Although most of his work does not address the nation-state, one of his articles in particular tackles the subject head-on. In "The End of Politics: Europe, the Nation-State, and the Jews," he explains why this Israel remains so unknown:

It is not the idea of tolerance that is in crisis in Europe today,
it is the idea of the nation-state, and the related concepts of
sovereignty and the use of force. . . . Many Western European
intellectuals, including those whose toleration and even affection for Jews cannot be questioned, find all this [the founding
of the state of Israel] incomprehensible. The reason is not anti-
Semitism nor even anti-Zionism in the usual sense. It is that
Israel is, and is proud to be, a nation-state—the nation-state of
the Jews. And that is profoundly embarrassing to post-national
Europe.[6]

The European problem with Israel, he insists, is not a problem with
Israel but a problem with Europe:

For many in Western Europe today, learning the grim lesson
of modern history has also brought with it a forgetting of all
the long-standing problems that the nation-state, as a modern
form of political life, managed to solve. The Zionist tradition
knows what those problems were. It remembers what it was to
be stateless, and the indignities of tribalism and imperialism.
It remembers the wisdom of borders and the need for collective autonomy to establish self-respect and to demand respect
from others. . . . Eventually Western Europeans will have to
re-learn these lessons, which are, after all, the lessons of their
own pre-modern history. Until they do, the mutual incompre-
hension regarding Israel between Europeans and Jews committed to Zionism will remain deep. There is indeed a new
Jewish problem in Europe, because there is a new political
problem in Europe.[7]

Lilla's point is ours precisely. The problem that the world has with
Israel is not the conflict, not the Palestinians, and not even necessarily the Jews. The problem is that Zionists remember statelessness and
the indignities that come with it. They know the need for borders.
But the very existence of borders is a challenge to what Europe *thinks*
it would like to become. So Europe assails the messenger, and because

Israel stands for nation-states and for difference, Israel has become the enemy.

This "problem in Europe," which we are preoccupied with in this book, is also the subject of Pierre Manent's brilliant book, *Democracy without Nations? The Fate of Self-Government in Europe*. Manent notes that the tide of public opinion has turned against difference not only in Europe, as Lilla and others have pointed out, but in the United States as well. The United States and Europe, with their mistaken directions, are our new twin towers of Babel.

In some ways, Manent admits, the United States and Europe are different. The U.S. model is committed to preserving nations and being willing to use force when necessary. Europe, on the other hand, is concerned less with nations than with the idea of pure democracy. But—and this is the critical point—as different as they are, the United States and Europe have one essential trait in common: they are "animated by a vision of a world in which no collective difference is significant." The United States and Europe, each a tower of Babel that would eradicate difference, may differ from each other, but they share a blindness as well: "We no longer appreciate the fact that separations between and among human groups cannot be entirely overcome. Nor do we see that this fortunate impotence is the condition of human liberty and diversity."[8]

"Fortunate impotence" is a strange notion, but Manent means it. We are fortunate, he is telling us, that we are unable to erase our differences, for differentness is key to liberty. Manent is right, and the European universalists are wrong. Human difference is not regrettable; it is the glory of humanity. Competing cultures need not lead to war. What leads to war is the absence of democracy and one people's desire to rule another and to snuff out the other's distinctiveness.

The world was right to be horrified at the unprecedented bloodletting of the twentieth century. But the world would be wrong to seek to prevent future bloodbaths by eliminating the nation-state, for if it succeeded in doing so, it would bequeath to subsequent generations a thin and anemic sense of identity (or worse, a sense of identity forged underground, heated in the fires of vengeance). Such a meaningless sense of identity is neither worth saving nor worthy of defense, and young people raised on the pale notion that human beings are all the same might not recognize attacks on their freedom until it is far too late.

There are signs everywhere that the sameness that the European Union seeks to force on the Continent is being met with resistance. Long before the financial crises in Greece, Ireland, and Spain put unforeseen pressures on the union, it was clear that a Europe devoid of difference was the dream of Europe's elites but not of the women and men who actually lived, worked, loved, and died in those countries. The fact of the European Union has done little to alter the sentiments of its citizens. Author Sidney Tarrow notes, "As the European Union was creating a single market and instituting a common currency, the proportion of those whose primary attachments were local or national remained more than 80 percent and hardly budged over time. Nor is there an overall trend toward greater European attachments, and these remain well below national or local identities."[9] Of course, one only has to look to the distinctly ethnic countries created in the aftermath of the fall of the Soviet Union and then Yugoslavia, and more recent headlines in Europe, dealing with debt crisis after debt crisis, to discover whether national identities have begun to fade away.

They have not, for as Lilla and Manent (and Zionism) understand, difference is essentially part of the human DNA. What Europe's elites seek to do is deny who we are. What Zionism seeks to do is recover who we are. That is the root cause of Europe's battle with the Jewish state.

Those who will triumph in this "brave" new (and supposedly post-difference) world—which is actually a cowardly new world—are those who refuse to give up on their identities, those who take pride in their heritage, and those who revere what they have been taught by their ancestors. In today's world, ironically, it is Islam that has taken this to heart. Long ago George Eliot wrote, speaking through the mouth of the character of Daniel Deronda, "A sentiment may seem to be dying and yet revive into strong life. . . . Nations have revived. We may live to see a great outburst of force in the Arabs, who are being inspired with a new zeal."[10]

She penned those words in 1876; how prescient she was. The Jewish state has had the misfortune of waging two battles at the same time. On the security-military front, geography has destined Israel to an ongoing struggle with its Arab neighbors, who, fueled by the zeal of which George Eliot wrote, have yet to reconcile themselves to the fact of Israel's existence. On the intellectual front, Israel has ineluctably taken on Europe's desperate desire to move beyond the very difference to which Israel is committed. Israel is thus at war not only because of geography but also because of ideology. Because the world has grown impatient with a conflict it cannot resolve, the international community holds Israel accountable for insisting on difference in an era of sameness; it thus blames Israel simply for being.

Just savor the irony. Rallying the world to the cause of democracy and toleration, Western intellectual elites have picked a beacon of democracy and toleration as their greatest enemy. To achieve their cause, they bypass democracy and call for intolerance, making common cause with the Middle East's most egregious defenders of authoritarianism and oppression.

The irony notwithstanding, we must be perfectly clear: whether Israel can survive matters not only for the Jews. As Manent and others have noted, the human difference that Israel now represents is essential to more than "mere" human heterogeneity. (Manent is a Catholic.[11]) It is ultimately about human freedom. If the world loses the former, it will also end up mourning the latter. Our freedom is ultimately about the right to be different. It is about the right to forge our own path, to make our own mistakes, and to go to hell in our own way, to paraphrase Yale professor Jed Rubenfeld.[12]

Ultimately, if we are just like everyone else, it will not matter who rules us. If we are not characterized by difference, there will be no need to defend our liberty, and in time we will allow it to be taken from us. We defend our liberty, and we send our sons and daughters to war at a horrific cost in the name of protecting it, because we believe that there is something unique about us that we dare not lose or let be taken away.

Whether human freedom survives depends on whether human difference survives. And to know what will happen with difference, we will have to see whether the world can cease its demagogic battering of the Jewish state. To many people, particularly in Europe's intellectual elites, Israel now represents a model that the world wisely wants to abandon but that the Jews refuse to relinquish. The challenge now facing Europe and the United States, however, is to rethink their instinctive dismissal of the Jewish state, and to learn to see Israel's insistence on the glory of human difference as critical to the ongoing battle to preserve freedom for people everywhere.

There is, however, an additional facet of universalism's betrayal of the Jews. Beyond the Jews' insistence on a nation-state and the difference that it entails, there is another ugly underbelly to Europe's hatred of Israel. Some of the hostility to Israel is, undeniably, hostility to the Jews. It's possible that the world could ignore a Kurdish nation-state, for instance, in a way that it cannot stop talking about the Jewish one.

The Israeli author Amos Oz has noted with irony that when his father was growing up in Europe, he saw signs that read YIDS, GO TO PALESTINE. And when his father finally arrived in Palestine, the signs read, YIDS, OUT OF PALESTINE.[13] In many ways, the world's rejection of Israel and Zionism is nothing but the new avatar of an ancient hatred.

Anthony Julius notes, "The blood libel has been revived, but as a variation on the blood libel."[14] It is in the context of the blood libel, he suggests, that we need to understand Suha Arafat's claim that Israel was using poison gas against the Palestinians or the common Palestinian claim that Israeli doctors have injected the AIDS virus into Palestinian children. All this, Julius argues, is simply hatred of the Jew in a new form. "Every call to boycott Jews or the Jewish State contains with it every previous such call. Anti-Semitism's discursive history makes this unavoidable. A poisoning allegation, a boycott call, can never be innocent."[15]

But no one really needs to even pretend innocence any longer. The hatred of Jews has become socially acceptable once again, just as it was in Europe in the early 1930s. Helen Thomas, the now infamous

White House press corps journalist, lost her job in 2010 for saying that the Jews should "get the hell out of Palestine" and go back to Poland and Germany (countries in which they had been exterminated, of course). Writing only a few days later, Shelby Steele of the Hoover Institution at Stanford University observed the following:

> This is something new in the world, this almost complete segregation of Israel in the community of nations. And if Helen Thomas's remarks were pathetic and ugly, didn't they also point to the end game of this isolation effort: the nullification of Israel's legitimacy as a nation? There is a chilling familiarity in all this. One of the world's oldest stories is playing out before our eyes: The Jews are being scapegoated again.[16]

Leon de Winter, a Dutch novelist, noted in the pages of the *Wall Street Journal* in 2010 that anti-Semitism had become socially acceptable once again. When he wrote those words, controversy about Gaza was raging, the Goldstone report was still creating a stir, and Israeli soldiers had recently battled members of a "humanitarian" flotilla headed for Gaza. (Goldstone ultimately repudiated many of his own conclusions; see chapter 3.) The international press was screaming that Israel was starving the Gazans, but de Winter noted that the world had simply turned on Israel for reasons having nothing to do with the Palestinians. In fact, he amassed some statistics that would surprise many readers of the world's most influential newspapers:

> Here are some more facts—lousy, stubborn facts. Let's look at the infant mortality rate in Gaza. It is a key number that says a lot about the state of hygiene, nutrition, and health care. In Israel the infant mortality rate is 4.17 per 1,000 births, which is about the same as in Western countries. In Sudan the rate is 78.1, that is, one in 13 infants die[s] at birth. In Gaza, infant mortality per 1,000 births is 17.71. Yes, that's higher than in Israel, but much lower than in Sudan. And Turkey's infant mortality rate? Well, that's 24.84. Yes, more infants die at birth in Turkey than in Gaza. . . .

The progressives don't care for any other group of poor or suppressed Muslims. They only cry for the "victims" of the Jews. Why is that so?[17]

Indeed, why is that so? De Winter proposed the following theory:

Europeans, who represent much of what goes for world opinion, have grown tired of carrying the guilt for the destruction of the Continent's Jews. They have started to long for some form of historical release. That comes in the form of Israel's military response to Islamist attacks and terror. The Europeans couldn't suppress the chance to defame the Jews and redefine Israel's defense measures as either "disproportionate" or outright aggression—war crimes, in other words.[18]

He concluded that "the media's wild indignation, an orgasm of hypocrisy, marks the next chapter in the long story of European hatred toward the Jews. It is *salonfähig* again to be an anti-Semite."[19]

Christopher Caldwell offered a slightly different explanation of Europe's "pile-on" of Israel:

With their own nationalisms off limits, many Europeans were tempted to embrace vicariously the nationalisms of others— particularly Palestinian nationalism, which, in its most radical versions, allowed Europeans to reconnect with a discredited strand of European nationalism, anti-Semitism. [20]

De Winter and Caldwell are both right. The collective sense of guilt after the Shoah has now abated, and formerly muffled voices are now reasserting themselves, clearly and loudly. Much of the world has joined the chorus, voicing its utter disgust with Israel with ever greater urgency and even anger, when it has really just tired of the Jews themselves.

In an era of nuclear weapons that can destroy the planet several times over, the notion that *ideas* are the most formidable weapon we have in our possession may sound strange. But it is true. Karl Marx wrote *The Communist Manifesto* in 1848; by 1905, Russia was rocked by revolutions that peaked in 1917 and overthrew the czar. Jean-Jacques Rousseau wrote his *Social Contract* in 1762; the French Revolution followed a mere twenty-seven years later. John Locke wrote *Two Treatises of Government* in 1690; less than a century later, the American Revolution changed the course of modern history. Mary Wollstonecraft penned *A Vindication of the Rights of Woman* in 1792; women's suffrage followed in New Zealand—the first country to give women the vote—almost exactly a century later. Theodor Herzl wrote *The Jewish State* in 1896, and, fifty-two years later, David Ben-Gurion stood in Tel Aviv on May 14, 1948, and declared Israel's independence.[21]

Without Marx, Rousseau, Locke, Wollstonecraft, or Herzl—to say nothing of Sigmund Freud and many others—our world and our ways of thinking about our world would be simply unrecognizable. And all that those people did, essentially, was to write books and disseminate ideas.

Ideas matter. They shape history. It is ideas, even more than wealth or territory, over which people go to war. Witness the conflict between radical Islam and the Western world today. That too is mostly about ideas. Islamic fundamentalists and terrorists do not seek the West's wealth. Nor are they (yet) trying to take its territory. What they are doing, especially in western Europe, is attacking European culture. Their battle with Europe is about values and ideas. So too is the world's battle with Israel.

To much of the world, Israel has become the embodiment of ideas that humanity should jettison. As noted briefly in the introduction, Jews drew very different conclusions from the horrors of the twentieth century than did much of Europe. After World War II, Europe began to despair of the nation-state, whereas for Jews, what suddenly mattered more than anything else was the creation of a country of their own. Europe began to speak in terms of transcending human difference, whereas Jews sought a home specifically for their own people.

Unlike the European Union, Israel has never pretended that borders don't matter. Instead of surrendering their identities in the aftermath of the Shoah and giving up on their future, Jews dreamed even bigger. They would have a state just as others did. They would chart the course of their own lives as other peoples did. And if Israel were successful, they imagined, the country that they were about to create could be the model of what countries could become.

Rather than pretend that all human beings were essentially the same, the Jews, thanks to their new country, would celebrate their differentness. In defiance of the world's insistence on the denial of difference, Israel insisted on the "dignity of difference."[22] Israelis chose Ben Yehuda over Zamenhof, Hebrew over Esperanto, and their own heritage over some imagined universal culture. Israel was a choice of difference over the ideal of sameness, a preference for the particular over the global, and for the Jews' own story over some anemic panhuman narrative. But in making that choice to be different, the Jews—even though they could not then have fully anticipated how this might come back to haunt them and their young state—were embarking on a path that was destined to put them at odds with the prevailing ethos of Europe and much of the rest of the world.

The real battle over Israel's survival is thus unfolding not in the skies over the Sinai desert or on the steep slopes of the Golan Heights. Terrorism certainly remains a threat, along with the possibility of old conflicts with Arab neighbors becoming reignited. But the real battle over the future of the Jewish state is now being fought in the court of public opinion. It is a battle not of tanks but of principles and of worldview; its weapons are not bullets but keyboards.

The decision to take the battle against Israel into the realm of ideas was a brilliant strategic move on the part of Israel's enemies. The Arab-Israeli wars of 1948, 1956, 1967, and 1973 proved to them that their standing armies were not going to be able to destroy the Jewish state. So they abandoned that tactic. Then the economic boycotts of the 1970s also failed. Although terrorism killed many people and filled the lives of many more with daily dread, it also failed to bring an end to the Jewish state or even to weaken it. On the ground and in battle, Israel could be wounded, but it could not be defeated.

So what did Israel's enemies do? Brilliantly, they discovered the power of ideas. It was ironic that the discovery of the power of ideas in the Arab-Israeli conflict would emerge from a culture so committed to repressing ideas in the populations that were its own citizens. But consciously or not, the Arab world—and subsequently, Israel's enemies all over the world—decided that Israel could be felled without warplanes, tanks, or bullets. They could demolish Israel simply by working to delegitimize it at every turn and, in more intellectual circles, by asserting that the very idea of a Jewish state was a mistaken notion.

Although they might not recognize it explicitly, the Palestinians and other Arab nations have come to understand that military or political events are an opportunity to provide the delegitimizers with more evidence of Israel's folly, or worse. If this alleged evidence is spun right, Israel could be destroyed not with fighter planes but with words.

The Palestinians, and Israel's enemies across the globe, have discovered that if you call Israel repressive or an apartheid state, then you can begin to do inestimable damage to the very idea of a Jewish state. "See," they tacitly argue, "a Jewish nation-state in our region is by its very nature repressive, discriminatory, and therefore illegitimate." That was why the Arab states pressured the United Nations to vote, in November 1975, on a resolution that asserted that Zionism is a form of racism. (The resolution passed, but it was revoked in 1991; no other U.N. resolution has ever been revoked.)

Taking a page from these Arab states, a growing group of individuals thus seeks to undermine Israel by undermining the very notion of the ethnic nation-state, the idea that is essentially Israel's foundation. They do more, of course. They suggest that Zionism should be tossed onto the garbage heap of history, as was done with discredited ideologies like apartheid and communism; they undermine Israel by claiming that the very notion of the nation-state has run its course. Once again, a universal ethic is turning on the Jews, this time on their state.

That is why the conversation about Israel's legitimacy must be expanded to include the profound ideas that are key to the sophisticated defense of the nation-state in general and of the Jewish state in particular. What is more critical than ever before is a renewed discussion of the ways in which the nation-state can heal the wounds of universalism; we need a conversation about the relationship between the nation-state and human diversity and, ultimately, about the relationship between the nation-state and human freedom. We must, before it is too late, recraft the discussion of Israel's future so that it is not merely about borders or violence but about human dignity and freedom.

Chapter Five

A BIBLICAL TUG-OF-WAR

It is necessary to promote a culture of peace
which does not reject a healthy patriotism
but keeps far away from the exasperations
and exclusions of nationalism.
                —Pope John Paul II, speaking in Croatia in 1994[1]

Popes do not often visit Albania. Indeed, when Pope John Paul II
went there in 1993, he was the first pope to do so since 1464. More
than five hundred years had passed since the previous visit. So why
did John Paul II consider it so important to go to this usually little-
noticed country? The answer had to do not with Albania but with
its neighbor to the north, Bosnia. The former Yugoslavia had already
exploded into sectarian and nationalist violence, and the battle threatened to spread to Albania, too. The pope wanted to urge Albanians
not to go that route.

Particularly interesting about the pope's visit was his warning
to the Albanians to steer clear of war. "True religious freedom
avoids the temptations of intolerance and sectarianism," he said. "Do
not let the sense of nationalism that you feel strongly at this moment
degenerate into the kind of intolerant and aggressive nationalism

that claims its victims still today and fuels ferocious hatreds in several parts of the world, some not far from here."[2]

Embedded in nationalism, the pope was saying, are dangers of intolerance and aggression. Although he spoke to a Balkan audience, the pope could easily have intended his advice for the Middle East; the suggestion that "intolerant and aggressive nationalism" is at the root of conflicts across the world could just as well have been meant as a warning that the conflict between Israel and its neighbors was also the result of nationalism run amok, and that with a more universal attitude on the part of the combatants, the conflict could be settled.

Although the pope was speaking in relatively recent times, the battle of ideas between the visions of universalism and particularism that he was echoing is ancient. It persists today in debates about the European Union and in arguments about the nation-state, but it actually originated long ago. Thus, in order to truly understand the battle of ideas in which contemporary Israel is trapped, to truly understand the long interplay between tribal attachments and government, we have to go back not just to the late nineteenth century but even earlier, to the world of the Bible.

We might be surprised that the Hebrew Bible (commonly called the Old Testament) addresses critical questions about nationalism and even the ideal state, but we shouldn't be. After all, the opening chapters of Genesis are all about the "big questions." The story of creation raises issues of the relationship between human beings and heaven, as well as the purpose of creation itself. The story of the Garden of Eden explores questions of temptation, sin, responsibility, and sexuality. The drama of Cain and Abel grapples with jealousy, anger, hatred, and murder, whereas the Flood deals with the inevitable imperfection of humanity. It is in these early chapters of Genesis that the Bible lays out the questions that are the core issue of what philosophers often call "the examined life."

The Tower of Babel is an integral part of this series of stories. The tale of the tower is meant to present a new idea, to say something about the Bible's politics. Indeed, it is here, in God's rejection of the

Tower of Babel project, that the Bible introduces the idea of universalism and rejects it; it is here that the germ of the idea of the nation-state first appears:

> Everyone on earth had the same language and the same words. And as they migrated from the east, they came upon a valley in the land of Shinar and settled there. They said to one another, "Come, let us make bricks and burn them hard." Brick served them as stone, and bitumen served them as mortar. And they said, "Come, let us build us a city, and a tower with its top in the sky, to make a name for ourselves; else we shall be scattered all over the world." The Lord came down to look at the city and tower that man had built, and the Lord said, "If, as one people with one language for all, this is how they have begun to act, then nothing that they conspire to do will be out of their reach. Let us, then, go down and confound their speech there, so that they shall not understand one another's speech." Thus the Lord scattered them from there over the face of the whole earth, and they stopped building the city. That is why it was called Babel, because there the Lord confounded the speech of the whole earth, and from there the Lord scattered them over the face of the whole earth.[3]

The opening verse, "Everyone on earth had the same language and the same words," may seem innocuous, but it is not. For immediately before this story, Genesis recounts the narrative of the Flood and its aftermath. The end of the Flood is the beginning of a new world order. After the waters have subsided, we are told, "These three were the sons of Noah, and from these the whole world branched out."[4] Indeed, this "branching out" seems so important that Genesis goes to great lengths to repeat it time and again, all in the space of a few verses. Even the names of some of the people in Genesis are intended to focus us on dispersion: "Two sons were born to Eber," we are told. "The name of the first was Peleg [Hebrew for "division"], for in his days, the earth was divided."[5]

What does it mean for these sons and their families to branch out? What is really occurring at this stage of biblical history is not the

departure of individuals from one another but rather *peoples* branching out, each people growing distinct from the others. "From these
the maritime *nations* branched out. [These are the descendants of
Japheth] by their lands, each with their language, their claims, and
their *nations*."[6] In other verses nearby, an all but identical formulation
is used to recap the genealogies of Noah's other two sons, Ham and
Shem. These are the first uses of the Hebrew word *goy*, or "nation," in
the Bible. And once it is introduced, the word appears over and over
again in the space of a very few verses.

The repetition leaves little room for doubt about what the Bible
wants the reader to learn from this story: the dispersion of nations, each
coalescing around its own common land, language, and lineage, is the
ideal condition for humanity after the Flood. As God refashions
the earth, humanity is very different from what it had been. Now
humanity is split into distinct groups, each with its own people, land,
and language. This division of humanity into peoples is no accident; division is the new ideal, a critical characteristic of this newly
re-created world. As the political philosopher Leo Strauss understood
the story, the solitary image of Noah's ark floating alone on the waters
of the flood is intentionally replaced by the image of a multitude of
nations: "The division of mankind into nations may be described as
a milder alternative to the Flood. . . . The emergence of nations made
it possible that Noah's Ark floating alone on the waters covering
the whole earth be replaced by a whole, numerous nation living in the
midst of the nations covering the whole earth."[7]

We can now begin to appreciate how significant the first verse of
the Tower of Babel story really is. If "everyone on earth had the same
language and the same words," then something had gone wrong. After
the flood, that is not how humanity is meant to live; not for nothing
did Esperanto fail. Without a multiplicity of languages, humanity loses
the variety of lenses through which it can think and imagine. Human
beings, the Bible insists, *are supposed* to scatter. They *ought* to have different languages, for languages are much more than mere means of
communication; as Ludwig Wittgenstein, a twentieth-century Austrian
philosopher, wrote, "The limits of my language mean the limits of
my world."[8] Our languages define how we see the universe; that

is why it was critical that different nations develop their individual worldviews not only by living in different locations but by speaking different languages.

But the builders of the Tower of Babel rejected this ideal. They wanted to build a tower that would bind them all together; they rejected the idea of territorial, cultural, and linguistic diversity that the book of Genesis sees as being critical to a flourishing human species. It was that refusal to disperse, to become different and heterogeneous—not the building of the tower per se—that was their real sin.[9]

God's response, therefore, was to thwart this enterprise by making it impossible for them to communicate with one another; God used language to force them to separate. "If, as one people with one language for all, this is how they have begun to act, then nothing that they may propose to do will be out of their reach. Let us, then, go down and confound their speech." And "from there the Lord scattered them over the face of the whole earth."[10]

Given this reading of the Tower of Babel story, it's clear that the concept of nationalism is not a new idea (even if nations were a good bit smaller back then). This image of distinct, particular group identities based on common languages and cultures did not originate with modern Europe, as some scholars claim.[11] Rather, these notions have been an integral part of Western civilization from its very beginning.[12] Much of the Bible is actually an attempt to explore this theme of the nation-state as an ideal way for human beings to organize themselves.

Once the Bible has made this basic claim about the importance of distinct nations, it zooms in on one particular people and its quest for a land of its own. Immediately after the Tower of Babel story, the Bible introduces Abram, later renamed Abraham, who will be the father of a family; that family will become a clan, which in turn will ultimately become the Jewish people. But in order for this future people to emerge, Abram is told that he must secure the one ingredient that every flourishing nation needs: a home in a specific land. Thus, the very first thing that God says to him is "Go forth from your native *land* . . . to the *land* that I will show you."[13] In exchange for this, Abram is promised, God will make his clan into a real nation: "I will make you exceedingly fertile, and make nations of you; and kings shall come forth from you."[14]

As readers of the Bible know, the future doesn't unfold quite that smoothly for Abraham's clan. He heads for Canaan, but in the years after his arrival, his family must head south to Egypt several times because of famine in Canaan. As the book of Genesis closes, the Israelites (only seventy in number at that time) have settled in Egypt. As the curtain rises on the book of Exodus, their situation becomes dire. The Israelites have increased to a thriving population of about six hundred thousand men, which might well have meant a total Israelite population of several million people; the pharaoh feels threatened by them and enslaves them.[15]

Once the Israelites are trapped in Egypt, the Tower of Babel's message is suddenly urgent. The builders of the tower had sought to remain in one place, but God's plan was that each people should seek its own territory. That is what the Israelites now want. The issue is not only their enslavement, as horrific as that is; it is also that as long as they reside in a foreign land, they cannot chart the course of their own future.

Because we commonly think of the pharaoh who enslaved the Israelites as evil, it is easy to forget that he is also deeply insightful: he is the one who first refers to the Israelites as "the *people*, the children of Israel," *am benei yisrael*.[16] He understands that they are more than a clan; they have become a nation, with the urge for independence that nationhood often entails. It is Pharaoh who introduces the notion of the Jewish people.

His instinct is to protect himself: "Let us deal shrewdly with them, so that they may not increase; otherwise, in the event of war they may join our enemies in fighting against us and go up from this land."[17] Note what Pharaoh fears. He is not concerned that the Israelites will topple his kingdom. He's too smart for that. He understands their basic human desire: it is the wish, as Israel's national anthem, "Hatikva," says to this day in its penultimate line, "to be a free people in our own land." Pharaoh knows that the Israelites will not try to conquer *his* land; because they are a nation, they are destined to seek a homeland of their own.

The story of the Exodus is therefore in some ways the fulfillment of the vision of the Tower of Babel. In the Tower of Babel story, humanity is instructed that distinctiveness, heterogeneity, and uniqueness are what they should seek; in the Exodus narrative, the additional requirements of freedom and independence are added—the Israelites become the Bible's model of a people desperately seeking to make that dream a reality.

Indeed, the link between the stories of the Tower of Babel and of the Exodus is beautifully hinted at in the Bible with one simple literary detail: the Hebrew word *leveinim*, or "bricks." The word *leveinim* appears in only two stories in all of the Five Books of Moses. It appears first in the Tower of Babel story, when the people discover their ability to make bricks and therefore to build the tower ("'Come, let us bake *leveinim* and burn them hard.' [So the] *leveinim* served them as stone."[18]) The second and only other time that the word is used is at the beginning of Exodus, in the recounting of the awful burdens of production placed upon the Israelite slaves: "Be off now to your work! No straw shall be issued to you, but you must produce your quota of bricks!"[19]

The appearance of the word *leveinim* in only these two stories is the Bible's literary way of telling the reader that the stories are intimately connected. The linkage between the tales makes a clear point: there are multiple forms of slavery. One is the standard form of slavery, a physical enslavement, typically enforced with brutality. It is the slavery that the Israelites endured in Egypt and to which Africans were subjected in the antebellum South. The other enslavement is not physical but is rather is about erasing identity. It is enslavement not to taskmasters but to a vision of a unified humanity. No force is needed to create this kind of slavery. All that is necessary is for people to abandon their differences, to have no conception of why they matter.

The Bible associates the Tower of Babel with the story of the Exodus because it wishes to note that both of these slaveries are utterly at odds with what human beings are meant to be. The Bible has an *ideal* for humanity, a vision in which each nation lives on its own land, with its own language and its own culture. With the Exodus, the Israelites embark on a journey to transform that universal dream into a reality. With the Exodus, the proverbial train of human history has left the station. The Israelites make their way to the Promised Land through the remainder of the Torah. Throughout the rest of the

Bible's historical books, they engage in the messy but necessary business of nation building.

An epilogue to the long biblical history of the Jews is found in the books of Ezra and Nehemiah. Here Cyrus, king of Persia, grants the Jews permission to return to their homeland and to rebuild the walls of Jerusalem and even the Temple itself.[20] The Bible's historical narrative thus ends not with destruction but with a reminder of the never-ending potential for rebuilding a people's sovereign state.

As if to stress the importance of Cyrus's decree and the critical significance of the Israelites' return to their ancient homeland, 2 Chronicles (the very last book of the Hebrew Bible) concludes with the same story of Cyrus urging the Jews to return to their land. Indeed, the very last paragraph of the entire Hebrew Bible reads as follows:

> The Lord roused the spirit of King Cyrus of Persia to issue a proclamation throughout his realm by word of mouth and in writing, as follows: "Thus said King Cyrus of Persia: The Lord God of Heaven has given me all the kingdoms of the earth, and has charged me with building Him a House in Jerusalem, which is in Judah. Anyone of you of all His people, the Lord His God be with him and let him go up."[21]

Just as the word *leveinim* linked the Tower of Babel to the Exodus, the very last word of the Hebrew Bible links the Exodus to Cyrus. Pharaoh predicted that the Israelites would seek to "go up" (*ve-alah*) from the land of Egypt. Now Cyrus encourages the Israelites to "go up" (*ve-ya'al*) to their ancestral land and to rebuild it. (It is no coincidence that in modern Hebrew, the language at the heart of Zionism, the same root yields the word *aliyah*, which literally means "going up" but is used to mean "moving to Israel.")

The Bible thus ends with a reminder of the message of the Tower of Babel. Seen this way, the Bible is an ancient argument for states and for boundaries, for human difference. Human beings thrive best, the Bible asserts, if they find a home and contribute to its cultural

enrichment. It is in that homeland that they will have their own language, their own heritage, and their own way of life. In their own lands,
the Bible believes, peoples have a chance at uniqueness. Armed with
that uniquity, they could well be on their way to genuine freedom.[22]

All of this raises some vexing questions. The Hebrew Bible is clearly a
critical document in the history of the West—the iconic literary critic
Harold Bloom uses the phrase "the shadow of a great rock" to refer to the
relationship between the Bible and Western civilization.[23] If the value of
human differentness and its expression in the nation-state is so central to
the Bible's worldview, how has this biblical ideal ended up on the defensive? How did a competing ideal, rampant universalism, so thoroughly
capture the hearts and minds of so much of the West? Why the antipathy
to the nation-state, which often finds expression as objections to Israel?

The answer is that while the Hebrew Bible did indeed have a
profound influence on the West, its impact was mitigated by the fact
that in Christianity it has been read through the prism of the New
Testament, which has a very different vision of humanity perfected.

Whereas the Hebrew Bible (the Christian Bible's Old Testament)
is a very political book, interested in nations, kings, wars, and power,
the New Testament is essentially apolitical. It does, of course, recognize that humanity is composed of diverse peoples. Paul speaks to the
people of Corinth, and what emerges is the First and Second Letters
to the Corinthians. He addresses the people of Rome, and his message
then makes up his Letter to the Romans. In the apocalyptic vision
of the Revelation of John, the narrator says, "After that I saw a huge
number, impossible to count, of people from every nation, race, tribe
and language; they were standing in front of the throne [of God]."[24]

But having an *awareness* of the existence of various peoples is very
different from *advocating* those divisions, or from seeing them as critical. The New Testament does not see the existence of multiple peoples
as necessary; rather, it believes that in its ideal state, humanity will
transcend these fissures.

These competing conceptions of the ideal human life are communicated in numerous ways when we compare the Hebrew Bible and

the New Testament. The Hebrew Bible devotes enormous swaths of text to the issue of land, including the promise that a particular people will inherit a specific land and the listing of the commandments that will be in effect when that people reaches its land. These concepts are entirely absent from the New Testament. In fact, references to land appear almost fifteen hundred times in the Hebrew Bible but only a few dozen times in the New Testament.

The two biblical worldviews are thus concerned with very different sorts of kingdoms. The word *kingdom* appears throughout the Hebrew Bible, but it refers to rule by kings of flesh and blood, not an otherworldly Kingdom of God. In the Hebrew Bible, God's plan for humanity is often set in motion through the actions of human rulers: kings and battles, victories and defeats. In the New Testament, in contrast, the realms of kings and God are entirely separate: "Render unto Caesar the things that are Caesar's, and unto God the things that are God's," urges the famous verse in the Gospel according to Matthew.[25] The New Testament is interested not in the kingdoms of men, but in the Kingdom of God, a phrase that never appears in the Hebrew Bible but appears in the New Testament more than sixty times, including almost fifty times in the three Synoptic Gospels (Matthew, Mark, and Luke) alone.

Some of this difference may have arisen from political strategy. The Hebrew Bible, say some scholars, was subversive, a document that urged the establishment of a society in stark contrast to the social and political orders found in the surrounding cultures of the ancient Near East (Egypt, Mesopotamia, Ugarit, and the Hittite Empire).[26] In contrast, scholars suggest, the New Testament may have purposely played down the parts of its message that were likely to arouse Roman ire. The strategy, they say, was to avoid conflict with Rome so that the Christian message could spread, which it did.[27] The New Testament thus stays away from issues of politics in order to make its message as compatible as possible with the existing power structures of its time.

Perhaps one of the most striking indications of the New Testament's uninterest in, or even antipathy toward, differences between nations is found in the Letter to the Galatians. There, Paul says, "There is neither Jew nor Greek, slave nor free, male nor female, for you are all one in Christ Jesus."[28] Because of the Christian apocalyptic emphasis on the Kingdom of God, the New Testament focuses on a vision of a wholly redeemed world rather than on the political and divided world that now exists.

To be sure, there was a long period when the Catholic Church was distinctly political, when it was deeply involved in territorial acquisitions and was in fact the most powerful imperialist force on earth. Beginning with Charlemagne in 800 CE and continuing for many centuries, the church was consumed with conquest.

There is a fine line between imperialism and universalism, for both fundamentally reject the importance of difference. Today, rather than endorsing imperialism, the church espouses positions that are much closer to the New Testament's original apolitical universalism. During a trip to Croatia in 1994 (during which he also made his stop in Albania), Pope John Paul II made the statement about "the exasperations . . . of nationalism" that opens this chapter.

Ironically, the pope was speaking about the "exasperations" of nationalism in a region that had been torn asunder after a failed attempt to artificially amalgamate several different ethnicities. Serbs, Croats, Bosnians, and Slovenes had no desire to be forced to unite in an artificial Yugoslavia, but the pope seemed to refuse to hear the human aspiration for independence and national individuality that lay at the core of Yugoslavia's demise. "We can almost see the footsteps on the way God wants you to follow in this difficult moment of history," he said, asking those assembled, "Has not history created thousands of unbreakable ties between your peoples? Your languages, although different, are they not so close that you can communicate and understand each other more than the peoples of other parts of Europe can?"[29]

In its own way, the pope's call for peace was a denial of the insights of the Tower of Babel. "Your languages are different," he essentially said, "but they're close enough for you to communicate. Why, then, not live together?" The answer is because that is not what peoples need, as the Hebrew Bible explains. It is contrary to each identity's DNA. What Pharaoh understood, the pope refused to hear. The differences between these warring peoples, the pope seemed to be saying, mattered much less than putting their history aside and learning to live together. That their desire to live apart from one another might stem from a profound yearning for uniqueness, for celebrating their cultures and seeking the flowering of traditions that they had nurtured for years, did not seem to cross his mind.

The debate around the concept of the nation-state—and, as a result, around the Jewish state—is thus the product of a long-standing tension between the Hebrew Bible and the New Testament. When the church was an empire, it conquered whatever and whomever it could in order to spread the word of God, combining one and all into a single kingdom. Now that the church is no longer an empire, it insists on peacemaking at all costs, even if that means advocating the preservation of countries that are breaking up because they had no good reason to exist in the first place. The peoples of those countries seek something different. They hope to restore their ethnic independence, precisely as the Hebrew Bible said they should, because nothing else will allow them the cultural richness they seek or the ability to derive the profound meaning that comes from inheriting a way of life from their ancestors and bequeathing it to their descendants.

There's an irony here that we dare not overlook. Some of the most strident critics of Israel and endorsers of this sort of universalism are secular professors from western Europe and the United States. They would scoff at the suggestion that they were forcing a Christian idea onto non-Christian peoples. But in at least some cases it is hard to see the matter any other way.

We can hear echoes of the implicit debate between the Christian and Jewish biblical worldviews in the ways that the United States and Israel defined themselves in their respective Declarations of Independence. The U.S. Declaration of Independence is well known, but it is worth reviewing for this discussion:

> We hold these truths to be self-evident: That all men are created equal; that they are endowed by their Creator with certain unalienable rights; that among these are life, liberty, and the pursuit of happiness; that, to secure these rights, governments are instituted among men, deriving their just powers from the

consent of the governed; that whenever any form of government becomes destructive of these ends, it is the right of the people to alter or to abolish it, and to institute new government.[30]

There is a *purpose* to the United States: to provide its citizens with the opportunity to realize their "unalienable rights" to "life, liberty and the pursuit of happiness." Despite the fact that God is found throughout the U.S. Declaration of Independence, Christianity itself plays no role in the document. Jesus is never mentioned. At least as far as the Declaration of Independence is concerned, the founders of the United States were severing their connection with the British monarchy for the sake of pursuing *universal* values of freedom and independence, not for the sake of a particular people. (As we will see in chapter 9, however, the matter was not quite that simple. The founders were all Protestants, and the United States was never as universalist as the Declaration of Independence suggests. Still, the founders of the United States intentionally did not describe their newborn country with reference to any particular people.) The U.S. Declaration of Independence is void of the particularism that the Tower of Babel story endorses and reflects to a much greater degree the values of the New Testament.

With that in mind, let's examine the Israeli Declaration of Independence, which we likewise cite only in part:

> The Land of Israel was the birthplace of the Jewish people. Here their spiritual, religious, and political identity was shaped. Here they first attained statehood, created cultural values of national and universal significance, and gave to the world the eternal Book of Books. After being forcibly exiled from their land, the people remained faithful to it throughout their Dispersion and never ceased to pray and hope for their return to it and for the restoration in it of their political freedom.
>
> Impelled by this historic and traditional attachment, Jews strove in every successive generation to re-establish themselves in their ancient homeland. In recent decades they returned in their masses . . . they made deserts bloom, revived

the Hebrew language, built villages and towns, and created a thriving community controlling its own economy and culture, loving peace but knowing how to defend itself, bringing the blessings of progress to all the country's inhabitants, and aspiring towards independent nationhood. . . .

This right is the natural right of the Jewish people to be masters of their own fate, like all other nations, in their own sovereign State. Accordingly we . . . hereby declare the establishment of a Jewish State in the Land of Israel, to be known as the State of Israel.[31]

The state of Israel, quite clearly, was created for a very different purpose from that of the United States. Ironically, God does not appear anywhere in Israel's Declaration of Independence. But the Jewish people, Jewish history, and the Jewish language are all mentioned time and again. Israel's Declaration of Independence, like Israel's purpose itself, is specific, particular, and all about the Jews.

This is the particularism that is at the heart of the Tower of Babel story and the entire Hebrew Bible. The debate between the Jewish and Christian biblical worldviews continues in the implicit dialogue between these two Declarations of Independence. It is a dispute about humanity, about how human beings ought to best organize themselves so that their lives can be most filled with meaning. What's really at stake is the question of what human life at its core ought to be about and of how people ought to govern themselves in order to foster lives that have the greatest possible meaning.

In light of all of this, the marginalized position in which Israel now finds itself does not seem terribly surprising. Consider how different the pope's worldview was from the way the early Zionists saw the world. The church's weltanschauung was distinctly apolitical; it saw politics and nationalism as obstacles in the way of creating a perfected world. Zionism, which (especially after the Shoah) eventually came to speak for most Jews, was consciously political. Given what the Jews had experienced in Europe, they had little faith in the vision of a united humanity. It was precisely in the politics of difference and the nation-state that the Jews imagined they might find their salvation (in the very physical sense of being rescued).

That is why Israel is destined to play a distinctly lonely role in the international arena. For as influential as the Hebrew Bible undoubtedly has been, Christianity's ostensibly apolitical message and its promise of universal access to salvation (in the otherworldly sense) have had a much wider influence. Thanks to Paul, Christianity's powerful message swept across the Western world with unprecedented alacrity. Once the emperor Constantine launched his groundbreaking toleration of Christianity (and quite possibly converted), it was only a matter of time until Europe adopted Christianity en masse. With that, the die was cast. The political views of the Hebrew Bible and the New Testament would forever be in tension.

This biblical tug-of-war has endured, often with ferocity. The Hebrew Bible's insistence on the importance of nationalism and sovereignty has endured, but so, too, has Christianity's vision of a world interested in other, more lofty matters. Particularly among the young and on the Left, these universal imaginings have claimed for themselves the moral high ground. Universalism is said to be a more advanced vision of humanity; it is, people say, a vision of a world that has outgrown the petty and often devastatingly murderous rivalries that nation-states invariably foster.

But Judaism has not ceded the moral high ground, even though many might like it to. Jewish thought rejects the claims of the universalists, and so does the Jewish state. Britain's chief rabbi, Jonathan Sacks, has described this eloquently:

> Judaism cannot but be seen as a revolution that reached halfway. It stands between two eras: that of the tribal cultures and local deities of the ancient world on the one hand, and on the other the universalistic cultures such as those of Greece and Rome and their religious successors, Christianity and Islam. Judaism was, as it were, born *in medias res* [in the middle of things]. . . . It was trapped in the parochialism of antiquity.[32]

Judaism's middle-of-the-road position is a desperately needed corrective.

Rabbi Sacks sees Judaism's emphasis on the particular not as a rejection of other cultures but as a celebration of them, each with its uniqueness and its own path to truth. He does not argue that Judaism is the embodiment of all truth. In fact, he was once roundly assailed by more traditional elements of British Jewry for implying in one of his books that different religions can be the bearers of different truths.[33]

What Rabbi Sacks said about different religions can also be true of different nations, peoples, and countries. Each has its own message, its own way of construing a life richly lived, its own set of traditions for fashioning a life filled with meaning that human beings can inherit and bequeath. It is the symphonic diversity of human perspectives that makes humanity great. For a marketplace of ideas to persevere, difference is critical. *That* is the one truth that Judaism insists on, in this regard; national difference, and the ability to express that difference through the existence of a variety of nation-states, is vital to the richness and flowering of all of humanity.

This is the crossfire in which the state of Israel now finds itself. To be sure, some of the hostility directed at Israel stems from anti-Semitism. Sad to say, anti-Zionism is in some ways simply the new manifestation of an ancient hatred. Some of the hostility directed at Israel stems from sympathy for the plight of the Palestinians, many of whom do, unquestionably, live extremely unenviable lives. And some is also undeniably due to actions that Israel takes that are immoral, foolish, or inadequately explained. But these factors are not a sufficient explanation. What is truly at play is an ancient battle over a vision of the roles of nations, states, nationalism, and nationhood. In that battle of ideas, much of the world sees itself arrayed precisely against the very ideas and ideals that Israel represents.

It is for that reason that we find this antipathy to Israel in reactions to Israel's Law of Return, as well. The Law of Return states that "every Jew has the right to come to this country as an immigrant."[34] It has become highly controversial in recent years; many people assert that as long as Israel gives primacy to *Jewish* potential immigrants, all other citizens of the nation (and particularly Muslim Israelis) will be made to feel second-class.

However, Israel is not alone in this approach; there are other countries that assert special relationships with their conationals living elsewhere, yet none of those other countries is subjected to the criticism that has become de rigueur for discussions of Israel. The sizable Armenian community now living in France has special status in the eyes of the Armenian government; even though these people are seen by France as French citizens in every way, Armenia looks at them differently and refers to them as "one of the communities belonging to the Armenian nation situated outside the homeland."[35] Similarly, the Irish Constitution states that "the Irish nation cherishes its special affinity with people of Irish ancestry living abroad who share its cultural identity and heritage."[36]

There are also European constitutions that give a unique place to individual religions. The Constitution of Norway says, "The Evangelical-Lutheran religion shall remain the official religion of the State [and] the inhabitants professing it are bound to bring up their children in the same."[37] Similarly, the Constitution of Denmark asserts both that "the Evangelical Lutheran Church shall be the Established Church of Denmark, and as such shall be supported by the State," and that "the King shall be a member of the Evangelical Lutheran Church."[38]

We find the same phenomenon in Latin America. The Constitution of Costa Rica declares that "the Roman Catholic and Apostolic Religion is the religion of the State," and according to the Constitution of Argentina, "the Federal Government supports the Roman Catholic Apostolic religion." Peru's Constitution notes that "the State recognizes the Roman Catholic Church as an important element of the historical, cultural and moral development of Peru."[39]

All of these countries and cases differ, but one point emerges clearly: Israel is far from the only country to put religion or ethnicity at the core of its self-definition. In a speech to the League of Nations in 1927, the Norwegian Nobel Peace Prize laureate Fridtjof Nansen said the following:

> The Republic of Erivan is nothing less than that to Armenians of every class and every party in whatever land they may now be. . . . [They] look not to Syria, not to Anatolia, not to South America, but to Erivan, the land at the foot of the eternal

snows of Ararat, as the place where the destiny of their nation must in future lie. There, year after year, they are striving to build up a new community, a political and social system which is Armenian through and through.[40]

Although he was speaking about the Armenians, he could just as well have been describing the Jews and the goals of the then-nascent Zionist movement. Could anyone have defined Zionism better? What is Zionism, if not for the desire to "build up a new community, a political and social system which is Jewish through and through"? What is Zionism's crime? Is it that unlike Armenia, Israel has been a huge success? That unlike Peru, the Jews started with nothing and built a first-world country? Or is Israel's problem that as the country rooted in the Hebrew Bible, it is simply at odds with the universalistic worldview of Christianity and thus with much of Europe?

This is not a new role for the Jews. This role was, to no small extent, the role of the biblical prophet. Vilified and rejected, despised and cursed, the prophet had the temerity to speak truth to power. That was the role of Isaiah and of Micah, of Hosea and of Amos. And it has, in many respects, been the role of the Jewish people from time immemorial.

The Jewish state represents in the contemporary world much more than a flag, a language, or borders—and certainly more than a conflict. Like the biblical prophets of old, the state of Israel represents a clear and unapologetic conception of the life well lived and the national environment that such a life requires. It is, in essence, a powerful argument to the world about the importance of difference, of the legitimacy—indeed, of the necessity—of the nation-state. Because that is what Israel stands for, it has aroused the ire of people all across the planet.

Chapter Six

THE INVENTION OF
THE INVENTION
OF NATIONALISM

A human life, I think, should be well rooted in some spot of a native land, where it may get the love of tender kinship for the face of earth, for the labours men go forth to, for the sounds and accents that haunt it, for whatever will give that early home a familiar unmistakable difference amidst the future widening of knowledge: a spot where the definiteness of early memories may be inwrought with affection.

—George Eliot, *Daniel Deronda*[1]

In the summer of 1977, an Israeli cargo ship bound for the Far East came upon a boat loaded with dozens of Vietnamese refugees who were out of provisions, including water, and whose boat was slowly leaking. Previous boats—of East German, Japanese, Panamanian, and Norwegian registry—had all passed the refugees but had ignored them. The Israeli crew, however, brought the refugees on board their ship and then to Israel, where Prime Minister

Menachem Begin ultimately granted them asylum and then citizenship. In the next several years, Israel absorbed another few hundred Vietnamese refugees.

In July 1977, about a month after the Israeli rescue of the first of these refugees, President Jimmy Carter and Prime Minister Begin met on the White House lawn. Carter opened what was to become a memorable and much discussed exchange:

> I was particularly impressed that the first official action of his [Prime Minister Begin's] government was to admit into Israel 66 homeless refugees from Vietnam who had been floating around in the oceans of the world, excluded by many nations who are their neighbors, who had been picked up by an Israeli ship and to whom he gave a home. It was an act of compassion, an act of sensitivity, and recognition by him and his government about the importance of a home for people who were destitute, and who would like to express their own individuality and freedom in a common way, again typifying the historic struggle of the people of Israel.[2]

After Carter spoke, Begin replied. His point was that what mattered about Jewish history was not *why* the Jews had suffered but *how* the Jews needed to act, given what had happened to them in their past:

> It was a natural act to us, Mr. President. We remembered, we have never forgotten, that boat with 900 Jews [the *St. Louis*], having left Germany in the last weeks before the Second World War . . . traveling from harbor to harbor, from country to country, crying out for refuge. They were refused. . . . Therefore it was natural that my first act as Prime Minister was to give those people a haven in the land of Israel.[3]

Indeed, Israel has always sought to become a place where the collective memories of a people, a sense of home, and a religious tradition all combine to create a distinct sense of obligation not only to Jews, but to humanity at large.

By the time the Israeli ship picked up the sinking Vietnamese refugees or Israeli planes took off to bring doctors and supplies to Haiti after the 2010 earthquake, this part of Israel's tradition was already well established. Golda Meir's appointment in 1956 as foreign minister of the young state of Israel was a case in point. One of the first things that she did was to explain to her staff that reaching out to newly founded African nations was one of her chief priorities. To many of her underlings, that sounded odd. What, after all, could these African nations do for Israel? Israel itself was struggling, and these other nations were even more tenuous and mired in poverty than Israel was. What purpose could there possibly be in reaching out to these impoverished nations? At a meeting of the Foreign Ministry, Meir explained as follows:

> We Jews share with the African peoples a memory of centuries-long suffering. For both Jews and Africans alike, such expressions as discrimination, oppression, slavery—these are not mere catchwords. They don't refer to experiences of hundreds of years ago. They refer to the torment and degradation we suffered yesterday and today. Let me read you something to illustrate the point.[4]

At that point, according to Yehuda Avner (later Israel's ambassador to England), who was in the room at the time, she picked up a copy of Theodor Herzl's 1902 classic book *Altneuland* and read an extensive passage:

> There is still one question arising out of the disaster of the nations which remains unsolved to this day, and whose profound tragedy only a Jew can comprehend. This is the African question. Just call to mind all those terrible episodes of the slave trade, of human beings who, merely because they were black, were stolen like cattle, taken prisoner, captured, and sold. Their children grew up in strange lands, the objects of contempt and hostility because their complexions were different. . . . Once I have witnessed the redemption of the

Jews, my own people, I wish also to assist in the redemption of the Africans.[5]

If Israelis did not have a sense of where they had come from, if they had no sense of identity (in the most profound sense of the word), they would have had no reason to take in the Vietnamese boat people. They would have felt no affinity with the Sudanese refugees they have taken in; they would not have seen the struggle of African nations as reminiscent of their own and therefore deserving of Israeli concern. It would never have occurred to them to reach out to earthquake-ravaged Haitians in ways that far exceeded what much larger, wealthier, and seemingly better equipped countries did.

Nationalism, like pride and like love, can take many different forms and evoke very different sorts of responses. In its ugliest forms, it can become chauvinism—and sometimes even fascism. But there is nothing about nationalism that means that it *must* become ugly or dangerous. Nationalism can simply be a community's expression of the self-esteem and sense of history that every human being needs in order to function, strive, love, and, ultimately, give. Despite the bad rap that nationalism has received in recent years, we should not lose sight of this: the love of one's country and the devotion to one's own narrative can, at its best, lead to reaching out to others, as both Meir and Begin did.

The sad irony about Israel's lonely place in the international arena is that the greatest obstacle to the Jewish state's future is a word: *nationalism*—a word that is so commonly interpreted to be negative that the world has lost sight of all of the good that it has brought and could continue to create.

This story about the Vietnamese who were picked up by an Israeli boat is important, because one of the most common objections to the argument on behalf of the importance of human difference and of the nation-state is that this focus on peoplehood, nations, particularism, and "one's own" must ultimately lead to a disengagement from the rest of humanity. People who are so focused on their own group, the objection goes, cannot in the end care about others. By that account, however, Israelis should not have been inclined to save the Vietnamese on the sinking ship, and their recently elected and politically embattled prime minister should certainly not have given them refuge.

All too often, examples such as these are simply discounted. In postwar academia, it has become fashionable to disparage nationalism as leading inexorably to war and injustice. Given the horrors that Europe suffered and perpetrated in the twentieth century, it is quite understandable that European scholars would seek to debunk the idea of nationalism. For if nationalism leads us to focus on ourselves and not on others, and if disregard for others is precisely what led Europe to become a blood-soaked hell for so long, then by all logic, nationalism must be the problem. Thus, many leading postwar academics have done whatever they can to deflate the very notion of nationalism.

Elie Kedourie is a prime example. A British historian, he became one of nationalism's great detractors. In his aptly titled book *Nationalism*, he asserted that nationalism might ultimately be surmountable because it was nothing but a "doctrine invented in Europe at the beginning of the nineteenth century."[6] Not only was nationalism not ancient, Kedourie argued, it was also dangerous. The importation of nationalism to the Middle East had turned that region into a "wilderness of tigers."[7] It would be almost impossible to exaggerate Kedourie's influence on the field; in its obituary for Kedourie, the *Independent* of London wrote, "Among his achievements was that of transforming our understanding of nationalism."[8] Virtually everyone who came after him has had to contend with his work.

As important as Kedourie's work has been, however, he has been outshined in popularity in recent decades by Benedict Anderson, whose *Imagined Communities* has become a much-read classic in universities across the United States and throughout the West. "[The nation] is *imagined* because the members of even the smallest nation will never know most of their fellow-members, meet them or even hear of them," Anderson wrote. "In fact, all communities larger than primordial villages of face-to-face contact (and perhaps even these) are imagined."[9]

Anderson argued that it was the printing press that made national-ism possible. Another scholar, Steven Kemper, has explained Anderson as follows:

> Nations had to be "imagined communities." Their size and complexity made the possibility of citizens knowing one another in a face-to-face way quite ridiculous. The spread of print technology made it possible for enormous numbers of people to know of one another indirectly, for the print-ing press become the middleman to the imagination of the community. . . . The very existence and regularity of news-papers caused readers, and thus citizens-in-the-making, to imagine themselves residing in a common time and place, united by a print language with a league of anonymous equals.[10]

Like Kedourie, Anderson (who began his training at Cambridge University and completed his studies at Cornell University), is inter-ested in the *origins* of nationalism. Although Anderson's interest in what made nationalism possible might sound like an arcane academic question of no import to the debate about Israel and the nation-state, nothing could be further from the truth. For like Kedourie, Anderson's interest in how nationalism got started is closely tied to his sense that there is something perverse about it. Like Kedourie lament-ing the "wilderness of tigers" that nationalism fomented in the Middle East, Anderson is similarly exasperated.

After all, he has argued, "The nation is always conceived as a deep, horizontal comradeship. Ultimately it is this fraternity that makes it possible, over the past two centuries, for so many millions of people not so much to kill as to willingly die for such limited imaginings." After asserting that nationalism has caused or fostered so much dying, Anderson asked what seems to be the natural question: "What makes the shrunken imaginings of recent history (scarcely more than two centuries) generate such colossal sacrifices?"[11]

Martha Nussbaum, a contemporary American philosopher who is in many ways equally critical of nationalism, is desperate to avoid those colossal sacrifices in the future, and she believes that American education ought to be reshaped for exactly that purpose: "I would like to see education adopt [a] cosmopolitan stance [and focus on] making world citizenship, rather than democratic or national citizenship, the focus of civic education."[12]

Kedourie, Anderson, and Nussbaum are part of a long and illustrious chain of academics. Many other scholars make similar arguments; some of them, like Ernest Gellner, argue that "nationalism is not a sentiment expressed by pre-existing nations; rather it creates nations where they did not previously exist."[13] Throughout this entire line of thinking runs a sense that there is something artificial about nationalism; indeed, the idea that nationalism is a modern invention is now all the rage.

The notion that nationalism is a modern invention is closely linked to the many calls for its end. Consider the following telling example of such a suggestion, written in 2006 by Thomas Bender, a professor of history at New York University:

I want to propose the end of American history as we have known it. . . . [National histories] are taught in schools and brought into public discourse to forge and sustain national identities, presenting the self-contained nation as the natural carrier of history. That way of writing and teaching history has exhausted itself. In its place, I want to elaborate a new framing for U.S. history, one that rejects the territorial space of the nation as a sufficient context and argues for the transnational nature of national histories.[14]

What this way of thinking does, of course, is to set the stage for projects like the European Union and to make movements like Zionism seem antiquated and fundamentally at odds with what we think we know about nations and their origins.

We would be wrong to cede the moral high ground to this position simply because it is in vogue. The scholars of nationalism have raised fascinating questions about the origins of nations. And they rightly point to the excesses to which nationalism can sometimes lead. Yet their claims that nationalism is a modern phenomenon seem at odds with the reading of the Tower of Babel story suggested in chapter 5. Doesn't the Hebrew Bible seem to speak about nations long before the nineteenth century? And didn't the Jewish people, scattered across the globe, cultivate a sense of nationalism long before the advent of the printing press? But no matter; these scholars' questions are interesting.

Yet the questions that these academics ask are not the only questions that make a difference. In addition to asking about the *origins* of nationalism, it is equally important to ask about the *impact* of nationalism. What has nationalism done for the flourishing of the human soul? What dimension of the human experience can be uniquely expressed only as part of a people or a nation? Those are questions that such discussions of the origins of nationalism simply do not address.

The Tower of Babel story is quite clearly interested in the human being, in a way of life that can give expression to the human soul, human aspirations, and human longings. Thousands of years later, political Zionism became interested in the same thing. Zionist leaders were not interested in the origins of the nationalist aspirations that coursed through their veins; they simply knew that they were desperate to save the Jewish people. Nor were they the first to intuit that much of the power of human life could be derived from the unique kind of belonging that the nation-state could make possible.

In *Daniel Deronda*, George Eliot suggested something very much akin to Zionism about twenty years before Herzl made his case to the world. The quote that opens this chapter is an extraordinarily compelling cry from the heart not only for Zionism but for nationalists worldwide. Eliot understood what creates a life pulsing with meaning. It is a sense of a native land, the "love of tender kinship for the face of earth," a place where "the definiteness of early memories may be inwrought with affection." It is a homeland, a place that a people can call its own. She would have been unmoved by the arguments of scholars like Kedourie and Anderson, for her interests lay elsewhere. She was interested not in origins but in potentials. She hoped that human beings would not simply understand but, more important, feel.

Certain places are home, and others are not. There are sounds and accents that are ours. Recognizing that, and taking pride in it, is part and parcel of being alive. To deny our particular attachments is to die. Seventy years before George Eliot, Walter Scott asked the following in his epic poem, "The Lay of the Last Minstrel":

> Breathes there the man with soul so dead
> Who never to himself hath said:
> 'This is my own, my native Land?'
> Whose heart hath ne'er within him burned
> As home his footsteps he hath turned, . . .
> From wandering on a foreign strand?[15]

It should therefore come as no surprise that Eliot was opposed to Esperanto, the lifelong project of Ludwig Zamenhof, which she said "has no uncertainty, no whims of idiom, no cumbrous forms, no fitful shimmer of many-hued significance, no hoary archaisms."[16] She, like the Hebrew Bible long before her and Herzl after her, understood the loss to human aspiration and the diminution of human greatness that comes with a homogenized conception of life, uprooted from ancient traditions and cultures, in which our differences are either ignored or diminished. She understood that the majesty of the human experience is to be found in those sounds and accents that haunt our native lands. It is to be found, in other words, in our differences, not in our sameness. It is to be found in what makes us unique, not in what we share with every other person under the heavens.

Eliot was right. And that explains why despite the work of Kedourie and his coterie, the idea of the nation and the pride in a homeland simply refuse to die. Is nationalism's tenacity a result of the obduracy of its advocates, or is it because nationalism, in its most enlightened form, speaks to a dimension of human life that goes to the core of who we are? I would suggest that it is the latter, without question.

Even in Germany, where the celebration of nationhood is understandably suspect because of the horrors of the Third Reich, an old-fashioned celebration of culture and uniqueness has reappeared among a generation no longer stifled by the crimes of the generations who came before them. Twenty years after Germany's reunification, the *International Herald Tribune* reported, a resurgence of national pride is evident "on the airwaves, where German songs are staging a comeback against the dominance of American pop, and in best-sellers about Goethe and Schiller or discovering Germany by foot, by car and by train from the Bavarian Alps to the Hanseatic ports on the Baltic Sea."[17] Even with all the complex history that German nationalism understandably evokes, something about the German national impulse refuses to die. That might be worrisome to many or comforting to others, but German nationalism (like many other nationalisms) appears here to stay.

There's nothing surprising about this. The desire to be heir to something larger than ourselves, to come from a tradition that we wish to bequeath, and to take pride in a narrative that is uniquely ours is hardwired into human beings—as long as we don't hyper-intellectualize ourselves into believing that we've become something that we're not or that we're no longer something that we still are. John Stuart Mill wrote that "the boundaries of government should coincide in the main with those of nationalities."[18] He was essentially making the same claim that George Eliot made in saying that "human life . . . should be well rooted in some spot of a native land."

Johann Gottfried von Herder, an eighteenth-century German philosopher, urged something very similar:

Nature raises families; the most natural state is therefore also *one* people with one national character. . . . Nothing, then, seems to run so obviously counter to the purpose of government as the unnatural expansion of states, the wild mixture of all types of races and nations under one scepter. . . . For the very statecraft that brought them into being is also the one that plays with peoples and human beings as with lifeless bodies.

But history shows sufficiently that these instruments of pride are made of clay, and like all clay on earth, they crumble and dissolve.[19]

Empires, Herder suggested, are intrinsically a violation of the freedoms and aspirations of individual nations. And nothing could be more natural than those nations, which are as much a part of nature as the human family is, he said.

This sentiment that a people approximates a family, that most of us have an instinctive desire to reach out and to protect those who are part of our larger whole, is what Israel consistently models to the world. When the international community discusses Israel, it would rather focus on the conflict in the Middle East than on what Israel has done to model the gifts that nationalism can bestow; but when it does so, it misses some of the extraordinary steps that the Jewish state has been taking since its independence. When approximately seven hundred thousand Jews were summarily exiled from Arab countries as the Jewish state was founded, Israel instinctively took them all in and made them citizens. Israel didn't have the money, the food, or the shelter that it needed for them, but they were taken in anyway.

This was Israel acting as a nation and a family, precisely as Herder described. Like many immigrants, these newcomers to Israel were not always treated as well as they should have been. But they were admitted and made citizens. Today their descendants are Israeli through and through, while the descendants of those Palestinians who fled are still pawns in a cynical international chess game in which no one wants them, in which Arab countries consciously keep them in limbo so as to be able to pressure Israel to take them in.

Whether it was the half a million Jews who fled the Nazis and came to Jewish Palestine and then Israel, the seven hundred thousand Jewish immigrants from Muslim Arab countries, or the approximately one million Jews (40 to 50 percent of whom may not even have been technically Jewish) from the Soviet Union, this commitment to welcoming immigrants was another reflection of Herder's insight that "nature raises families" and Eliot's claim that we live most fully in a "native land [with] the love of tender kinship."[20]

Israel demonstrated the power of this sense of kinship in 1991, when Israeli pilots, mostly of European descent, landed lumbering, converted C-130 jets on narrow airstrips in Ethiopia in the midst of a civil war and airlifted fourteen thousand Ethiopian Jews to Israel in just over a day in one of the greatest rescue operations in all of human history. The scholar Ernest Gellner famously claimed that "two men are of the same nation if and only if they share the same culture, where culture in turn means a system of ideas and signs and associations and ways of behaving and communicating."[21]

However, the Israelis and those Ethiopian Jews had very little in common. Even though the Ethiopians were Jews, that community had fled Judea in the face of the Babylonian onslaught two thousand years earlier and had headed south to Africa long before Jewish tradition as we now know it had even developed.[22]

For thousands of years, Ethiopian Jews were completely cut off from Jewish life in Babylonia, Palestine, Europe, and North Africa, so they preserved a Jewish way of life that was now entirely anachronistic to Jews everywhere else. They did not have a common language with the rest of world Jewry. Their only Jewish text was the Torah and some of the other biblical books (in their own language); all of the rabbinic texts were foreign to them, since those texts were written long after the Ethiopians' ancestors had fled to Africa. The postbiblical Jewish holidays and the beliefs and practices that emerged from rabbinic texts were all unfamiliar to that community. They knew nothing of the Talmud, of Purim and Hanukkah, of the Shoah, or of any dimension of the rest of Jewish experience in the past two millennia. So different were they, in fact, that when they finally arrived in Israel, the Israeli chief rabbinate undertook long discussions to determine whether they were actually Jewish according to Jewish law.

The tremendous difficulties, and sometimes even social and cultural barriers, that the Ethiopian community has experienced in acculturating to Israeli life are often seen as a source of shame for Israel. To be sure, no one can deny that Israel has not always handled the Ethiopian community sensitively or wisely. But that same difficulty is also testimony to how radically different these people were from any other Jews that Israelis had met before. That these people knew nothing about Israel and spoke no Hebrew was the least of it. That their Judaism was so unrecognizable made matters more complicated. That they knew nothing of electricity, running water, or modern technology (some tried to light fires in the planes carrying them to Israel because they were cold) just added to the challenge. This was an immigration project unlike anything Israel had ever attempted before.

Nonetheless, despite the challenges, the vast majority of Israelis were convinced that bringing the Ethiopian community to Israel was the right thing to do. They intuited that there was a sufficient amount that they shared with these new immigrants—an ancient past, a sacred text, a yearning for a homeland, and a sense of being part of the same people—to warrant seeing them as a branch of their extended family.

Jewish experience has demonstrated this inclination time and again. It has demonstrated the power of belonging and the ability of sovereignty to foster that belonging, not only to Jews but to the world at large. Those familiar with the ways in which nationalism has inspired hope, purpose, and even selflessness in Jewish history understandably find it difficult to square this experience with the scholarly claims about nationalism that obsess over racial and cultural purity or even a tendency to fascism. There are times that actual experience trumps the wisdom of even seemingly great scholarship. The Jewish people's history is just such an instance.

It's important that we not overlook one of the most common responses to the defense of nationalism: Doesn't such a deep commitment to one's own people invariably come at the expense of caring about others? We noted the Vietnamese refugee example above, but it's important to restate the point. The British Jewish philosopher Isaiah Berlin wrote that there is no reason that "one community, absorbed in the development of its own native talent, should not respect a similar activity on the part of others."[23] Wishing that others also flourish can be the noblest form of particularity.

Besides the Vietnamese refugees whom Begin admitted, witness Israel's extraordinary efforts in Haiti after the earthquake; the freedoms accorded to Israeli Arabs (although these still need to be better enforced), which are far in excess of what they would have in any of the Arab states bordering Israel; or the many Sudanese refugees who were given sanctuary in Israel.

What is it that leads Israel to do these things? How is it that Israel's focus on Jews and Judaism does not preclude these commitments? The answer is simple: there are elements of our humanity that come to the fore precisely when we conceive of ourselves as part of a more limited family, nation, religion, or state. If we are part of an enormous human mass, we make no real difference. We matter, we feel, and we become determined to act precisely when we are part of something small, more unique, with a message. And when being part of a particular people has taught us to care about individuals other than ourselves, we can extend that sympathy and reach out to others who are not part of our nation.

It is for that precise reason that other philosophers, often called *communitarians*, have begun to articulate an array of reasons for celebrating human difference and for defending the institution of the nation-state as a guarantor of that difference. Charles Taylor and Michael Sandel are among those at the heart of these discussions. In many ways, these philosophers' ideas are just twentieth-century versions of some of the insights about humanity that we have argued were already implicit (at the very least) in the Hebrew Bible, but they have added much to the conversation.

Sandel made the basic point magnificently in *Liberalism and the Limits of Justice*:

> We cannot regard ourselves as independent . . . without . . . understanding ourselves as the particular persons we are—as members of this family or community or nation or people, as bearers of this history, as sons and daughters of that revolution, as citizens of this republic. Allegiances such as these are more than values I happen to have. . . . They go beyond the obligations I voluntarily incur and the "natural duties"

I owe to human beings as such. They allow that to some I owe more than justice requires or even permits, not by reason of agreements I have made but instead [by] virtue of those more or less enduring attachments and commitments which taken together partly define the person I am.

In a clear dig at the antinationalists and postnationalists, he added the following:

To imagine a person incapable of constitutive attachments such as these is not to conceive an ideally free and rational agent, but to imagine a person wholly without character, without moral depth. For to have character is to know that I move in a history I neither summon nor command, which carries consequences nonetheless for my choices and conduct. It draws me closer to some and more distant from others; it makes some aims more appropriate, others less so.[24]

Note the extraordinary parallels between Sandel's words and Israel's experience. His notion that the people he describes owe "to some . . . more than justice requires or even permits" is an important part of the debate surrounding Israel. The Law of Return, which we discussed earlier, grants Jews anywhere the automatic right to settle in Israel and become citizens; for that reason, it has been decried by some as inherently discriminatory. Why should the members of one people be given preferential treatment over others in obtaining citizenship? Does it make any sense that American Jews, perfectly comfortable in New York, Boston, or Los Angeles, should have automatic rights to Israeli citizenship that they don't technically *need* (because they are living quite well without it), when refugees from Darfur or other genocides cannot obtain it?

From a purely universal or liberal perspective, the policy makes no sense.[25] But when we recognize that being part of a people, a state, a heritage, or a culture means that we owe a particular allegiance to those who share that, Israel's policy makes much more sense. It may not be popular in the court of international opinion, but Sandel makes clear that the Law of Return speaks to a profound human attribute, to the source of our ability to love and to reach out to others.

That Israelis reach out to Vietnamese boat people or to Somali refugees is no accident. The sense of obligation to others stems from first learning an obligation to one's own family, community, and people. Without question, one of the most powerful dimensions of Israeli life is this sense of shared enterprise to which Sandel refers. It's part of Israeli life that crops up regularly, often when one least expects it.

I recall, for example, a moment the day after the Israeli soldier Gilad Shalit was captured by Hamas in June 2006. I was driving, stopped in the middle lane at a red light. There were cars both to my left and my right. The announcer on the radio interrupted the program and read aloud a letter to Shalit from his parents that had just been released to the press.

There was nothing surprising in the letter, but it was heartbreaking nonetheless. At that point, with Shalit just captured and apparently wounded in the attack that also killed several of his comrades, no one could have had any idea how long he would languish in captivity. So his parents wrote to him that they hoped he was physically well or at least recovering. They told him how worried they were about him, that they hoped he was being strong, and that his family was waiting anxiously for his return.

There was something agonizing about hearing that letter being read on the radio, and as I listened to it, I found myself fighting back tears. For no particular reason, I happened to look first to my left and then to my right, and I saw both other drivers, one a man and one a woman, both still sitting at the red light, wiping tears from their eyes as well. I have never forgotten the power of that unanticipated moment, the feeling of shared enterprise that, I must confess, I don't recall ever having felt in the forty years that I lived in the United States. The power of these moments is not incidental to human life; they evoke a sense of belonging that profoundly enriches our sense of who and what we are.

Those of us who were in Israel in October 2011, when Shalit was finally released after more than five years of captivity, will never forget the streets lined with thousands of people who did not know him but who saw him as their own son and who wanted to be part of the process of welcoming him home. When he returned, by helicopter and car, to his home in Mitzpe Hila, the dancing on his street continued long after he'd entered his house and closed the door. Men and women, religious and secular, young and old, those who'd grown up with him and those who'd never met him were united at that unforgettable moment. There was a powerful euphoria in Israel that night, not only because an individual soldier had been freed but because Israelis rediscovered that distinctly Israeli capacity to bond together, to feel the extraordinary power that comes from being part of a larger whole.

Another moment comes to mind. I was at the market one morning about twenty years after the Israeli airman Ron Arad had been shot down over Lebanon and had disappeared. I was picking up some milk and some bread, and I was standing in the checkout line next to pile of newspapers when I noticed Arad's picture on the front page. The lead story claimed, based on some allegedly newly acquired intelligence, that after his plane was shot down, Arad might have been alive for quite some time, and that after an attempted escape, he had apparently had both his legs broken by his captors. I didn't pick up the paper but merely stood, immobile, reading what I could on the top half of the front page.

Behind me in line, a woman also began to read the paper, and she actually dropped the items she was about to purchase as she put her hands to her face in horror. When her items fell, I turned to look at her, and she turned to me. We exchanged not a single word, but we didn't need to. Just looking at each other, bonded over the horror of what we had read, we surely felt what Sandel was writing about when he said that we "move in a history [we] neither summon nor command, which . . . draws [us] closer to some and more distant from others."

I no longer recall what the front page of that paper looked like, but even though years have passed, I still recall what her eyes looked like at that moment. Encounters like that, even wordless ones (perhaps especially wordless ones), make Israeli life different from life in many other countries. That is what draws students and tourists to want to return to Israel. Even with all the anguish and pain that Israeli life can entail, these people feel a magnetic draw to a country that is not actually their home. As devastating as these feelings can be, they pull people in because they reflect "attachments and commitments" that help to make us the people we become in a country like Israel.

Moments such as these are what distinguish Israel from other countries that are not ethnic nation-states in quite the same way. In fact, from the very moment that Gilad Shalit was kidnapped by Hamas, and for all the years that he was held in captivity, his name became a household term both in Israel and among Jews everywhere. Israeli newspapers counted the days of his captivity, and Israel was paralyzed for a week in the summer of 2010, when tens of thousands of people joined his parents in a hike from their home in the north to Prime Minister Benjamin Netanyahu's house in Jerusalem to demand that he do more to secure the young man's release.

At the very same time, an American soldier was being held captive in Afghanistan. His name was Private First Class Bowe Bergdahl, and he had been held by the Taliban since June 30, 2009.[26] Like Shalit, Bergdahl was born in 1986. Like Shalit, he was being held by an Islamist terrorist organization. But unlike Shalit, his name was hardly a household term. Indeed, an event staged to urge his release attracted only fifty participants.[27] The similar event for Shalit had brought tens of thousands to the march.

This is not meant as a criticism of American society. Bergdahl's parents had their own reasons for keeping a low profile and for trusting that the U.S. Army would get their son back. But most American college students to whom I mentioned Bergdahl in those years had never heard of him; I doubt that there was a single Israeli at that time who did not know who Shalit was.

Those facts are just a small indication of the profound difference between the Israeli and the American experiences, of the senses of attachment and obligation that can arise in the sorts of communities about which Sandel writes. When we read Sandel and reflect on Shalit, Arad, and Bergdahl, it is difficult not to conclude that whether or not Benedict Anderson's theory about the spread of nationalism is correct, what matters for our conversation is not the history he describes but the attachments about which Sandel writes. Those are what defines us. Those are central to what many of us believe is at the core of the very meaning of our lives.

Sandel's teacher, the Canadian philosopher Charles Taylor, once coined a wonderful term that captures part of what makes the Israeli experience so powerful. He called it "inescapable horizons":

> The agent seeking significance in life, trying to define him- or herself meaningfully, has to exist in a horizon of impor- tant questions. That is what is self-defeating in modes of contemporary culture . . . which *shut out* history and the bonds of solidarity. These self-centered "narcissistic" forms are indeed shallow and trivialized; they are "flattened and narrowed." . . .
>
> Otherwise put, I can define my identity only against the background of things that matter. But to bracket out history, nature, society, the demands of solidarity, everything but what I find in myself, would be to eliminate all candidates for what matters. Only if I exist in a world in which history, or the demands of nature, or the needs of my fellow human beings, or the duties of citizenship, or the call of God, or something else of this order *matters* crucially, can I define an identity for myself that is not trivial.[28]

It is not insignificant that Taylor mentions "the call of God" in his list of duties that shape us. Although Taylor was not specifi- cally writing about Israel, he could have been. In Israeli society, history combined with the duties of citizenship (such as universal military service) and the call of religious tradition create a sense of belonging and obligation that is unusual in Western, highly devel- oped countries.

It is commonly said that Israeli society is highly secular. Despite the high profile of the politically volatile ultra-Orthodox population in Israel, the argument goes, the typical Israeli is secular and unin- terested in religion. On one level, that is true. The overwhelming

majority of Israelis define themselves as secular, do not attend synagogue, and do not send their children to a religious school.

But what does *secular* mean? According to the Avi Chai
Foundation's 2000 portrait of Israeli society, 5 percent of Israeli Jews
defined themselves as Haredi (ultra-Orthodox), 12 percent as religious, 35 percent as traditional, 43 percent as nonreligious, and 5 percent as antireligious. But according to that same study, 98 percent of
Israeli Jews have put mezuzahs on the front doorposts of their homes,
85 percent always participate in Passover seders, 71 percent always light
Hanukkah candles, and 67 percent fast on Yom Kippur.[29] Thus, the
percentage of people who engage in these supposedly religious customs
is far larger than the combination of the Haredi, religious, and traditional categories. Many "nonreligious" people are clearly participating
in what seem like religious rituals. How can one explain that?

From a purely rational or theological perspective, those statistics
make no sense. But what Israelis intuitively understand is that theology and classic religious reasoning are not the only criteria by which
one makes judgments about religious behaviors. Part of what is at play,
far beyond theology, God, or commandments, are the demands of history and of belonging— "inescapable horizons"—the very demands
of which Sandel, Taylor, and others write so eloquently. That is what
leads so many seemingly secular Israelis to engage in what appears to
be distinctly religious behavior, and it is part of what gives Israel its
unique quality as a society of engaged belonging.

Engaged belonging can assume highly unanticipated forms.
I recall a late-night visit to the music store at Ben-Gurion Airport just
before I was about to board a flight. A staffperson came over to me
to offer some help; the first thing that I noticed about him was that
he was pierced in more places than I could count. In Israel, this is an
unmistakable signal that a person is *highly* secular. "Just browsing,"
I told him, not really imagining that this human colander and I were
going to share a taste in music.

"Do you have this?" he persisted, picking up a CD I'd not seen
before.

"What is it?" I asked.

"It's Etti Ankri, singing the songs of Rabbi Yehudah Halevi," he said. Ankri is one of Israel's most popular female vocalists, and Rabbi Yehudah Halevi was an important medieval Spanish Jewish poet and philosopher. "It's awesome; our best-selling CD," he continued. "I can't stop listening to it. You won't be sorry if you buy it. In fact, if you don't like it, I'll personally buy it from you the next time you're at the airport."

I was so stunned that I bought the CD without looking at it very carefully. Moments like that capture the sense of belonging and the sense of shared history that surface differences might camouflage. There I was, obviously a religious Jew, speaking to this punk-looking salesman, speaking about the poetry of Rabbi Yehuda Halevi and about the singer Etti Ankri, who'd more or less started in his community and was then moving, more or less, toward mine. Theology didn't matter then. Neither did politics. There was no doubt at that rather strange moment that we were part of something very, very powerful.

The Kedouries and the Andersons of the world have given us much to think about, but Sandel and Taylor urge us into conversations about the innermost chambers of our lives. Following in Plato's tradition, we can seek to *define* love, or we can reflect on the way it shapes our lives. We can, in the spirit of a *Time* magazine cover story from the 1990s, explore the biochemical changes that take place in our bodies when we feel sexual attraction.[30] Or instead we can reflect on the strange fact that even though falling in love makes us vulnerable, most of us understand that life without that vulnerability is a life much less richly lived.

Nationalism and love are similar in that respect. In both of these spheres, we can, if we wish, explore the origins of the feeling (history or biology). Alternatively, we can acknowledge that what matters as we shape our own humanity is the power of commitment, the nobility of selflessness, and the sense of purpose that comes with charting a vision for our lives.

Sandel and Taylor can lead us there. Kedourie cannot. Studying what Israel has done to and for the Jewish people, including how it has transformed Jews' sense of contributing to the world, can lead us there. Relentlessly assailing the Jewish state for a conflict it cannot end on its own leads us nowhere.

Chapter Seven

DIVERSITY IS THE KEY TO HUMAN FREEDOM

Occupied with building our twin towers of Babel, we no longer appreciate the fact that separations between and among human groups cannot be entirely overcome. Nor do we see that this fortunate impotence is the condition of human liberty and diversity.
—Pierre Manent, *Democracy without Nations?*[1]

In 416 BCE, as the Peloponnesian War raged, Athens attacked the tiny island of Melos. The Athenians had claimed suzerainty over the island a few years earlier but had not pressed the attack. This time, however, they made it clear that they were serious. Melos could sign a treaty, join the Delian League, and pay tribute to Athens, or Athens would destroy it. The Melians refused, preferring death to losing their freedom by submitting to the conquering Athenians. Thucydides relates their famous response to the Athenians:

> Our resolution, Athenians, is the same as it was at first. We will not in a moment deprive of freedom a city that has been inhabited these seven hundred years; but we put our trust in the fortune by which the gods have preserved it until now, and

in the help of men, that is, of the Lacedaemonians; and so we will try and save ourselves. Meanwhile we invite you to allow us to be friends to you and foes to neither party.[2]

All of the ingredients of contemporary resistance movements are in this ancient speech. There is a sense of personal honor, a profound sense of history, and a belief that the Melians' freedom is dependent on preserving their memory and experience. They would not submit to the Athenians and pretend to be people with values and a past different from those they had inherited; they might as well have decided to alter their DNA.

The Melians believed that without the preservation of their unique identity, life was not worth living. Athens could conquer them and even kill them, they insisted, but it could not erase who they were. Athens could take their lives but not their freedom. The Melians were willing to die for the freedom to live the lives they believed they were meant to live—and they did.

What motivates a people to resist in that way? Why do people— whether they are Melians battling Athens, Jews resisting Rome on Masada, or members of countless other groups who have refused to surrender—not simply put survival first? Why not capitulate and live to see another day?

The reason is that life itself is not really our ultimate value. When John Stuart Mill, the British philosopher best known for his conception of liberty, urged people to support the North during the American Civil War, he acknowledged that war and the horrific price that defending a nation can exact are sometimes necessary and even worthwhile:

War is an ugly thing, but not the ugliest of things; the decayed and degraded state of moral and patriotic feeling which thinks nothing worth a war, is worse. A man who has nothing which he cares more about than he does about his personal safety is a miserable creature who has no chance at being free, unless made and kept so by the exertions of better men than himself.[3]

Certainly we all share a deep human instinct to stay alive and protect those we love. Underwater, running out of air, we will do anything humanly possible to get to the surface. Our children can be only hours old, with no personalities or values yet, to speak of, but we intuit that even then we would give up our own lives to save theirs. These are among the most basic of human instincts. We are hardwired that way.

But mere survival is not, in the end, people's most profound desire. It is not a purpose. The great resisters of history, and many other unknown people, did not *wish* to die when they did. But they preferred death over a willingness to erase or deny who they were. They preferred death over the loss of their freedom. Freedom often matters more than life.

The essence of this freedom has something to do with living our lives in a manner that fulfills who we believe we were meant to be. The Greeks had a notion similar to this; they called it *eudaimonia*. Eudaimonism is the theory that the highest ethical goal is happiness and personal well-being, something akin to what scholars call the "flourishing life."[4] In our world, the Greeks' focus on virtue and living in accordance with the gods—all of which are implicit in *eudaimonia*—is not what most people have in mind when they speak about living in accordance with the culture they have inherited. Nonetheless, that Greek notion of fashioning a life well lived with our own history and culture at its core still speaks volumes to many of us today.

For most of us, flourishing requires, first and foremost, freedom. But freedom is much more than a matter of not being enslaved or imprisoned. The freedom at stake for many of those who have resisted the foreign powers that sought to take them over is the freedom to chart the course of their own lives; human flourishing demands the opportunity to take the culture that our ancestors nurtured and then bequeathed and to cultivate it further in order to pass it on again, to our own children.

The conception of human fulfillment at the core of this book is about much more than breathing our next breath or acquiring more possessions. It is ultimately about spiritual and historical freedom, the liberty to leave our own unique mark on the world that we inhabit for a very short period. Without the ability to somehow shape the world according to *our* views, *our* values, and the tradition that *we* have inherited and that *we* wish to bequeath to those in *our* family, clan, or people who will come after *us*, what point can there be to all our toil? Without leaving some unique legacy behind us, we blend into the mass of humanity. We are everyone—and we are no one. We leave no fingerprint on the world; it is as though we were never here. We do not matter. We become slaves to invisibility and insignificance. Without the option of being distinct, there can be no meaningful freedom. For all intents and purposes, there can be no freedom at all.

At first blush, this link between human differentness and human freedom can easily seem far-fetched. The notion that our differences are also what fuels our drive to remain free is not how we usually think about freedom. If anything, a world *without* difference seems more likely to be a world without conflict, a world at peace. Wouldn't a world at peace be much more likely to create freedom for everyone?

But the universalism that can seem so appealing is actually infinitely more dangerous than a world built on difference. Few people have explained why this is so as eloquently as Rabbi Jonathan Sacks:

> Universalism is an inadequate response to tribalism, and no less dangerous. It leads to the belief—superficially compelling but quite false—that there is only one truth about the essentials of the human condition, and it holds true for all people at all times. If I am right, you are wrong. If what I believe is the truth, then your belief, which differs from mine, must be an error from which you must be converted, cured and saved. From this flowed some of the great crimes of history, some under religious auspices, others—the French and Russian revolutions, for example—under the banner of secular philosophies.[5]

Ironically, the desire to suppress the other's view, the need to destroy its voice and to eliminate all difference is the result not of a world built on a variety of different cultures but precisely the opposite: a world in which people can claim that there is only one truth. That is a world built on universalism.

Isaiah Berlin made a similar point in a brutally frank fashion:

Few things have done more harm than the belief on the part of individuals and groups (or tribes or states or nations or churches) that he or she or they are in *sole* possession of the truth. . . . It is a terrible and dangerous arrogance to believe that you alone are right. . . . The belief that there is one and only one true answer to the central questions which have agonized mankind and that one has it oneself—or one's Leader has it—was responsible for the oceans of blood: But no Kingdom of Love sprang from it—or could.[6]

Where will humanity find protection from the view that any one group has a monopoly on insight or truth? This is the critical point: the safety that humanity needs will be found in a world of competing truths and alternate narratives. What we need is a world in which multiple nation-states populate the planet's "public square" with different conceptions of what human life should be about and of how we can best protect and cultivate the traditions to which we are heirs. Our challenge is to foster a world in which different nation-states flourish so that they might cultivate the cultures and different visions for humanity that lie at their core.

Philosophers across the spectrum have recognized this danger. Even Immanuel Kant, considered by some to be the father of postnationalism, worried that an international governing body could become a "soulless despotism."[7] John Locke made much this point when he wrote, "For the end why people entered into society being to be preserved one entire, free, independent society, to be governed by its own laws, this is lost whenever they are given up into the power of another."[8]

Similarly, Jean-Jacques Rousseau, writing in *Émile* in 1762, understood this well. "I shall never believe I have heard the arguments of the Jews until they have a free state," he said. "Only then will we know what they have to say."[9] Rousseau wrote these words one hundred and thirty years before Theodor Herzl began his efforts at building a Jewish state, but his words are perhaps the very best possible formulation of why Zionism matters. States are platforms, Rousseau believed; it is when peoples have sovereignty that they can proclaim the messages of their own culture to humanity at large. That is why Israel and its model of the ethnic nation-state matter, not just to the Jews but to human beings everywhere. The world would be far better off if more peoples could have their own Israel.

It is alarming that human difference is endangered today in ways that it may never have been before. Many observers have noted that what plagues Europe in our era is precisely an insufficient willingness to defend its various ancient cultures from outside threats. Natan Sharansky—the former Soviet dissident, political prisoner, and human rights activist and one of the genuine Jewish heroes of the twentieth century—is one of those voices of alarm. He insists that Europe has absorbed, almost without reaction, an ongoing and unabashed assault on civilizations cultivated over centuries. Europe has lost the will to recognize and fight for the cultural heritages that once made the Continent great.

Sharansky believes that the "triumph of post-identity ideology among the intellectual classes in Europe and its permeation into mainstream discourse" has made fighting back "all but impossible."[10] For him, an epitomic indication of Europe's lost willingness to defend its cultures is its funding of imams who actively preach hate against the very countries that serve as their hosts. We should not misconstrue Sharansky; he surely understands the value of free speech. His point is not about the right to speak but about the inability of a majority culture to defend itself from those who preach hatred against it. When Europe's majorities have nothing to say in response to those who assail them, Sharansky asserts, we are sad witnesses to a culture no longer believing in itself.

There *was* a time when human beings did believe in their own cultures, did resist, and did see the battle to preserve their identities as a battle for freedom itself. Human beings who genuinely believe in the value of their heritage will inevitably struggle to preserve it and will refuse to live in a world in which they are denuded of what has made them distinct. That was what animated the Melians in their resistance against Athens. And that was the central factor in the decision of the zealots of Masada who, when they realized that Rome was about to defeat them, decided to commit collective suicide.

We can readily understand why the Masada myth was so compelling an image in the early years of the Zionist revolution. The collective suicide of the Masada zealots in 72 CE communicated the same message that motivated the early Zionists: if their identity was going to be erased, then Jews had no reason to stay alive. It is thus no accident, as one scholar has put it, that "the first manifestations of widespread Jewish interest in Masada coincided with the rise of Zionism during the early decades of the twentieth century."[11] It made no difference whether the threat was the Roman Empire, European assimilation, or anti-Semitism. Whatever the threat, if they were not going to be able to live as Jews in the manner that they chose, staying alive was worse than meaningless.

The Masada narrative has fallen into disfavor among many Israelis in recent years, because the glorification of suicide seems wrong in a country committed to a renewed Jewish *life*. Still, Masada's continued popularity as a tourist site, both for Israelis and for foreigners, suggests that something about the story—the will to live only if one can remain free and be oneself—remains very compelling for many people.

History provides examples of such rebellions almost without limit. The Indian revolt against the British East India Company, also known as the Sepoy Rebellion, was ignited by the British suppression of Indian culture. Chief among the causes of the mutiny was the fact that by 1858, soldiers who were largely Hindus and Muslims became convinced that the company was seeking to undermine their religious identity and convert them to Christianity.[12]

The Pattern 1853 Enfield rifle was the proverbial straw that broke the camel's back.[13] Loading the Enfield rifle required that soldiers bite the cartridge in order to open it. When rumors spread that the cartridges were coated with pig fat, forbidden to Muslims (and to those Hindus who are strict vegetarians), the soldiers' resentment of their British commanders reached the boiling point.[14] With that, a group of Sepoys declared a mutiny against the British East India Company, sparking a wider rebellion across much of northern India.

The power of identity and of religious symbols became horrifically apparent in the darkness of the Nazi assault on the Jews. There were numerous instances in which Jewish prisoners in Nazi death camps, starving as they were, hoarded the bread they received on Thursday and saved it for Friday so that they could have the symbolic two pieces of "challah" on Friday evening in accordance with Jewish tradition. On the verge of death, they were clearly under no religious obligation to have those two pieces of bread on Friday night. What they were experiencing could in no way be called a Sabbath, and hoarding bread was sometimes punishable by death.

What possible point could there have been to doing something so dangerous and seemingly meaningless, even foolish? The answer is simple: they were actually creating their own form of freedom. Hoarding bread for Friday night was these inmates' way of imposing *their* order on the world the Nazis had created; it was about creating freedom even in the depths of depravity and slavery. It was the ultimate act of defiance. It might not keep them alive; indeed, it could easily have led to their deaths. But even if it did lead to their execution, they would die knowing that they had imposed *their* heritage and *their* way of life on the very system that had been designed to destroy them. They could not escape the barbed-wire fences or the hell into which they had been herded, but in some small yet profoundly meaningful way, they could create a form of freedom by insisting, even in the camps, that their sense of who they were had not been erased.

The demise of the Soviet Union is another example, perhaps the clearest case in point. Despite their unceasing efforts, the Soviets were ultimately unable to snuff out the desperate yearning for independence of the many nations they had forced to become part of the USSR. Methodically and relentlessly, the Soviet leadership did everything in its power to transform those unwilling citizens into "real" Soviets, outlawing their original languages, erasing their religious heritages, their holidays, and their histories. But it was all to no avail. The various Soviet peoples' desires to preserve their cultures proved more formidable than the entire enormous Soviet fear-generating apparatus.

When the USSR finally collapsed, fifteen nation-states emerged, each hoping to provide its own people with something akin to what Israel has afforded the Jews. The collapse was inevitable not only because the Soviet economic system had been an unmitigated failure and the cause of widespread poverty but also because the human desire to be free, to preserve difference and heritage, is simply inextinguishable.

Jan Palach, a twenty-year-old Czech student who set himself on fire in protest of the Soviet invasion of Czechoslovakia in 1968, was motivated by very similar sentiments. In the words of Jaroslava Moserova, a physician who tended to Palach in the hospital and later became a Czech senator, Palach's suffering and subsequent death were not ultimately about the Soviet presence in his country. Palach's act was about something even deeper:

> It was not so much in opposition to the Soviet occupation, but the demoralization which was setting in, that people were not only giving up, but giving in. And he wanted to stop that demoralization. I think the people in the street, the multitude of people in the street, silent, with sad eyes, serious faces, which when you looked at those people you understood that everyone understands, all the decent people who were on the verge of making compromises.[15]

Palach did not want those average citizens making compromises, giving up on who they were. There was something grand about Czech history, identity, and difference that was about to be snuffed out, and he would make the ultimate sacrifice to remind his fellow citizens of the importance of what was at stake.

The significance of these and many other paradigmatic examples should not be overlooked. Resistance, wherever and whenever it unfolds, often has a shared underlying cause. Whether French partisan resistance to the Nazis, which we still celebrate, or Vietcong resistance to French and then American encroachment on their independence, which still evokes horribly painful memories for Americans, the desire to preserve a people's culture and way of life has often led to the fight for freedom.

Ultimately, what matters is our differentness, our knowledge that we are *not* interchangeable with everyone else on the planet. Our differences and our uniqueness not only provide pride and purpose but actually lead us to resist others who would seek to rule us, control us, and erase our distinctiveness. It is our differences, not our sameness, that relentlessly spur our drive to be free of oppression and, ultimately, free to express the identities we've inherited.

For many people, as we have seen, difference is suspect. A focus on differentness, after all, seems almost selfish. Isn't a focus on *our* particularity and *our* uniqueness likely to make us more concerned about ourselves than about others? What will happen to empathy if we focus on what makes *us* different?

It's a natural worry but ultimately misplaced. In the inimitable words of Rabbi Sacks, "There is no road to human solidarity that does not begin with moral particularity—by coming to know what it means to be a child, a parent, a neighbor, a friend. We learn to love humanity by loving specific human beings. There is no short-cut."[16] Identity and particularism are not obstacles to caring about others; they are the road to empathy, and from there they are the path to partnerships that labor for freedom.

Michael Walzer, a great American political philosopher, puts it beautifully:

> Societies are necessarily particular because they have members and memories, members with memories not only of their own but also of their common life. Humanity, by contrast, has members but no memory, and so it has no history and no culture, no customary practices, no familiar life-ways, no festivals, no shared understanding of social goods. It is human to have such things, but there is no singular human way of having them. At the same time, the members of all the different societies, because they are human, can acknowledge each other's different ways, respond to each other's cries for help, learn from each other and march (sometimes) in each other's parades.[17]

Natan Sharansky's experiences as a refusenik and his time in a Soviet prison are living proof of Walzer's point. The Soviets had tried with all of their might to extinguish Jewish identity. By the mid-twentieth century, Jewish knowledge and literacy in the Soviet Union were effectively just a memory. Hebrew and Yiddish were largely forgotten. Synagogues were virtually unattended. Most Jews hid their Jewishness whenever they could. Yet despite all this, the Soviets failed. They were unable to erase the deep and pervasive sense among these Jews that even though they now knew very little about what being Jewish *was*, it was still the very essence of who they were and where they came from, and they couldn't ignore it. The same was true of the other peoples that the Soviets had conquered.

It was the Six-Day War of June 1967 that reawakened the still flickering ember of Jewish consciousness in the souls of Soviet Jews. The revival of Jewish consciousness began, for Sharansky and for others (like that couple my wife and I visited in Moscow in the 1980s), when news of the Jewish victory over multiple Soviet-backed Arab armies created a resurgent sense of pride that the Soviets could never have expected. That, in turn, led to the beginning of the Soviet Jewish refusenik movement, of which Sharansky quickly became a leader.

Yet this revival of Jewish identification among Soviet Jews had an impact on more than the Jews' sense of themselves. Soviet Jews came to feel empathy for the struggles of others, as well. Sharansky has written that he learned something very powerful about identity, pride, and the yearning for freedom during his days in a Soviet prison:

> I discovered that only by embracing who I am—by going back to the *shtetl*, by connecting to my own people, by building my own particular identity—could I also stand with others. Far from negating freedom, identity gave me both inner freedom and strength to help others. When Jews abandon identity in pursuit of universal freedom, they end up with neither. Yet when they embrace identity in the name of freedom, as Soviet Jews did in the 1970s, they end up securing both.[18]

To resist communism, Sharansky wrote, it would not have been sufficient for him to have seen himself as a universalist, a member of the entire human family. He had to be *different* from the masses of humanity. He had to know himself before he could struggle to be free, and he had to *be* himself before he could summon the strength to help others. "Far from cutting me off from others, . . . by deepening my own identity I became connected to others in a more profound way. Instead of dividing me from those in other communities, my identity enabled me to join them in a common struggle."[19]

And the same was true in reverse. The people who helped Sharansky most were not necessarily those who were like him. Rather, they were people whose own sense of identity, no matter how different from Sharansky's, enabled them to feel a certain shared sense of solidarity:

> It was only in prison that I began to truly appreciate the feeling of solidarity that can develop between those who are deeply committed to their identities. I would learn how even those with vastly different identities—without a sense of common past or even shared future—can profoundly inspire one another. I would learn how the deep attachments others feel to their people, traditions, and history resonate with those who feel similar attachments and build mutual respect.[20]

Proof of the power of identity is this: what ultimately disappeared was not Judaism but the Soviet Union.

The lessons that were relearned by the refusenik movement, however, were never only about the Jews. Here too the universal ramifications of the identity that comes with particularism showed themselves to be irrepressible. When the Egyptians overthrew President Hosni Mubarak in February 2011, many Israelis were nervous about the possible threat to the thirty-year-old Egyptian-Israeli cold peace that Mubarak's fall might have signaled.

But there was one prominent Israeli who celebrated what was happening in Egypt. It was the voice not of a left-wing leader but rather of a person very clearly associated with the moderate political right; it was the voice of Sharansky, who by then had long since been released from the Soviet prison and had moved to Israel, becoming a politician, a writer, and a powerful symbol of human rights worldwide. In an interview with the *Jerusalem Post*, he noted that the nervousness was understandable but somewhat misplaced. "Maybe," Sharansky said, "this is the moment to try to put our trust in freedom."[21]

Sharansky did acknowledge that he was worried about the Muslim Brotherhood, and he knew that Israel could never drop its guard or lose its military edge. Yet it was his own experience under Soviet rule that led him to see real possibilities in Egypt. His ability to recognize the profundity and power of the sentiment sweeping across Egypt gave him hope that, legitimate worries aside, there could be great possibilities in what was transpiring just south of Israel's border. Sharansky was far too wise to imagine that democracy and freedom would progress without serious setbacks; he understood that freedom-seeking Egyptians had (and still have) a long and difficult road ahead of them.

So what led Sharansky to be the only major Israeli leader who actually celebrated the Egyptian revolution, who saw cause for hope in a sea change that most Israelis saw only as worrisome? It was his personal experience. And that experience was not universal. It was Jewish. It was ethnic. Sharansky had suffered under the Soviets precisely because he was different. He had been supported by others who cared about him because *they* were different. It was precisely their differences from him that made them his partners in fighting for freedom.

This is the great irony: there is a universal dimension to the quest for particularism. It sounds strange, but it is true. The more we strive to highlight what is different about us and our clan, people, nation, or state, the more we discover shared values and commonalities with other people who are doing precisely the same thing, no matter how different from us they may be. As we discover our own particular identities, we uncover something universal. What we learn is that no matter how different our identity may be from that of others, if they, like we, treasure their identity and vow to protect it, we have a tremendous amount in common.

I have often felt much greater affinity to Christians of faith than I have with members of my own Jewish people for whom Jewishness is utterly unimportant. Those Christians, like me, know what it is to stand for faith in a world that sometimes sees religion as foolish superstition. They too know what it means to labor to maintain faith in a world that is too often cruel and inexplicable. They too know the power of belonging that can come from worship. They too know what it is to commit oneself to timeless values and to give up on more immediate satisfactions that to much of the world are the very reason for being. All of our differences notwithstanding, they and I share a great deal. What has been most interesting, at times, is that they have understood our decision to live in Israel better than many of my unaffiliated Jewish acquaintances.

Pierre Manent's observation, quoted at the beginning of this chapter, that "separations between and among human groups cannot be entirely overcome" is no cause for sadness, as far as he is concerned. Our inability to overcome our differences is actually a "fortunate impotence," an inability we should celebrate, for our differences are, as he says, "the condition of human liberty and diversity."

More than any country in the world, Israel represents the celebration of that "fortunate impotence." It is the Jewish state that reminds the world of the importance of difference, of uniqueness, of the power of our own cultures. It is, therefore, the Jewish state that has turned into a clarion call to humanity, begging human beings everywhere not to give up the conditions that freedom requires. Does the world really detest Israel so deeply that it would destroy the Jewish state and, with it, the very symbol of difference that makes human freedom possible?

Chapter Eight

THE ONLY THING WE SHOULD NOT TOLERATE IS INTOLERANCE

The windows of the soul are infinite, we are told. . . . One's destination is never a place, but rather a new way of looking at things.

—Henry Miller, *Big Sur and the Oranges of Hieronymus Bosch*[1]

A s different as human cultures are from one another, there are still some dimensions of our lives that are virtually universal. A simple human smile, like a tear, conveys a sentiment that we all understand, regardless of the milieu in which we were raised. The wonder evoked by a newborn baby is universal.

So too, it seems, is the human yearning to travel. Human beings have been traveling for the simple thrill of it for millennia, and for almost as long, they have been sharing stories of what they saw. The fascination with new places and different kinds of people is as old as civilization itself. Whether expressed in Homer's fictional accounts in *The Odyssey* or in the thousands of travelogues posted every day on the Internet, the yearning to go to new places and to share what we have seen seems virtually hardwired into the human condition.

What is the source of this innate desire to see the world? In part, many of us travel simply to see new places. But there is more to it than that. After all, we could see these places from the comfort of our home in photos, on the Web, in a movie, or on TV travel shows without having to endure the heat or the cold, the crowds and the security, the long flights and the great expense. So why do so many of us still put ourselves through the hassle of actually getting to these places?

We travel to get away from our daily routine, of course, but also to encounter remarkably different cultures. "Traveling," Descartes wrote hundreds of years ago, "is almost like conversing with men of other centuries."[2] Real travelers, not mere tourists, venture to new places to watch people eat and laugh, to observe how they worship and mourn, and to see the role that food and religion play in their lives. We want to hear their music, drink their wine, and see their dress. We travel to see how others create a life well lived.

The wonder of traveling to the Italian province of Tuscany, for example, is not only to see the hills and the castles, to taste the wine and the bread, or even to listen to the lilt and rhythm of a different language. The true magic of Tuscany emerges when all of these disparate, sensuous experiences combine to create a transcendent understanding of how the Tuscans have chosen to organize their lives. Visiting the small villages that dot the Tuscan landscape, each built around a central piazza with a church and a tower that are surrounded by concentric circles of shops and homes, we come to realize that these villages are not accidents of urban planning. Rather, they are the product of a unique people's history, culture, and understanding of how human life ought to be lived. Putting a public gathering place and a house of worship at the center of every town says something extraordinary about what Tuscans believe ought to be at the core of their lives.

There is no way that a plasma screen can ever communicate this. We have to be there to take it all in, and once we do, we return home with a very different sense of the place and culture into which we were born and that had always seemed to us as natural as the rising of the sun. What we really discover when we travel is not a *foreign* culture, but a new way of seeing the world that our own ancestors have constructed for us and for those who will follow us.

David Mitchell, the British novelist, captures the sense of wonder that we often experience when seeing firsthand a culture dramatically different from our own. He was eighteen, on his first real journey, traveling through India and Nepal. He recalls: "I was standing on a busy interjunction in New Delhi with the traffic and the din and the scooters and the bikes and the elephants and the cows, and I remember thinking: These people have got something that we've lost. Our traffic rules and sanitation and systems make life easier and more convenient, ensure longer lifespans and perhaps a fairer society. But these things come at a cost, and the cost is what I felt there. There's a velocity and density of life there that you don't get in the West, and that I found oxygenating."[3]

Descartes and Mitchell are making essentially the same point: what travel really does is afford us a different lens through which to observe the world we call home. What we come to understand better is not only how *others* live and what *they* believe in, but how *we* live and what we've decided is important to *us*.

But what will preserve this ethnic diversity, this mosaic of human life, in a world that is so rapidly being homogenized? One powerful contributor is the nation-state. With countries that have distinct cultures at their core, we have some hope, at least, of preserving both the French *chanson* and the German *lieder* (types of songs). We might even manage to preserve some of the many languages still surviving the onslaught of the Internet. Distinct ways of life can be tended to and cultivated—not by accident, but because that could be the very purpose of the countries that make up our world.

That is why people tend to travel to destinations where they can genuinely encounter the cultures they are visiting. When my wife and I went to Moscow in the 1980s, there were hardly any other American tourists there. In part, of course, going to the Soviet Union was still frightening. But the real reason that most Americans did not consider venturing forth to Russia was that they knew, on some intuitive level, that they would not be exposed to the real

Russia. The Soviet Union, at that time, created a fictitious Russia for tourists to see; it was certainly not the sort of place where native Russians were going to share their genuine worries, concerns, hopes, and fears. What tourists were going to encounter wouldn't be real, unless their meetings with refuseniks, like ours, had been carefully prepared by people "in the know." We want to be part of something unique and distinctive ourselves, but when we meet others, we want to learn about the unique and distinctive culture of which *they* are a part. That wasn't possible in Soviet Russia in the 1980s, so that made travel to the USSR seem virtually pointless. Almost no one went.

Very few people go to North Korea today. It is probably a bit dangerous and more than slightly unwelcoming. But the real reason is that potential tourists know that what they encounter will not be a culture that is ready to share itself; if we were to encounter North Koreans, we would want to learn about the distinct way of life and of thinking that is uniquely theirs. That is what would make the trip interesting. But that's not possible in North Korea today, so people have little desire to go.

Compare that to the great irony of the many American tourists to Vietnam today. Not many decades ago, Americans were fleeing to Canada in order not to get sent to Vietnam as soldiers; today, Americans are anxious to visit Vietnam as tourists. What is the attraction of Vietnam? It's certainly beautiful, different, and even exotic, but it's more than that. The attraction is in no small measure a result of the fact that Vietnam occupies a special—and painful—place in the American psyche and memory, and the country is now reasonably accessible.

Memory, pain, curiosity, and openness are factors in getting people to visit new places. For in locales replete with painful memories and associations, we are virtually urged to see what our own lives might have been like had history unfolded differently, and we can wonder about our own culture and how it ever saw *that* culture as the enemy. (It's remarkable that Auschwitz-Birkenau is Poland's number one tourist attraction; pain and attempts at healing are often at the core of our decisions of what we choose to see.) We travel to figure all this out, to see the myriad ways in which different countries are actually about different ways of constructing a view of what constitutes a meaningful life.

If the grandeur of human life is to be found in its diversity, and if this differentness is the key to human freedom, what should be our attitudes toward societies that do *not* value freedom? Throughout this book, I've been advocating the importance of Israel precisely because Israel models the value of difference. But should we honor difference even when other states do not share the commitment to a free press or to freedom of association? Does the value of difference trump the value of these types of freedom?

Should the goal of the United Nations be to impose some form of Western democratic life on the entire world? That seems to be what the United States did to Japan at the end of World War II and what it sought to accomplish in Iraq recently. Isn't that attitude not simply an imperialism of its own, an intolerance clothed in the garb of freedom?

We must tread lightly here, for the questions are thorny. Does the United States have the right to impose democracy on Syria? How much do elections in Gaza really matter if a repressive regime like Hamas is elected? Who are we to say that our way of life is truly better than others'? If the people of Saudi Arabia wish to live under a repressive regime that allows no diversity of religion and no rights for women (not even, so far, the right to drive a car), is that our business? Should we stay out of their affairs, or should we seek to impose our sense of freedom even on societies that do not seem to be seeking it?

One can make a compelling case for not intervening. Indeed, even the Hebrew Bible—which has many negative things to say about the idolatrous nations that lived around the Israelites—does not give the Israelites carte blanche to take territories away from those peoples. Quite the contrary, in fact. Even peoples whose ways of life may seem repugnant (idolatry is an absolute evil in the eyes of the Bible) are not to be conquered. Relative to the size of Israel today, the Israelite kingdom of old might seem rather large. But the critical point is that it was limited—not by the Israelites' lack of military might but by God's explicit biblical command as the people drew near its Promised Land:

> You have been skirting the hill country long enough, now turn north. . . . You will be passing through the territory of your kinsmen, the descendants of Esau, who live in Seir. They will be afraid of you; be very careful not to provoke them. For I will not give you of their land so much as a foot can tread on; I have given the hill country of Seir as a possession to Esau. . . . Do not harass the Moabites or provoke them to war. For I will not give you any of their land as a possession; I have assigned it to Ar as a possession. . . . You will then be close to the Ammonites; do not harass them or start a fight with them. For I will not give any part of the land of the Ammonites to you as a possession; I have assigned it as a possession to the descendants of Lot.[4]

In addition to everything else that concerns the Hebrew Bible, diversity is also a prime value; so is peace. And to promote both diversity and peace, imperialism must be curbed. The Israelites are not to take over one nation after another in order to impose their truth on everyone else. There is value in the existence of others, even if we disagree with them about the most critical issues.

So perhaps we ought to put it this way: our goal must be to produce not a world filled with democracies but a world characterized by tolerance for difference. It may be true, as Winston Churchill said, that democracy is the worst form of government, except for all the others. The world may gradually migrate toward universal democracy; but we should keep in mind that it is not *democracy* that is the ultimate goal; the goal is tolerance, diversity, and freedom. Those are the values that the free world must export to whatever extent it can.

If democracy follows, it will be because people desire freedom with such desperation that they finally break the shackles of their oppression; it will be because they decide that nothing will guarantee their rights to live as they wish better than a government that they themselves elect. Democracy will come when they are willing to fight for their right to a free press, for the rights of minorities, for the right to assemble, and for all of the other liberties that liberal democracies typically afford their citizens.

How much should we intervene to guarantee those types of freedom? Should the West have imposed those values on Egypt? Should it impose them on Syria? Should it impose them (if it even could) on other repressive Arab regimes? It probably cannot do so. There are limits to what we can impose on others, no matter how just our cause. Even freedom-loving countries will have to abide the lack of freedom in other places.

But we should be clear about the difference between what we can accomplish and what we believe in: we *do* believe that freedom is an ultimate human value. We cherish democracy because it invariably fosters freedom better than other forms of government do, and we value the nation-state because the nation-state is the best guarantor we know of the difference that ultimately makes freedom both valuable and possible. (A discussion of whether the United States is a nation-state is found in the next chapter.) Other societies that do not share this freedom are different, and they are less worthy than ours. Our commitment to tolerance and open-mindedness need not lead us to abdicate our true beliefs. Some societies are better than others; there is simply nothing that we can do to make all of them better.

There is a commonly heard objection to this notion: a world of nation-states might well promote difference and human diversity, but it will also lead to war. Isn't that a very high price to pay for heterogeneity, no matter how much we may value it?

As we have stated repeatedly, though, the notion that a multiplicity of nation-states will inevitably lead to war is wholly unfounded. What leads to war is imperialism, not democratic nation-states. Michael Doyle, a Columbia University scholar and international relations expert, noted in two articles (which are still classics nearly thirty years later) that liberal democracies do not go to war with each other.[5] (Contemporary scholars like Michael Walzer of the Institute of Advanced Studies at Princeton have called Doyle's thesis "one of the relatively few well-founded 'findings' of modern political science."[6])

Imperialist countries, which *can* be democracies on paper, do declare war on those who are not like them. Germany until Hitler was a prime example, and so is Gaza under Hamas. But can you think of a single instance in which a genuine liberal democracy declared war on another genuine liberal democracy? It's virtually impossible to come up with an example.

The problem with imperialism is that it usually denies the legitimacy of difference. That is why it seeks to destroy or subdue societies that are not like it. Despite all the assaults on the notion of nationalism after World War II, it is not nationalism that leads to conflict. It is not nationalism that is the cause of land grabs. When a country is not a liberal democracy, nationalist rhetoric can indeed become a tool with which a country's leaders justify expansionism. But when nationalism is coupled with liberal democracy, it does not lead to land grabs.

Quite the contrary, in fact. Although imperialism might seem to create a simpler international map, it is a multiplicity of liberal democratic nation-states that brings genuine peace. Nation-states create a more complicated map and, on the surface, a less stable international community. But when they are true liberal democracies—not just with elections, but with transparent institutions that guarantee the rights of expression and association, a free press, and the like—they are ultimately the source of freedom.[7]

Our ultimate goals ought to be human difference, human expression, and human freedom. Humanity has discovered no better system for promoting those than the liberal democratic state. Spreading democracy, though, is not an end in itself; it is a means of protecting and promoting human differentness. How hard we should push to encourage the spread of democracy will never be an easy question to answer. But whatever we decide, we ought to recall that what we are truly seeking to preserve and enhance is human freedom—and we have discovered no better way of doing that than through flourishing liberal democratic nation-states. (See chapter 9 for a discussion of the United States in this regard.)

For whom, though, does the ethnic nation-state create freedom? Does it bestow freedom on everyone or just on those who belong to the majority culture? If the purpose of the nation-state is to promote the flowering of a particular culture, what happens to minorities in that state who are of a different culture? How will *they* live out their identities? Will they not get caught in the majority's tendency toward a desire for ethnic purity?

Nation-states have an absolute obligation to protect the rights of the minorities who live within their borders. That is the whole point of diversity and tolerance. If we were to argue for the nation-state as a protector of diversity, but only among different countries and not within them, our argument would be a sham. When ethnic nation-states adopt policies of ethnic cleansing, they become the enemy rather than the embodiment of the principles that this book advocates. If difference is valuable—indeed, sacred—it matters everywhere. Even when difference is a challenge, as it often is within the borders of a single state, it ought to be recognized for the positive role that it plays even inside an ethnic society.

Israel and its significant Arab minority are a case in point. For Israel to remain both Jewish and democratic, it clearly needs to have a significant Jewish demographic majority. Otherwise, Israel will either have to give up on democracy (in which case it loses its moral legitimacy) or on its Jewishness (in which case it surrenders its very reason for being).[8] For that reason, the Arab minority in Israel, which constitutes about 20 percent of Israel's citizens, is often perceived as a serious challenge to Israel remaining the kind of country that it seeks to be.

That challenge is real (although Israeli demographers debate how imminent the threat is, with a few even claiming that the tide has begun to turn in favor of an enduring *Jewish* majority).[9] But even while Israeli strategists seek to mitigate the challenge of a growing Israeli-Arab population, they would do well to recognize that Israel is a richer society for having citizens who see its history differently, who possess a different narrative about the land, and who have different ways of showing their attachment to it. Israel is richer for having an internal countervailing voice to its predominant narrative—a voice that reminds Israelis that not everyone sees the events of 1947–1949 in quite the same way, a voice that reminds Israelis that contemporary Israel is not immune to the danger of the abuse of power.

This is not to suggest that Israeli Jews ought to capitulate in the face of that other voice, but it *is* to say that in a society of genuine dialogue, Israel will be a richer society with a more profound worldview the more Jewish Israelis both defend their state *and* feel enriched by dialogue with fellow citizens who have a very different weltanschauung.

Israel does not engage in ethnic cleansing, and it is far from ethnically pure. But Israel does unquestionably suffer from a parochialism born of a lack of sufficient intellectual diversity, or put otherwise, a lack of tolerance for the great diversity of its citizens. The causes of Israel's occasional xenophobia are many. Israel was created in the shadow of the Shoah and was populated at first by people who knew what it was to have the world betray them. Having been at war for the better part of a century, too many Jewish Israelis are incapable of seeing Arabs as anything but enemies. Israeli universities are technically excellent, but they do not provide the broad liberal arts education that many Americans take for granted. Unlike in the United States, where most rabbis first go to college before training for the rabbinate, Israel's rabbis are trained almost exclusively in yeshivot, with virtually no exposure to the outside world.

At times, some Israeli leaders—be they religious, political, or cultural leaders—express views that simply make many of us shudder. Some examples are Foreign Minister Avigdor Lieberman's push for loyalty oaths among Israeli Arabs, a letter from rabbis urging Jews not to sell or rent property to Arabs, and hard-line rabbinic resistance to IDF conversions that were designed to usher many Russian immigrants into the Jewish community.[10]

A Jewish state committed to the values that this book endorses needs to do much better than that. Having different sorts of people—of various ethnicities, religions, and cultures—inside Israel will contribute much to widening the worldview of typical Jewish Israelis and, one would hope, to deepening their tolerance. For that to happen, Israeli leaders, along with those who support Israel and care about its future, must focus on the idea that is at the core of this book. Differentness is a value because it leads to cultural humility and to human freedom.

That is precisely why true lovers of Israel and genuine believers in the ideal of human difference ought to favor the creation of a Palestinian state. Reasonable minds can and do disagree about under what conditions such a state should be recognized, and they can differ bitterly about what its eventual borders should be. Those disagreements are perfectly legitimate, even healthy. But we will know that Zionism has succeeded in shaping Jewish identity and intellectual commitment when Israel's most passionate defenders also understand that if Jews deserve a chance at the self-expression that sovereignty affords, so too do other peoples, including the Palestinians.

It is difficult to speak that way about one's enemies, but that makes the challenge all the more important. When we hear people say, "There already *is* a Palestinian state—it's called Jordan," we know that they are either appallingly ignorant about contemporary Jordan (which oppresses its Palestinian majority, often brutally) or that they are concerned with only the flourishing of one particular people: their own.[11] Ultimately, that argument does not defend Zionism; rather, it sells short the profundity of the ideas that are at the core of the Jewish state.

Zionists will have internalized the great insight of Zionism when their passion for the Jewish state and what it has done for the Jewish people translates into a similar concern for the aspirations and flourishing of other peoples as well.

If our claim about the nation-state is correct, must then all the peoples of the world who are seeking such states be granted them? That would seem to be the undeniable conclusion. "Either the theory is right, or it is wrong," one might argue. "If it is right, then the Jews should have Israel, but the Basques should have a country, and so should the

Chechnyans, the Roma, and many others." The Palestinians would then hardly be the only state-seeking people in question.

There are Native Americans who still want some of their land back from the United States. Some of the tribal nations were removed from their lands so recently that their grandparents were the ones who "lost their freedom" this way.[12] If the Jews get a state, this view suggests, then so too must the Mohawk Indians of Akwesasne, for instance. Native Americans are considered quasi-sovereign nations within the United States, theoretically, but they do not have anything remotely approaching the rights a fully acknowledged nation-state would have. Shouldn't they too be given states? But what if that is simply impossible? What does that do to our theory?

Obviously, not every people who currently seeks a nation-state has a reasonable chance of creating (or re-creating) one. As was the case with Israel, finding (or recovering) territory is invariably difficult. And there are usually other complicating factors. The American South wanted its sovereignty (and its slaves), but the North was not willing to give up on the viability of the Union and therefore fought a war to prevent the South's secession from becoming permanent.

The Kurds of northern Iraq want a sovereign Kurdistan, a country that would comprise territories from several different presently existing states. The Iraqi Kurds just happen to be sitting on a great deal of Iraq's oil, however, so Iraq is not going to willingly relinquish that territory anytime soon. Nor do Turkey, Iran, or Syria seem particularly willing to give up their respective pieces of Kurdistan.

We must therefore distinguish between an ideal and the possibility of its implementation. The principles about human diversity and freedom that are embodied in Zionism should have something to say about the Roma, the Chechnyans, the Tibetans, and even the Palestinians. What can and cannot be implemented is another issue. But as a matter of principle, what Zionism ultimately means is that any time the creation of a state for an open, tolerant people can actually be negotiated, it would make the world a better place.

This may appear to be saying, "You can want it, but it may never happen as it did for us," and that may be frustrating. The frustration is real, but that does not weaken Zionism's claim. There is simply no reason to claim that just because not every people who deserves a state can have one, then no one should.

When the Internet Corporation for Assigned Names and Numbers, the international body responsible for domain names on the Web, announced in 2009 that it would begin making it possible for people to register Web addresses in languages other than Latin script, many people in the West barely noticed.[13] But Manu Joseph, a popular writer from India, wrote to the *New York Times* praising the Internet Corporation's decision to allow different cultures to assert their linguistic identity in a cyberspace that had previously been organized exclusively in English. The "world does not want to be unified," Joseph wrote. "What is the value of belonging if you belong to all? [Ours] is a fragmented world by choice."[14]

This notion that the world is fragmented by design, that our differences are to be celebrated and not overcome, has been precisely one of the great insights that the Jewish tradition and now the Jewish state have sought to communicate to the world. It is often an unpopular notion, at odds with the prevailing intellectual currents of much of the world. The universalism in vogue today leaves no room for the particularism that has long been at the core of Judaism and the Hebrew Bible's vision of a life well lived. This ideological clash is part of what has led to Israel's marginalization, so it is part of what must be squarely brought to the table and discussed.

What too many people today do not understand is that the Jewish tradition and Israel make a bold claim. It is the claim made by Rabbi Sacks, which we quoted in chapter 7, that we learn to love humanity by loving specific human beings. Although universalism and erasing difference might *seem* to create a more harmonic world, the Jewish tradition and the Jewish state have long argued that the absence of difference devalues human life and ultimately endangers freedom. "If I am not for myself," the rabbinic sage Hillel asked, "who will be for me?" First we must be for ourselves. First we must know who we are. Only once we know why *we* matter and why *our* freedom is important will we have the fortitude to reach out and help others strive for theirs.

It is for this reason that critics of the nation-state are incorrect when they argue that it must invariably lead to ethnic cleansing. The ethnic nation-state is about the flourishing of a particular people, but true national flourishing ought to lead to empathy for others in search of their own flowering. Our own sovereignty must be an opportunity to assist others in their quest, not to subvert them. That is what must happen in Israel, which needs to accord greater rights and opportunities to its Arab citizens. Some appreciable measure of what statehood has done for the Jews must also extend to the substantial minorities who live in its midst.

Safeguarding the rights of minorities and affording them opportunities to strengthen their culture is precisely what every nation-state ought to be about. Once we genuinely appreciate the value of human differentness and heterogeneity, loyalty to our own group need not condemn us to triumphalism or to attempts to subvert the flourishing of others.

Without instinctive loyalty to our own group, whoever we may be, we cannot stand for ourselves, for anyone else, or for anything at all. When we stand for nothing, it makes no difference who rules us. When we cannot articulate what is unique, important, and worth preserving about our own culture, we can make no argument for freedom or for the courage that defending it will require. We must love ourselves and our own tradition, or we will love nothing, and eventually we will be nothing. Without a burning sense that we have something critical, insightful, and sacred to pass on, we will have no cause to defend the freedom that many of us now take entirely for granted. Either we acknowledge that both our culture *and* other cultures must survive, or freedom itself has no future.

Chapter Nine

A COUNTRY WITH THE SOUL OF A CHURCH

Providence has been pleased to give this one connected country to one united people—a people descended from the same ancestors, speaking the same language, professing the same religion, attached to the same principles of government, very similar in their manners and customs, and who, by their joint counsels, arms, and efforts, fighting side by side throughout a long and bloody war, have nobly established liberty and independence.

—John Jay, "Federalist #2"[1]

More years later than I care to recall, I can still remember how uncomfortable I felt in Mrs. Brown's seventh-grade social studies class.[2] We studied mostly U.S. history that year, and we started at the very beginning: the *Mayflower* and Valley Forge, Fort McHenry (the birthplace of the national anthem), and later the Alamo. These were the stories of the founding of the United States of America, and she taught them with a pride and an urgency that I still recall—and that I still remember not feeling.

I didn't tell my parents about the discomfort I felt, and I certainly didn't tell her. But the feeling was palpable. The more she drilled those stories into us, the more I couldn't help but feel that they were really not *my* stories. After all, *my* ancestors hadn't been anywhere near the *Mayflower*; actually, they wouldn't have been allowed on it. My ancestors never stepped foot in Valley Forge or at the Alamo. When all of that was happening, I knew (even as a kid), my ancestors were in eastern Europe.

It was not only an uncomfortable year for me in social studies class, it was also an awakening of sorts. I was supposed to feel something that I just didn't feel at all. And I wasn't supposed to be feeling what it was that I did feel: that I had a different narrative, a different history that had shaped who I was and am. But I kept all that to myself; being in an American social studies class meant having to pretend that my ancestors could have been on the *Mayflower*, even when I knew that they could not.

There is a price, and an underbelly, to the extraordinary welcome that the United States has extended to its immigrants. We saw it in the story of the parcels of religious objects dropped into the oily waters of New York Harbor (see the introduction). It has to do with pretense, with the price of entry, with the erasure of self that the United States, like all host countries, has invariably required.

Lady Liberty has certainly afforded unparalleled freedom and promise to the tired, poor, huddled masses that yearned to be free, but *she did so at a cost*. Without a doubt, these immigrants were financially much better off and physically more secure than they would have been had there been no United States to welcome them. That goes without saying. But we need to be aware of the cost no less than we are aware of the promises made and kept. There *is* a cost to "making it" in America, and it is often a painful one.

The cost, for many people, has been having to give up a large measure of their identities. Those satchels nonchalantly dumped into New York Harbor, where they sank unceremoniously to the bottom and disappeared, were a symbol of much more than the religious items they contained. They symbolized entire ways of life, centuries of tradition, and sometimes sacred practices, which immigrants to the

United States had to live without if they were going to "make it" in their new homeland.

Jews are hardly the only people who have made this painful accommodation. In many ways, the United States was *about* making that accommodation. In 1914, Woodrow Wilson told a group of immigrants to the United States, "You cannot become thorough Americans if you think of yourself in groups. America does not consist of groups. A man who thinks of himself as belonging to a particular national group in America has not yet become an American."[3] At times, Wilson was even more vehement that to be an American meant to be absolutely nothing else:

> If the immigrant who comes here in good faith becomes an American and assimilates himself to us, he shall be treated on an exact equality with everyone else, for it is an outrage to discriminate against any such man because of creed, or birthplace, or origin. But this is predicated upon the man's becoming in very fact an American, and nothing but an American. . . . There can be no divided allegiance here. Any man who says he is an American but something else also, isn't an American at all.[4]

Wilson was hardly alone. Erasing difference became a central American ethos of the early twentieth century. Sometimes this goal was communicated in ways that would strike us today as utterly absurd, totally lacking in sensitivity or tact. In the early 1900s, for example, workers at the Ford Motor Company were required to attend an Americanization school. There they studied proper English, learned American manners, and were taught to shed the distinctive characteristics they had brought with them to the United States. As they completed their studies, the students participated in a graduation ceremony in which the following occurred:

> All the men descend from a boat scene representing the vessel on which they came over; down the gangway . . . into a pot . . . which represents the Ford English School. Six teachers, three

on either side, stir the pot with ten-foot ladles representing nine months of teaching in the school. Into the pot 52 nationalities with their foreign clothes and baggage go, and out of the pot after vigorous stirring by the teachers comes one nationality, [namely,] American.[5]

What these "Americans" coming out of the pot understood, of course, was that to be Americans, they had to give up the portions of their identities that they'd brought with them from the "old country." Is it any surprise that there is a sadness attached to the success that many have achieved?

Look and listen carefully to the quiet musings of other immigrant groups, and some of that sadness, their version of the bundles dumped in the harbor, surfaces time and again. The details are different, but the story is the same. This sadness, loss, and dislocation are rampant in the world of American immigrant literature, particularly among the generation of writers who have been American just long enough to feel sufficiently secure to acknowledge what their parents or grandparents had to abandon for the success these writers now enjoy.[6]

It might seem strange to discuss American immigrant literature in a book about the idea of the nation-state, but there's a reason for this: as fictional as literature might sometimes seem, it often conveys truths that are no less profound than the truths of philosophy, for example. That, of course, is why we read serious literature. We seek in great works of fiction not just memorable characters or plots that surprise or intrigue but also insights into who we are as human beings and what we ought to seek.

The philosopher Martha Nussbaum has noted, "Storytelling and literary imagining are not opposed to rational argument, but can provoke essential ingredients in a rational argument."[7] Indeed, there are, as she writes elsewhere, insights that cannot be gleaned any other way: "Certain truths about human life can only be fittingly and accurately stated in the language and forms characteristic of the narrative artist.

With respect to certain elements of human life, the terms of the novel-ist's arts are alert winged creatures, perceiving where the blunt terms of ordinary speech . . . are blind."[8]

With Nussbaum's explanation in mind, it is worth turning to several samples of American immigrant literature that lay bare the profound loss that immigration to the United States has entailed, despite the opportunities it also presented. Chang-rae Lee, a widely lauded novelist who teaches at Princeton, seems the ultimate U.S. immigrant success story: he is widely published, venerated in literary circles, and serves on the faculty of one of America's greatest academic institutions.

What is truly fascinating about Lee's characters is the internal emptiness that accompanies their apparent success. In *A Gesture Life* (1999), Franklin Hata, the main character, seems to be the embodi-ment of the American dream. A Korean adopted by Japanese parents, he later immigrates to the United States. He builds a business, is respected throughout his community, and lives a quiet but honorable life in retirement. His is the life to which many Americans seemingly aspire.

Just beneath the surface, however, Hata is stranded and miser-able. His material success means nothing in the face of his soul-suffocating emptiness. He is at odds with his adopted-from-Japan "American" daughter, uncomfortable and inept in his relationships with women. Despite his lifetime of success, the United States is still fundamentally a puzzle to him. "Fitting in Perfectly on the Outside, but Lost Within" was how the *New York Times Book Review* described *A Gesture Life*.[9] Franklin Hata is the walking dead— essentially waiting quietly in the suburbs to die alone and, most likely, unnoticed.

Chang-rae Lee's point is clear: many Koreans have succeeded in the United States, but at a tremendous price. They left their ethnic homeland for America, seeking financial opportunity and freedom, but parts of their souls had to be surrendered to "make it" in their adopted home. They did achieve success—as long as happiness and contentment are not thrown into the equation. Was it worth it? That is the question that Lee's work forces us to ask.

Franklin Hata's ambivalences and struggles are similar to those portrayed in the works of Jhumpa Lahiri, an Indian American author whose first book, a collection of short stories entitled *Interpreter of Maladies,* won the Pulitzer Prize for fiction. Lahiri's work is filled with the same intense dislocation and emptiness experienced by Franklin Hata: many of her characters struggle with the profound ramifications of coming to the United States and abandoning their unique cultural identities in search of success in their new homeland.

One of the most poignant short stories in Lahiri's book is "When Mr. Pirzada Came to Dine," which traces the evenings that Mr. Pirzada, a Pakistani botanist studying New England foliage for the year on a government fellowship, spends at the house of ten-year-old Lilia and her Indian family during the Bangladesh Liberation War in 1971. Lilia's parents, feeling alone in their new country and estranged from their culture, seek out individuals like Mr. Pirzada who share their cultural heritage and national memories: "The supermarket did not carry mustard oil, doctors did not make house calls, neighbors never dropped by without an invitation, and of these things, every so often, my parents complained. In search of compatriots, they used to trail their fingers, at the start of each new semester, through the columns of the university directory circling surnames familiar to their part of the world."[10]

Yet although Lilia's parents sometimes bemoan their present condition, they happily make these sacrifices to provide a better future for their daughter. Lilia's father, dismayed that she has not learned about the 1947 partition of India and Pakistan—her *own* cultural and national history—asks, "What exactly do they teach you at school?" Her mother bluntly responds, "Lilia has plenty to learn at school. . . . We live here now, she was born here."

"She seemed genuinely proud of the fact," Lilia describes, "as if it were a reflection of my character. In her estimation, I knew, I was assured a safe life, an easy life, a fine education, every opportunity. I would never have to eat rationed food, or obey curfews, or hide neighbors in water tanks to prevent them from being shot, as she and my father had."[11]

But this security comes at a deep cost to Lilia. Lilia doesn't "learn about the world," about her own background and culture, or about her own identity and history, in the United States. All she can do, when asked by her father whether she was "aware of the current" events in India and Pakistan, is to nod her head, completely "unaware of the situation."[12]

Instead, in school Lilia learns about a distinctly *American* history, a distinctly *American* culture and ethos, which she cannot necessarily connect with: "We learned American history, of course, and American geography. That year, and every year, it seemed, we began by studying the Revolutionary War. We were taken in school buses on field trips to visit Plymouth Rock, and to walk the Freedom Trail, and to climb to the top of the Bunker Hill Monument. We made dioramas out of colored construction paper depicting George Washington crossing the choppy waters of the Delaware River, and we made puppets of King George wearing white tights and a black bow in his hair. During tests we were given blank maps of the thirteen colonies, and asked to fill in the names, dates, capitals. I could do it with my eyes closed."[13]

But "no one at school," Lilia recalls, "talked about the war followed so faithfully in my living room"—no one talked about *her* cultural identity and history. Even at the young age of ten, Lilia recognizes that there is something profoundly lacking in her American upbringing. One afternoon, while in the school library doing research for her presentation on the British surrender at Yorktown, she realizes that she "could not concentrate" on this history that was not hers and "returned to the blond-wood shelves, to a section . . . labeled 'Asia,'" where she found a book about Pakistan.[14]

Lilia grows so engrossed in *Pakistan: A Land and Its People* that she does not realize that her teacher, Mrs. Kenyon, has come to the library to monitor her research. "Is this book part of your report, Lilia?" Mrs. Kenyon asks after she "glanced at the cover." The answer, of course, is no. "Then I see no reason to consult it," Mrs. Kenyon said, replacing the book on the shelf. "Do you?" Of course Lilia sees an intense and urgent reason to consult the book: it is a book "filled with photos of rivers and rice fields and men in military uniforms."[15]

It is a book about the conversations that occupy her parents and Mr. Pirzada every evening, a book that focuses not on an American identity that is conspicuously not hers but on some part of her *own* ethnic, national, and historical background. But ten-year-old Lilia does not yet possess the skills to express these profound emotions; she does not yet have the vocabulary to resist the cultural assimilation and loss that America forces on her immigrants.

In the deep sense of loss that she experiences, Lilia is not alone in Lahiri's book. In another story, "A Temporary Matter," Lahiri describes how when the protagonist, Shukumar, was a teenager, he "preferred sailing camp or scooping ice cream during the summers to going to Calcutta." It was only when he began to "study [India's] history from course books," without passion, "as if it were any other subject" that he started to feel the full burden of never having fully experienced his Indian culture. With his marriage faltering and his dissertation on Indian agrarian revolts in shambles, he begins to wish that "he too," like his wife, "had his own childhood story of India"—that is, had his own connection to a culture and a country that his parents left when they moved to the United States.[16]

In a third story, "The Third and Final Continent," the protagonist (and unnamed narrator of the story) is a Bengali immigrant to the United States. He and his wife, Mala, fully understand that their son, a Harvard undergraduate, must give up the richness of his Bengali heritage in order to succeed in their new country: "Mala no longer . . . weeps at night for her parents," her husband describes, "but occasionally she weeps for our son. So we drive to Cambridge to visit him, or bring him home for a weekend, so that he can eat rice with us with his hands, and speak in Bengali, things we worry he will no longer do after we die."[17]

"Eloquent and assured," says one review; "direct [and] translucent," says another.[18] Each reviewer used slightly different language to describe Lahiri's sharp and incisive writing style and beautiful prose in her debut work of fiction, but all seemed to agree that at the heart of her stories pulses a heavy sense of dislocation, lost moorings, and sadness for the price paid to enter the United States—in her words, a "diffuse, watered-down, eclectic place."[19] All agreed, in the words of

Caleb Crain in his review in the *New York Times Book Review,* that "Lahiri's stories are rendered more powerful by the sense of cultural transition and loss" upon moving to America that permeates her collection of short stories.[20]

We see this all-consuming worry even with Nicole Krauss, the Jewish American author. Even though she is an extraordinary example of the typical U.S. immigrant-family success story, there is something about the world her family left behind that she cannot escape. Her novel *The History of Love* is consumed with loss, the long and dark shadow of the Shoah, and missed opportunities for loving and parenting. Love, book manuscripts, relationships, secrets—many things disappear in Krauss's novel. In what is perhaps a very telling decision, Krauss dedicates the book to "My Grandparents, who taught me the opposite of disappearing."[21] Does being an immigrant mean dropping so many parcels of memory into the harbor waters that newcomers risk disappearing altogether?

With Junot Diaz's extraordinary *The Brief Wondrous Life of Oscar Wao*, a new plot twist becomes very important: the protagonist, Oscar, returns to the land from which he came. In his Pulitzer Prize–winning novel, Diaz also highlights the intense sense of dislocation that immigrants feel when they come to the United States. But Diaz juxtaposes this dislocation with the acute sense of belonging that his characters feel when they return home to the Dominican Republic. Diaz himself is Dominican, and much of his novel traces the history of his country under the tyranny of the dictator Rafael Trujillo.

Oscar's mother leaves the Dominican Republic to escape Trujillo's tyranny, but in America, Oscar is adrift. He is obese, socially awkward, and, noticeably to his hypermasculinized Dominican American peers, still a virgin. After graduating from college and reaching rock bottom, Oscar decides to spend the summer in the Dominican Republic—to listen to his "elder spirits" and to return "home."[22] It is only when he returns to the Dominican Republic—when he, as Diaz describes it, "goes native"—that Oscar finally finds himself and gets "some power of his own."[23] While there, he falls in love with Ybon, a woman who is utterly wrong for him and is dating a jealous Dominican police captain. To be more precise, though, he falls in love not only with Ybon but with the Dominican Republic, the country from which he had supposedly been liberated.

After a near-death experience with the vengeful captain and his milieu, Oscar returns to the United States. But having experienced the freedom of belonging in Dominican society, he can't reacclimate to his watered-down American identity. Despite the protestations of his family and his friends, he makes the Dominican Republic his home, even though he understands on some level that this will mean his death, which comes a few weeks later. Ybon, fearing for his safety, begs Oscar to "go home." But Ybon, with her entreaties, misses the point entirely. Oscar has to explain it to her: "But beautiful girl, above all beautiful girls . . . *this* is my home."[24]

This intense feeling of belonging that people experience when they return to their ancestral homelands is not only the province of great fiction. It figures in nonfiction as well. No one would have seemed less likely to experience a sense of otherness in the United States than Barack Obama, perhaps the quintessential American immigration success story. (Obama was born in the United States but spent his formative years in Indonesia.) Obama often mentioned his biracial background and his unusual childhood based in several far-flung homes, and said, "In no other country on Earth is my story even possible." That was certainly true. But while Obama is no Oscar, he and Oscar share the power of going to a land which is, in some ways, more "home" than is America. For Oscar, that land was the Dominican Republic; for Obama, it was Kenya, the land from which his ancestors had come.

In a much discussed comment, Obama, when asked if he believed in American exceptionalism, replied, "I believe in American exceptionalism, just as I suspect that the Brits believe in British exceptionalism and the Greeks believe in Greek exceptionalism."[25] Why was it that this president, so obviously aware of what it was that his country has provided him, could not more enthusiastically endorse an ideology that has long been a strong element of American mythology?

A hint, I believe, can be found in his first book, the autobiographical *Dreams from My Father*, in which Obama reflects on what it was like to go to Kenya, as he searched for his roots:

> For a span of weeks or months, you could experience the freedom that comes from not feeling watched, the freedom of believing that your hair grows as it's supposed to grow and that your rump sways the way a rump is supposed to sway. . . . Here the world was black, and so you were just you; you could discover all those things that were unique to your life without living a lie or committing betrayal.[26]

That is an extraordinary statement of belonging—in a country to which he had profound ties of culture and heritage but in which he had never lived—written five years after Obama had been elected president of the *Harvard Law Review*. It is a powerful acknowledgment that even Obama, who by the time he wrote his book was an emerging American success story, felt the loss that comes with a pervasive, constant awareness of otherness. It is the loss that comes from not being truly at home in the way that Jews can be in the Jewish state, that Obama could be in Kenya, and that many African Americans have undoubtedly felt upon visiting Africa. It is the loss that comes from living in a country in which your race or culture is not the norm, in which you feel like an exception that at best must be accommodated and at worst is merely tolerated.

There is a power to going "home," even when that is a place in which one has never made a home. Thousands of Jewish American college students visiting Israel on programs such as Birthright experience this when they land in Israel and travel the road from Ben-Gurion Airport to Jerusalem. What they are shown as their bus winds its way up the narrow highway to Jerusalem are the caves of the Maccabees, which the Jews used as bases as they fought to expel the Syrian Greeks from Judea more than two thousand years ago. They pass the carefully preserved remains of the jeeps and trucks that Jewish resistance fighters used in 1948 to try to break the Arab siege on Jerusalem. They pass the memorial to these fighters, the *portzim* ("those who broke through"), and to Yitzhak Rabin, who at age twenty-four took it upon himself to lead the charge.

All it takes is a good explanation of what lies alongside this road to transform these young Americans' sense not only of Israel but of Jewishness itself. Suddenly, these descendants of the immigrants who dropped treasured parcels into the harbor find themselves driving through a story that is truly theirs, wondering how they can recover the knowledge that they intuit is required to fully appreciate the culture that they are just now encountering in all its power.

Barack Obama's experience is actually much more universal than he might have imagined. Take any of us back to our "Kenya," and suddenly we will "experience the freedom that comes from not feeling watched." That is the freedom that makes home.

Therefore, no matter how welcoming the United States may be to its immigrants and their descendants, even though it can provide financial opportunity unlike any other country, it cannot provide the sense of belonging and the full identity that people's ancestral homelands afforded them. It cannot give them what happens when, as described in Genesis, peoples branch out "according to their clans and languages, by their lands, according to their nations."[27] There is a power to one's ancestral homeland, a sense of belonging that the nation-state can provide that even a country as magnificent as the United States cannot except to those who were its founding core.

Does the United States really have a founding core? A common claim is that it does not, that the United States is not a nation-state. Rather, the argument goes, it is a flourishing society with a real sense of peoplehood, but it has no particular ethnic core. Doesn't that undermine this book's argument for the importance of the nation-state model?

That claim however, is oversimplified. For even though we do not often think of it in this manner, the United States *is* in some significant ways a nation-state; it is a nation-state of the white Protestant Europeans who came to the New World seeking the freedom that they could not then enjoy in England. Those Protestants eventually extended their freedom to the many others who joined them (or who were imported to work for them, like African Americans). But the core of the society they formed did not greatly change. It was Christian, and Christianity remains the dominant religion today.

It was Christian, but more. It was also about a particular group of people (Anglo-Saxons), and my ancestors would not have been welcome to join them. That was what I intuited in social studies class when I was growing up.

The very notion that there is an ethnic or religious core that remains at the heart of the United States is controversial. Millions of immigrants have found shelter and promise on America's shores, in what has traditionally been described as a "melting pot." Is there really some particular essence to the United States that is more powerful and durable than the mélange of cultures that these immigrants brought with them? Many people say that there is not. Jews, for example, continually stress that the United States is not a Christian nation, that Jews are just as much a part of the core of America as Christians are. What was once heralded as the "Judeo-Christian" core of the United States has now been expanded to include Muslims and others. It has become de rigueur, of late, to deny the very notion of this core.

Let us, then, put the claim as starkly as possible: there was (and is) a nation at the core of the United States. That nation was white and Protestant. Religious tolerance certainly flourishes in America, and the American Jews have done better than Jews have ever done anywhere else in the diaspora. Nonetheless, despite the fact that (as mentioned in chapter 5) the U.S. Declaration of Independence does not mention any particular ethnic group as being the core of the country, in many significant respects, the United States is the nation-state of the European Protestants who founded the country several hundred years ago.

John Jay, the first chief justice of the U.S. Supreme Court, clearly asserted that the United States was a nation-state of a very particular sort, as the quote that opens this chapter indicates. Does Jay's description not sound like Genesis's description of Noah's sons after the Flood? Is it not a picture of the nation-state par excellence? Note too that Jay referred not only to ancestors, language, principles of government, manners, and customs but also to religion. Although the passage does not use this exact terminology, Jay's point is clear: The United States is a nation-state; at its core it might be many other things, but it was especially English and Protestant.

Though John Jay died almost two centuries ago, much of what he wrote remains true. Even the massive immigration of millions from dozens of different countries, it may be argued, has not changed the essential character of the United States that he described. John McCain, the Vietnam War hero and Arizona senator who was the 2008 Republican presidential candidate, said this: "I would probably have to say 'yes,' that the Constitution established the United States of America as a Christian nation," he said. "But I say that in the broadest sense. The lady that holds her lamp beside the golden door doesn't say, 'I only welcome Christians.' We welcome the poor, the tired, the huddled masses. But when they come here they know that they are in a nation founded on Christian principles."[28]

Supreme Court Justice Antonin Scalia has written passionately about the religious ethos at the heart of the United States in a dissenting opinion worthy of being quoted at some length:

> Presidents continue to conclude the Presidential oath with the words "so help me God.". . . The sessions of this Court continue to open with the prayer "God save the United States and this Honorable Court." Invocation of the Almighty by our public figures, at all levels of government, remains commonplace. . . . As one of our Supreme Court opinions rightly observed, "We are a religious people whose institutions presuppose a Supreme Being." . . .
>
> Who says [otherwise]? Surely not the words of the Constitution. Surely not the history and traditions that reflect our society's constant understanding of those words.[29]

Scalia, one must admit, did not assert that the United States is a *Christian* nation; he merely said that it acknowledges a Supreme Being. But his reference to "the history and traditions that reflect our society's constant understanding of those words" reflects his sense that there is a core set of beliefs that make America what it is.

Note how Samuel Huntington, the enormously influential scholar and political scientist, has also described the United States. "America has always had its full share of subcultures," he said. But then he added the following:

> It also has had a mainstream Anglo-Protestant culture in which most of its people, whatever their subcultures, have shared. For almost four centuries this culture of the founding settlers has been the central and the lasting component of American identity. One has only to ask: Would America be the America it is today if in the seventeenth and eighteenth centuries it had been settled not by British Protestants but by French, Spanish, or Portuguese Catholics? The answer is no. It would not be America; it would be Quebec, Mexico, or Brazil.[30]

Jhumpa Lahiri, the short-story writer mentioned above, understands this dynamic well. In her story "This Blessed House," she chronicles Sanjeev and Twinkle's first weeks as a married couple in their new house. While cleaning and preparing the new house, Twinkle uncovers Christian paraphernalia hidden in various places throughout the house and insists that they put their discoveries on the mantel. Sanjeev, who attempts to elucidate the absurdity of Twinkle's actions because "we're not Christian," watches as all of Twinkle's "curiosity centered around discovering the next treasure."[31]

Finally, while raking the lawn one fall weekend, Twinkle finds "a plaster Virgin Mary as tall as their waists, with a blue painted hood draped over her head in the manner of an Indian Bride" and suggests that they put it on the lawn. "All the neighbors will see [and will] think we're insane" because "we're not Christian," Sanjeev objects.[32] But Twinkle, a graduate student at Stanford University whose parents live in California, understands what Sanjeev, an MIT-trained engineer whose parents live in Calcutta and who, while at MIT, "would walk each evening across the Mass. Avenue bridge in order to order Mughlai chicken with spinach from his favorite Indian restaurant," cannot: "Why [would they think we're insane]," Twinkle asks, "for having a statue of the Virgin Mary on our lawn? Every other person in this neighborhood has a statue of Mary on the lawn. We'll fit right in."[33]

Twinkle and Sanjeev, new to the United States, may not know much about the differences between Protestants (who would not have a statue of the Virgin Mary on their yard) and Catholics (who would). But Twinkle is astute enough to recognize that America is a country "with the soul of a Church," and she draws immediate conclusions about what it will take to fit in.[34]

Despite the many immigrants, and despite our nation's diversity, white Protestant Christianity (of a genteel, European sort) still lies at the very heart of what the United States has become. "The American Creed, in short, is Protestantism without God," Huntington says.[35] Note Huntington's implicit endorsement of the idea of a nation-state, a country created when peoples branch out "according to their clans and languages, by their lands, according to their nations."[36] "America," he says, "was created as a Protestant society just as and for some of the same reasons Pakistan and Israel were created as Muslim and Jewish societies in the twentieth century."[37]

How, then, has a United States that is white and Protestant at its core been able to accommodate the influx of so many people of such different ethnic, religious, and cultural backgrounds? How has a country with a white Protestant core so successfully made space for so many other peoples? In part, it has done so by demanding that those peoples drop their parcels in the sea as they land. People could be different, but they were expected to not be *too* different.

Yet it is not only the immigrants who have had to make profound and often painful accommodations. In some ways, America itself had to make profound accommodations; it too had to drop some metaphorical parcels into the waters of oblivion. In order to make a space for people of so many different sorts, the United States has had to constrain its notion of what public life should be about. How does one fashion a collective whole out of Indians and Pakistanis, Mexicans and Poles, Germans and Irish, Nigerians and Chinese? How does one create a functioning unity of Jews and Christians, Buddhists and Hindus, Muslims and atheists?

In the United States, that is accomplished largely by limiting the sphere of the collective. The shared American experience is denuded of religion, cultural richness, and the specificity and profundity of ancestral languages. In the United States, the unity required for keeping the enterprise afloat is created by limiting it to the political sphere and little beyond it. There is no American parallel to the piazza and cathedral at the center of all the villages in Tuscany that we discussed in chapter 8. Today, there are few U.S. parallels to the Israeli phenomenon of an entire country slowing down on Friday afternoon as the Sabbath sets in or of highways that are so devoid of cars on Yom Kippur that pedestrians can and do walk down them in the middle of the day.

There is no U.S. parallel nearly as widespread as Israelis' periodic quoting of biblical or rabbinic Jewish law, as there was in January 2004 when Israelis argued whether to pay Hezbollah's demands for the return of the bodies of three Israeli soldiers and Elhanan Tenenbaum, a businessman captured while abroad.

Nor is there a U.S. parallel to the paralysis that overtakes Israel as the air raid siren sounds on Yom ha-Zikaron, the memorial day for fallen soldiers, which creates a moment of indescribable existential unity. The United States is in some respects a hybrid, and not always a thoroughly fulfilling one. It has a core that was, and largely remains, white and Protestant, but its impressive heterogeneity simultaneously precludes it from having the profundity within its public square that other nation-states can boast.

Why does the United States not exhibit all of the characteristics of a nation-state? The size of the country is certainly a factor. The United States is physically enormous, whereas Israel is tiny (about the size of New Jersey). Although the United States is now home to nearly 315 million people, whereas Israel's population is roughly that of metropolitan Los Angeles, what really matters is more than population. Michael Walzer explains this with extraordinary insight:

Different people gathered in different parts of the country, but they did so by individual choice, clustering for company, with no special tie to the land on which they lived. . . . If the immigrants became Americans one by one as they arrived and settled, they did só only in a political sense: they became U.S. citizens.[38]

The people who became citizens of the United States did not feel the instinctive tie to the land that Jews felt to Palestine, that Italians feel to Italy, or that the French feel to France. (There *were* people who felt this was about the land that is now the United States, of course: Native Americans. But they have been moved and removed and then boxed onto reservations that are a far cry from the source of pride that the land-writ-large once held for them.) The United States, Walzer says, is essentially "an association of citizens."[39] The U.S. Constitution may begin with the words "We the People," but these people are fellow citizens, not a people in the sense that the Jews have been a people since time immemorial.

Gordon Wood, a U.S. historian and the prizewinning author of *The Creation of the American Republic, 1776–1787*, notes that in order to not be a wholly and overtly Christian nation, the United States has had to dilute the ethos of its shared public space:

Because the United States is composed of so many immigrants and so many different races and ethnicities, we can never assume our identity as a matter of course. The nation has had to be invented. At the end of the Declaration, the members of the Continental Congress could only "mutually pledge to each other our Lives, our Fortunes, and our sacred Honor." There was nothing else but themselves that they could dedicate themselves to—no patria, no fatherland, no nation as yet. In comparison with the 235-year-old United States, many states in the world today are new, some of them created within the fairly recent past. Yet many of these states, new as they may be, are undergirded by peoples who had a preexisting sense of their ethnicity, their nationality. In the case of the United

States, the process was reversed: We Americans were a state before we were a nation, and much of our history has been an effort to define that nationality.

In fact, even today America is not a nation in any traditional meaning of the term. We Americans have had to rely on ideas and ideals in order to hold ourselves together and think of ourselves as a single people.[40]

Huntington has made a similar point: "Americans may sing 'Oh beautiful for spacious skies,' 'The land we belong to is grand,' or 'This land was made for you and me,' but what they celebrate is an abstraction, not a particularity . . . the connection to the land is often expressed in terms of belonging or possession, not in terms of identity."[41]

Now, it must be acknowledged, Israel has also asked its immigrants to drop their parcels into the sea in a variety of ways; Israelis do not always live up to their own standards of tolerance. I recall a harrowing description that a colleague of mine recounted of his coming to Israel from Russia as a child. He told a group of us that upon their arrival to a kibbutz, the Russian kids were told to strip naked and were marched into a shower. (For Jews with even a smattering of Jewish historical awareness, the mere image of herding young Jews into a shower is chilling.)

Russian children, he told us, *never* (unlike Israeli children) undressed in front of one another, even at their relatively young, preadolescent age. The whole episode was extremely humiliating. But it got worse: when they emerged from the showers, they found their Russian clothes in a pile, ablaze, and they were given new "Israeli" clothes to don. It was, quite obviously, the Israeli parallel to that skit at the Ford Motor Company a century earlier.

There are countless examples of such stories in Israel. Ethiopian Jews have become much more like the society that airlifted them to freedom; they changed not precisely because they *wished* to, but because they understood that this would be part of the price of entering the promise of Israel. The institution of the *kes*, their religious leader, lost ground to the standard rabbi of Israeli society. Amharic and Geez quickly gave way to Hebrew. Similarly, Yemenite and Iraqi Jews slowly dropped the unique cultures they brought with them, both because those cultures were difficult to maintain as a small minority and because their children consciously wished to be more like everyone else.

Shared history also matters a great deal. In the aftermath of the Dolphinarium discotheque (Tel Aviv) suicide bombing of June 2001, in which 21 teenagers, mostly Russian immigrants, were killed and more than 130 were injured, Israeli television interviewed countless parents and relatives of those who'd been murdered and maimed. One woman whose child had been hurt sobbed into the camera and asked Israeli society, "Now that we've also been attacked, will you begin to think of *us* as Israelis, too?" It was harder to know what was more painful at that moment: the loss of those children or the feelings of close to a million immigrants that it took *that* to make them genuine Israelis.

This price of entry is not limited to those who are usually seen as more marginal, like Russian immigrants. My own family experienced it, too. It was May 2002, during the height of the Second Intifada. Jerusalem was being blown up left and right, on what felt like a daily basis. People were being incinerated in buses, and going to a restaurant meant taking your life in your hands. Jerusalem hunkered down. People stayed home, held their breaths, and prayed that it would all end one day.

In the midst of this, our eldest child, Talia, was in high school, and something was clearly awry. Even considering the surly uncommunicative style that is often part of adolescence, she was distant and shut down in a way that became very worrisome. She refused to talk to us about it. "Nothing" was the only response that we got when we asked what was wrong.

Eventually, beyond worried, we scheduled an appointment with her high school principal, a woman we knew she liked. Perhaps the principal could give us a sense of what might be going on. But when we described what we were experiencing, the principal actually seemed relieved. She apparently had expected that we might actually be there to tell her about a serious problem. She could see that we were not mollified by her calm, so she explained.

"Look," she said, "Tali's fine. That's the bottom line. She's fine. She's an immigrant, though. And she's been working incredibly hard to make it here. Her Hebrew's now perfect. She's got a wide circle of friends. She fits in. Most days, it's almost as if she can forget that she's only been here a few years.

"But then," the principal continued, "there are days like the Jenin massacre. Every girl in this high school has a cell phone, and suddenly, without warning, every phone starts ringing. Because all these students have brothers in the army. Or fathers. Or a sister's boyfriend. Or an uncle. Someone. They hear a rumor that fourteen soldiers have been killed in one incident, and there's too high a chance that someone in this school is going to be affected. So there's a low level of panic, and cell phone pandemonium erupts.

"Tali's phone, though, doesn't ring. You haven't been here long enough. She doesn't have a father in the army. Or a brother. Or a boyfriend. Everyone in her life is okay, and she knows it. Yet when she looks at what's going on at her school, instead of feeling relieved, she feels left out. Because she's finally come to understand: she's not going to be fully Israeli until she's inside the circle of death."

It is dangerous to oversimplify, but there *is* an unofficial core of Israeli society, too. You're "in" if you're white, of European descent, an army veteran (and better to be an officer), well educated, and not too religious. If you become too religious, you're out one ring from the inner circle. Yemenite Jews and Jews of North African extraction are farther out. Russians are even farther out, at least in some ways, because many of them are not technically Jewish. Ethiopians, in a terrible instance of Israeli racism, are farther out still. You're "in" if you've lost someone in a war or to terrorism.

Much of this is an aspect of Israeli society that has to be fixed. But still, even with all the many serious imperfections, there's a dramatic difference between these concentric circles and those of the United States. For in Israel, these immigrants were *sought*. The Israeli government *brought* them to its shores. In the United States, the only immigrants the country actually sought were those they would turn into slaves.

Part of the very purpose of Israel was the ingathering of exiles. Ethiopians were airlifted to Israel in daring air force missions called Operation Moses (1984) and Operation Solomon (1991). The Israeli government worked on behalf of Soviet Jews for decades and then admitted even those who were not technically Jewish, simply because they qualified under the broad definition of Israel's Law of Return (which includes the non-Jewish family members of Jewish immigrants). Immigration is a prominent theme of Israel's Declaration of Independence, and the Israeli government has a Ministry of Absorption.

When the responsibility for encouraging immigration was largely moved from the Jewish Agency to a nongovernmental body called Nefesh be-Nefesh, many Israelis were scandalized. Promoting immigration was a *government* function, they said. Being part of a society in which immigration was seen as a *purpose* of the country made immigrants heroes, in some small way.

Added to that sentiment was the fact that even though Yemenite, Russian, and Ethiopian Jews all brought their own cultures and heritages to their new homeland, there was a shared core that was much richer and thicker than what the United States can express, and it was a core to which many Israelis could resonate. The ancient Hebrew language, now revived thanks to Eliezer Ben Yehuda, was more than a means of communication. It made each of these people linked to the others in ways that English or Spanish or French could never have done. There were religious and cultural traditions—holidays, history, national commemorations—to which they could attach themselves and join the body politic.

None of this is to suggest that the hardships have not been real or that they have been excusable. But even these hardships have not obfuscated the pulse of a shared ethos, even in a country as divided as Israel. The army has taken on the role of converting the Russians who wish to convert without fighting the rabbinate; having them feel fully part of the collective is so important that the military has taken on this unusual role. In many combat units, one finds soldiers of white European extraction alongside those from North Africa and Ethiopia. Walking around Jerusalem, one sees new recruits standing in the Old City not far from the Western Wall, listening to a lecture as part of their basic training. And the message is clear: "This place and this story belong to all of you. Polish, Russian, Moroccan, or Ethiopian—all of your communities trace their roots right back to this place. That's why we're here. It's why you're in this unit."

It is, to be honest, a very far cry from Mrs. Brown's seventh grade social studies class. And it *is* more powerful. Israel is obviously not the only model of governance and society that can work in our world. And there are advantages to the U.S. model: it can make a place for virtually everyone, at least in one of those concentric circles. One would absolutely not want the U.S. model to disappear, leaving the ethnic nation-state as the only remaining model.

Nothing about the claims throughout this book should be read as an indication that Israel is a perfect implementation of the ideal of the nation-state. Israel is a frustrating and deeply flawed country. It can legitimately take pride in many successes, but that is no justification for ignoring its failures. For me, the most painful part of having moved to Israel has nothing to do with the periodic frightening moments during wars or terrorist attacks, or even the knowledge that moving to Israel has put our children directly in harm's way, primarily as soldiers. It's not the very real pain of having left much of my family far behind, living in a much smaller home, having one car instead of two, or anything of the sort.

For me, the most painful part of living in Israel is the daily encounter with its profound flaws. There are the occasional comments about Arabs that are undeniably racist, uttered by members of my own religious community. Israel's unwillingness to take the necessary steps to stop the trafficking of women or the occasional Jewish violence against Arabs (mostly in the West Bank) are huge failures. So too are the continued discrimination against Ethiopian Jews, a lack of openness to non-Orthodox forms of Judaism, the crumbling educational system, and much, much more. Adopting a homeland that *should* be (and is, in many ways) a light unto the nations but falls so far short of the ideal is deeply painful.

This book makes no claim that Israel is an impeccable example of anything at all. Rather, the claim is this: as the world discusses Israel and evaluates its successes and failures, part of what must be recognized is that Israel is a different sort of project from the United States, the country to which it is most often compared. Israel must not be seen as the Jewish attempt to re-create the United States in the Middle East. Israel's particularistic Declaration of Independence is not different from the U.S. Declaration of Independence by accident. Israel's focuses on the Jews—their history and their destiny. The situation of Arabs in Israel is not analogous to the status of Jews or any other minority in the United States. The separation of church and state that makes the United States great would undermine Israel's very essence and reason for being. These are entirely different projects.

Israel is not simply a Hebrew-speaking version of the United States. It sees the United States as the model of many great things, but it does not seek to become the United States. Lady Liberty could not have been stationed outside the port of Haifa—for although Israel has welcomed millions of immigrants and has, indeed embraced many tired, poor, and huddled masses yearning to be free, those were, by and large, Jewish tired, Jewish poor, and Jewish masses yearning to be free in a distinctly Jewish setting. If you use the United States as the model of what a modern country should be, Israel falls terribly short. But if you use the standard of the nation-state—its focus on heritage, culture, religion, tradition, and ongoing conversation in the public square—as the goal, then Israel is not only an extraordinary success, but even more, it is a model from which the international community could learn a great deal. It is even a model to which thoughtful Americans might look as they ponder both the successes and limitations of their own society.

Israel has given Jews what they have never been able to have anywhere else, even in the United States: a chance to live a robust Jewish life on their ancestral land. They speak their reborn national language, observe their own calendar, and celebrate the fact that it, and not someone else's calendar, sets the tone of the national rhythm of time. In Israel, Plymouth Rock is replaced by Jerusalem, the Alamo is the Gilboa Mountains, and the national stories are the Jews' stories, the stories of the Bible and of subsequent Jewish history. Only in Israel is the air that is breathed the air of robust Jewish life and identity.

The historian Barbara Tuchman has noted that of all the peoples who lived in the Western world three thousand years ago, it is only the Jews who live in the same place, speak the same language, and practice the same religion now as they did then.[42] That is more than an idle curiosity. It is a reflection of the fact that the Jews have regained a kind of authenticity and vitality that very few peoples can claim. A hundred years ago that claim would not have been true. It is true today because of the revolution called Zionism, a revolution whose most important fuel was the power of an idea. It is, in large measure, the idea that was first expressed with the Tower of Babel.

The United States is an extraordinary country, and it too is built on the foundation of a profound, world-altering idea: Jeffersonian democracy. But Jefferson's ideal is not the only idea that can lie at the core of a great country.[43] And Jefferson's ideal cannot provide for Jews what Israel does, precisely because the United States *does* retain elements of being a nation-state, but created by and for a different nation.

The challenge for Jews, regardless of where they choose to live, is to recognize what it is that Israel does to change their lives. The challenge for the world is to celebrate Israel for the model of human flourishing that it represents. For Israel continues to provide a model of cultural and historical renaissance—not only for Jews but for human beings the world over. As it does so, Israel actually affords it citizens a richness of life and identity that America, despite its extraordinary successes, is simply not equipped to foster.

Chapter Ten

A STATE UNTO THE DIASPORA

For several decades, the Jewish establishment has asked American Jews to check their liberalism at Zionism's door, and now, to their horror, they are finding that many young Jews have checked their Zionism instead.

—Peter Beinart, "The Failure of the American Jewish Establishment"[1]

Why do Jews lie at the Passover seder? Across the world, be they Russians or Americans, Iraqis or Canadians, almost all Jews participate in a Passover seder and recite the famous line "Next year in Jerusalem." But seated in the comfort of their homes in New York or Los Angeles, how many American Jews actually mean it? The vast majority clearly have no intention of being in Jerusalem for the next Passover. They certainly do not plan to live there permanently, which is what the liturgy really means. Why, then, proceed with the charade? On this pivotal night of the year, when Jews recall their beginning as a people and reflect on the meaning of freedom, why misrepresent what their lives are ultimately about? Why would one celebrate freedom by uttering a lie?

Truth comes in different forms. "Next year in Jerusalem" is not about a plan, it's about a dream. Saying "Next year in Jerusalem," even if one does not expect to be physically present in Jerusalem next year, has long been the Jewish people's way of keeping an ethereal ideal in mind. It was a national yearning that bound the Jews together, regardless of their actual intentions. There was a place that served as a compass: for praying, but even more important, for dreaming, for flights of national fancy. For two millennia, as Jews imagined their people's future, one place occupied center stage, even when they knew that they would never see it with their own eyes: Zion. It was in Zion that they imagined a revitalized Jewish people. It was in Zion that they imagined they would experience true freedom. It was in Zion that they believed the greatest days of Jewish history were yet to unfold.

The times, however, are changing. Ours is the first generation in which the central role of Zion in Jewish dreams is beginning to fade. It is fading rapidly, and we know why. For too long, Israel's supporters have framed their conversation about the Jewish state in terms of the conflict with the Palestinians. Even among knowledgeable and commit-ted Jews, an oral "Rorschach test" in response to the word *Israel* evokes responses such as "checkpoints," "occupation," and "settlements"—as though the conflict were most of what Israel is about.

When the revival of Jewish sovereignty evokes only images of war, when the restoration of a people to its ancestral land (even with all its complications) evokes no pride, when the ingathering of exiles after two thousand years does not strike a chord of sheer awe, Jews have lost sight of the real significance of Israel's re-creation. When Jews the world over do not recognize that the delegitimization of Israel affects them, that they too have a personal stake in what happens to and in Israel, a renewed discourse is desperately needed. It is time for a new way of thinking about the Jewish state and how it models something new and dramatic not only for Jews but for human beings everywhere. That is the conversation to which this book has been dedicated.

The evidence that a new conversation is long overdue is every-where. Signs of a distancing between diaspora Jews (mostly, but not exclusively, American Jews) and the Jewish state can be found at every turn. A recent study asked American Jews whether the destruction of

Israel would be a personal tragedy for them. The study asked about the *destruction* of Israel, not its gradual disappearance or a slow withering away of the state. Among Jewish Americans sixty-five years of age and older, more than 80 percent said that Israel's destruction would indeed be a personal tragedy for them. But among those thirty-five years of age and younger, a full 50 percent said that Israel's destruction would not would not be a personal tragedy.[2]

Similarly a 2011 study of American Jews showed that the younger the cohort, the lower the level of support for Israel.[3] The same phenomenon began to surface even among young rabbinical students; outside the Orthodox community, mainstream Zionist rabbinical students began to report that expressing support for Israel on their campuses had become a lonely proposition.[4]

At one well-known rabbinical school, prayer services on Israeli Independence Day included two options: a prayer service that included the recitation of the celebratory prayer (known as Hallel) in honor of Israel's reestablishment, and a prayer service that omitted the recitation. A decade earlier, offering a formal option for those who did not wish to celebrate Israel's re-creation would have been unthinkable.

What has changed? Why, in an era in which American Jews can hold their heads high and espouse any political position they wish, have many young American Jews begun to turn away from Israel? Why has Zion suddenly found itself shifted away from the core of their national sensibilities and dreams? The most obvious reason, as I stated earlier, is the ongoing conflict with the Palestinians. These young people have no memory of an era in which Israel was fragile or of a time prior to the international community's endorsement of Palestinian national aspirations. Israel's re-creation and even the 1967 and 1973 wars, in which Egypt and its allies pledged to "push the Jews into the sea," are ancient history.

What these students see is what appears to be an imbalance of power. One side has an internationally recognized state, nuclear weapons, a world-class army, a robust economy, and a liberal democracy that affords its citizens a vast array of rights and protections. The other side has none of these. These students' earliest memories of Israel are of the Palestinian Terror War (commonly but incorrectly called the Second Intifada), of heavily armed Israeli soldiers arrayed against Palestinian boys who were "only" throwing rocks. Sensitivity to the underdog and a deep-seated belief in fairness has led them to believe that the scales must be balanced. The Palestinians need to get a state.

Palestinian statehood, however, has been slow in coming. To be sure, some of these young American Jews (though not all) understand that the lion's share of the impasse stems from the Palestinian refusal to accept the fact of Israel's existence. Palestinians are also still unwilling to create a genuine and transparent democracy and continue in their insistence that any political settlement with the Israelis has to allow for the return of the now millions of people classified as "refugees" by the U.N. Relief and Works Agency for Palestine Refugees in the Near East. Israelis, in turn, understand that allowing the original refugees and their descendants to enter Israel would end the Jewish character of their state—which, they assume, is precisely what the Palestinians intend.

Nevertheless, these young Jews also intuit that the Palestinians are not going to change. Therefore, they believe, *something* has to give— and that something has to be Israel. If Israel refuses to budge, then it is Israel that is responsible for the occupation (which began in 1967 when Israel captured land belonging to Egypt, Jordan, and Syria after those countries attempted to destroy the Jewish state). Israel is the occupying power, these young Jews believe, the side with the military might and the party with the morally unjustifiable stance. Therefore, faced with a choice between loyalty to their humanitarian values or to their parents' Zionism, they have chosen the former. No one put it more pithily than Peter Beinart, a widely read voice of the younger generation of the American, liberally inclined, Jewish intellectual elite. His assertion in the quote at the beginning of this chapter was preceded by the following explanation:

Among American Jews today, there are a great many Zionists, especially in the Orthodox world, people deeply devoted to the State of Israel. And there are a great many liberals, especially in the secular Jewish world, people deeply devoted to human rights for all people, Palestinians included. But the two groups are increasingly distinct. Particularly in the younger generations, fewer and fewer American Jewish liberals are Zionists; fewer and fewer American Jewish Zionists are liberal.[5]

But something else has changed as well. To be sure, the conflict with the Palestinians is a significant cause of the shift in American Jewish attitudes. Beyond that, however, these young Jews have also come to believe that they simply do not *need* Israel any longer. Although their parents' and their grandparents' generations were shocked by the Shoah or perhaps still feel marginal and vulnerable in the United States, these young people do not. American Jews are no longer marginal or subject to anti-Semitism, they believe. So of what importance is a Jewish state to *them*? Why express fealty to a country that they do not need and that often makes them feel shame?

Ironically, as much as this perspective sounds like a radical shift (which it is), the seeds of this view had been planted many centuries earlier, even as early as the redaction of the Bible. Some of the confidence that predominantly young Jews have in believing that they do not need Israel as much anymore is the result of a strategic decision that the creators of the Jewish tradition made long ago. Faced with the realization that the Israelites might soon lose their sovereignty in their ancestral homeland (which is precisely what happened), those who shaped the Judaism that we now take for granted began to teach that even though Jewish sovereignty was fragile and might not last, the continued flourishing of diaspora Jewry, and therefore of the Jewish people as a whole, was possible even without autonomous Jewish life in the land of Israel. The scholar Jacob Wright of Emory University suggests the following:

> Anticipating the coming doom and destruction, these authors set about the task of their people's preservation. They did so—subtly yet critically—by unhinging the concept of "nation" from that of "state." Hence, while defeat may have destroyed Israel's *state*, it came to play a key role in the creation of Israel's identity as a *people*.[6]

Wright knows that most ancient national narratives were constructed around great victories. But, he asks, "What was it that caused the biblical literature to crystallize during this period? Was it those rare moments of hope, when the political status quo seemed likely to persist? Or was it, instead, the growing awareness that the entire political entity was on the brink of destruction?" It was the latter, he suggests: "It was not the moments of peace and prosperity, but rather the experiences of catastrophe that produced the strongest impetus for the composition of the magisterial history found in Genesis–Kings and the profound, disturbing messages of the prophets."[7]

The Bible's take on Jewish history was a preparation for exile. The Jewish sovereign state may well not survive, the Bible essentially says, but the nation can.[8] Even as the prophets warn the Israelites about the doom to come, they also reassure them that their *people* will not end. The *state* may be doomed, and the suffering to follow will perhaps be immeasurable. But the *people* Israel is eternal, as Jeremiah notes:

> For I will forgive their iniquities and remember their sins no more. Thus said the Lord who established the sun for light by day, the laws of moon and stars for light by night, who stirs up the sea into roaring waves, whose name is Lord of Hosts. If these laws should ever be annulled by me—declares the Lord—only then would the offspring of Israel cease to be a nation before Me for all time.[9]

In its time, this move was a stroke of genius. It may well have been this worldview that equipped the Jews for survival throughout two thousand years of statelessness. Today, however, the Jews *do* have a state. Yet that state is maligned and marginalized, and it needs the Jews' support more than ever. Ironically, therefore, that ancient biblical strategy is now showing its dangerous, even paralyzing, side. For what it has done is to convince many Jews that even though the loss of the state of Israel would be horrible, it would not spell the end of the Jews.

Zionism is thus more revolutionary than we commonly imagine, for Zionists rejected the notion that the Jews could survive as a nation without a state. The biblical strategy of preparing the nation for defeat may well have served a critical purpose long ago, they essentially claimed, but today it has become not only counterproductive but dangerous. It is no longer the case that the Jewish nation can survive in any meaningful way without the Jewish state. The Zionists were right.

Political Zionism did not emerge from Europe because Jewish life in Europe was idyllic. Quite the opposite was the case. Zionism emerged under Theodor Herzl because Jewish life in the diaspora, despite pockets of flourishing and great intellectual and cultural achievement, was basically, to borrow from the seventeenth-century English philosopher Thomas Hobbes, "poor, nasty, brutish, and short."[10] The Jews had become Europe's victims on call.

"But," some will protest, "that was Europe, and that was then. The United States today is different." That confidence is quite similar to the confidence that the Jews of Cordoba had—until they began to be forcibly converted, burned alive at the stake in the Spanish Inquisition, and summarily evicted. The Jews of Berlin in 1930 also believed that they had found the ultimate home, that German society was so enlightened, so cultured, and so scientific that there was no danger of returning to the dark days of Europe.

Germany's highest-ranking Orthodox rabbi actually wrote legal opinions urging Jewish conscripts to the German army not to desert, even though staying in the army would oblige them to violate the Sabbath and eat nonkosher food. Germany was going to be the new great home of the Jewish people, he assured them at the turn of the twentieth century; Jews should do everything they could to earn the trust and admiration of their German hosts.[11]

A few decades later, of course, German Jewry was gone.

Jewish history is replete with examples of communities that believed, as many American Jews do today, that they had finally found the one place in the diaspora where Jews would be safe, presumably forever.

The argument here is *not* that what happened in Spain, Germany, or elsewhere could also happen in the United States. Not for nothing did the Jewish tradition insist that after the destruction of the Temple, the role of prophecy was taken away from prophets and given instead to fools and children.[12] No one can know what is in store for Jews anywhere, not even in the United States.

Philip Roth's magnificent *The Plot against America* (2005) does a masterful job of imagining the United States with a very different past. In it he describes an alternate U.S. history in which Franklin D. Roosevelt loses the 1940 presidential election to Charles Lindbergh, a fascist and a known anti-Semite, who then shapes the country to his liking. Perhaps Roth intended to issue a warning about American Jewish complacency and the American Jewish future, perhaps not.

That, however, is not the essence of *this* argument. The claim here is not that the United States might someday turn on the Jews and end the Jewish golden age that we now take for granted. The point here is about Israel, not about America. What matters for us is not that a new Charles Lindbergh may emerge in the United States but that the very Jewish life that American Jews take for granted is actually a product of the existence of a Jewish state—the very state from which many young Jews are now distancing themselves.

Here is what too many members of the younger generations of American Jews simply do not understand: American Jewish life as it now exists would not survive the loss of Israel. Consider the following two sets of three nations: the Spanish, the French, and the Russians, on the one hand, and the Tibetans, the Chechnyans, and the Basques on the other. In many respects, these six ethnicities or nations have much in common. Each of them has its own language, music, litera-ture, cuisine, and religious beliefs and practices—all the makings of a rich national culture. Yet no one has any difficulty knowing in which category each of these nations belongs. Dividing these six nations into two groups is an exercise in the obvious.

The Spanish, the French, and the Russians belong in the same group because they have sovereign ethnic nation-states in which their heritages flourish, in which their national memories can be cultivated, and through which they express their worldviews and act as players in history. The Tibetans, the Chechnyans, and the Basques, in contrast, do not have (and in some cases have *never* had) nation-states. Because they have no sovereign states, they are not significant actors on the world stage; as a result, they must constantly battle to preserve their cultures. Nor are they secure: they tiptoe around the world, looking anxiously over their shoulders to see what history has in store for them next. These are peoples to which history happens, not peoples who shape history.

There was an era in which American Jews did the same thing; they, too, tiptoed around America, nervously trying to stay under the radar. They were reminiscent of the ten spies who reported back to Moses when they returned from scouting out the Promised Land: "We looked like grasshoppers to ourselves, and so we appeared to them."[13] American Jews who believe that they could survive the loss of Israel do not remember that era. They take it as entirely natural and wholly unsurprising that thousands of American citizens feel comfortable ascending the steps of the Capitol with their heads held high and with a sense of absolute entitlement (in the best sense of that word) on the day that the Policy Conference of the American-Israel Public Affairs Campaign (AIPAC) devotes to lobbying. Never do they ask themselves why virtually no one ascended those very same Capitol steps between 1938 and 1945 to demand that the United States do something to save the Jewish people from extinction.

There were millions of Jews in the United States during that horrific period, and they knew what was happening. But American Jews lacked the confidence and the sense of utter belonging in the United States that this generation of students now takes for granted, so they did virtually nothing. Aside from the famous "Rabbis' March" of October 1943, in which some four hundred mostly Orthodox rabbis marched on Washington (President Roosevelt refused to meet them and departed the White House via a rear door), there were almost no mass protests, sit-ins, or long lines of buses making their way to Washington to demand that the United States do *something* to save the Jews.[14] That was a different era in Jewish history and in American Jewish history. The confidence that today's American Jews take for granted was largely absent in those years.

Today, young American Jews think nothing of the fact that if they so chose, they could wear a *kippah* to a job interview on Wall Street or Madison Avenue, inform the interviewer that they do not work on the Sabbath and must leave work early on Friday, and still have every chance of being awarded a position. At Ivy League schools, where Jews are disproportionately represented, the fact that not so long ago these schools had quotas on Jewish admissions strikes today's students as quaint. They have no sense whatsoever how tenuous American Jews felt before there was a Jewish state, far across the ocean.

When asked in which category of peoples—the Spanish, French, and Russians or the Tibetans, Chechnyans, and Basques—the Jews belong, most Jews would naturally assert that they are part of the former group. Jews no longer think of themselves as a people who must tiptoe around the globe. Soviet Jews reawakened and decided that they wanted out of their national prison, so the state of Israel made their rescue a national project. When an Air France flight filled with Jews was hijacked to Entebbe, there was a country that rescued them. When Ethiopian Jews were caught in the crosshairs of a deadly civil war, there was someone to whisk them out.

What all these have in common, of course, is the state of Israel. What Israel has done is to change the existential condition of Jews everywhere, even in the United States. Without the state of Israel, the self-confidence and sense of belonging that American Jews now take for granted would quickly disappear.

It is Israel that has transformed the Jews from "Basques" to "Spaniards" or from "Chechnyans" to "Russians." Now, just a few decades after they achieved sovereignty, the Jews have a setting in which their heritage is cultivated and is the norm, a land in which their language thrives and thus colors everything from high literature to daily conversation. They have a society in which their worldview—their conception of what is worth remembering, what merits mourning, and how to engage in that memory and mourning—is the focus of the educational system, the country's landmarks and monuments, and even of the army.

Israel may be under threat from Palestinian terrorism and Iranian nuclear ambitions, but Jewish culture, memory, and language thrive now as they never did before Israel was re-created. The world has taken note of how dramatically Israeli independence has altered the condition of one of the world's oldest peoples. That is the source of the profound change in the self-perception of American Jews, but many simply do not realize it.

That is why what is unfolding now in American Jewish life is particularly troubling and ironic. The very sense of belonging and utter security that leads many American Jews to believe that they do not need the state of Israel is a product of the state of Israel. The confidence they feel that enables them to critique Israel is a product of the very state they now dismiss. And in moving away from devotion to the Jewish state, occasionally even opposing or undermining it, they are actually weakening the very source of the confidence that makes their political work possible. There is a precedent for the Jews having an utterly defeatist attitude about themselves. It could return.

In November 1947, as the U.N. General Assembly voted to create Israel, as Jews held their breath and listened to the roll call, it would have been virtually impossible to imagine what was about to happen next. Who could have guessed that the painful complexities of actually having that state, and the long and relentless conflict with Israel's neighbors, would begin to undermine the dream that had united and animated the Jews for so long? Who could have imagined that young American Jews, pained by the conflict, would begin to abandon the country for which their great-grandparents had yearned?

David Ben-Gurion, Israel's first prime minister, began to sense the chasm between Israeli Jews and the diaspora even in the early days of the state. When American Jews failed to move to Israel in the numbers that he had expected, he said, "For hundreds of years, a question-prayer hovered in the mouths of the Jewish people: Would a country be found for this people? No one imagined the frightening question: Would a people be found for the country when it would be created?"[15] Little could he have imagined that a mere trickle of immigrants would be the least of those problems.

The state of Israel has had yet another seldom noticed effect on American Judaism. Even as Israel becomes more controversial among American Jews, even as the American Jewish community becomes ever more split in a bitter and often uncivil war of words between those who support AIPAC and those who align with J Street (a left-wing pro-Israel lobbying group that is controversial because, unlike the more traditional lobbying groups like AIPAC, it considers open disagreement with Israeli government policies to be a form of support), or between those who see support of Israel as a sacred Jewish obligation and those who believe that support of Israel unfairly requires that they compromise their social and liberal values, Israel remains virtually the sole topic that has the capacity to arouse the passions of American Jews.

An often overlooked but important question: without Israel, what would remain that would make Jewishness anything more than an anemic form of ethnic memory of the sort that long-ago immigrants like most young Polish Americans or Irish Americans now have? What else in contemporary Jewish life provides an anchor for Jewish engagement, discussion, pride, and activism? Ironically, without Israel, Jews who seek survival could well find themselves "wishing" that the hostile and intolerant environments of medieval and early-modern Europe weren't a vestige of the past. At least those threats, they might wistfully note, had kept the Jews united and driven.

About what else in Jewish life besides Israel do contemporary Jews actually feel outrage? They become passionate when Israel is abused in the international media or when it is attacked; even those who are critical of Israel will often react swiftly when a critique of Israel crosses some hard-to-define line to become unfair. Conversely, American Jews also feel profound shame and even anger when Israel does things that they consider inexcusable. Disagreements about whether a J Street representative should be permitted to speak at a given synagogue often evoke more passion than any other synagogue-policy decision.

What else evokes such immediate passions? Conflicts between denominations don't. The policy of whether Jewish community centers should be open on the Sabbath matters to very few. In 2011, a proposed ban on circumcision in San Francisco had clear anti-Semitic overtones.[16] Yet even this did nothing to evoke the passions that a naval raid on a flotilla thousands of miles away did in 2010.[17]

There is clearly something about Israel that continues to provide the real electric energy of American Judaism, even when many

American Jews believe that the loss of Israel would not be tragic. Just as American Jews recite the phrase "Next year in Jerusalem" even when they have no intention of moving to Israel, they become incensed when Israel's chief rabbinate or an Israeli political party threatens to declare all Reform and Conservative conversions invalid even though that policy will have absolutely no bearing on their own lives. They insist that their own future would be secure even without the state, yet they care deeply about what Israel's leadership says about their own denomination. When the conversion issue erupted once again in 2010, Alana Newhouse, a leading Jewish writer and intellectual, wrote the following in the *New York Times*:

> If this bill passes, future historians will inevitably wonder why, at a critical moment in its history, Israel chose to tell 85 percent of the Jewish diaspora that their rabbis weren't rabbis and their religious practices were a sham, the conversions of their parents and spouses were invalid, their marriages weren't legal under Jewish law, and their progeny were a tribe of bastards unfit to marry other Jews.[18]

Newhouse was far from alone in issuing a rallying cry around the proposed bill. She was right that the bill was a shortsighted and foolish provocation. But the number of American Jews who have been converted by Reform or Conservative rabbis and then seek to emigrate to Israel (and be accepted as Jewish by Israel's chief rabbinate) is minuscule. Why, then, the overwhelming rage on the part of American Jews? Many believed that the state of Israel was telling them that they were not authentic, and even though they had no intention of ever living there, their connection to Israel made that feeling simply unbearable.

A similar reaction takes place when Israeli authorities clamp down on groups such as Women of the Wall. Women of the Wall is a grassroots women's organization designed to secure the rights of Jewish women to hold an organized prayer service (that is, to pray as a group rather than individually, as women now do) at the Western Wall; this includes the right to hold a Torah scroll, which the mainstream Israeli rabbinate insists is an activity reserved for men. The Israeli police occasionally arrest these women, because a woman's holding a Torah scroll at the Western Wall is technically a violation of Israeli law.[19]

When that happens, American Jewish leaders are often quick to respond. There are some extraordinarily sophisticated female Reform rabbis, for example, who ordinarily might not be at all inclined to worship at the Wall. Why, then, do they feel a need to protest the religious policies of a locale at which they would otherwise have no desire to pray? They have staked out this issue because what Israel says about women's roles, even when they themselves live in the United States, matters to them deeply. It is more than an issue of access. It is a matter of being accepted by the entity (the state of Israel) that provides them with enormous meaning, even as they feel rejected by some of its policies.

This is the phenomenon of which we should take note. Despite the proclamation of some American Jews that Israel is no longer as central to their identity as it once was, and despite the fact that half of young American Jews claim that Israel's destruction would not be a personal tragedy for them, Israel still gets under their skin in a way that no other Jewish issue does. Being angry is actually a good sign, for it indicates investment. And there can be no denying that much of what ails American Judaism today, beyond unprecedented Jewish illiteracy, is a simple lack of passion.

Ironically, it is Israel that provides what is left of that passion. As strange as this may sound to the younger American Jewish generations, without Israel, American Jews' future might be much less secure than they imagine. And undoubtedly, without Israel, Jews' sense of self could revert to that of Chechnyans and Basques faster than anyone might imagine. But most important for this conversation, without Israel there would also be the additional danger that the primary source of energy and passion in the Jewish world could simply disappear. Without passion, there is simply no way that the Jewish people could persevere.

To be sure, what happens to Israel affects most directly the Jews who live there. And, as this book has insisted, Israel is a model of ethnic flourishing for peoples everywhere—it is thus a "state unto the nations." But in addition to those two roles, Israel is also the source of the vitality of Jewish communities around the world. It is Israel that gave rise to the Soviet Jewry movement. It is Israel that is central to the identity of the ten thousand Polish Jews who are the remnant of the four million who lived in Poland before the Shoah. In France and in Britain, Zionism and devotion to Israel are in many ways the glue that binds each of the Jewish communities together. In ways that are not sufficiently appreciated, Israel is also a "state unto the diaspora."

A sovereign state being a state unto its diaspora is not only a Jewish phenomenon. This is one of those instances in which what Israel models can serve as an inspiration to others. One need only examine the experience of the Armenian American community to see how the establishment of a sovereign ethnic nation-state can imbue its diaspora with new vitality. Armenia was the first of the non-Baltic states to secede from the Soviet Union. It declared its independence in August 1990 and proclaimed itself a country about a year later.

What sort of difference did national sovereignty make for Armenians throughout the world? Consider the following. Armenians have deep roots in American society and developed their first social-service and political organizations more than a century ago, but as Heather S. Gregg observes, it is only within the last two decades that "Armenian lobby groups in the United States have achieved considerable success in gaining political and material support from Congress."[20] In 2011, forty-three of the fifty American states recognized that the atrocities committed by the Ottoman Empire against Armenians during World War I were acts of genocide; before Armenia's independence, however, only six states did so.[21]

Similarly, no congressional caucus existed to advocate for issues concerning Armenian Americans and Armenia until 1995, but by the 112th Congress in 2010, the Congressional Caucus on Armenian Issues boasted 134 members. And in 2008, senator and presidential candidate Barack Obama proclaimed that "the facts are undeniable. An official policy that calls on diplomats to distort the historical facts is an untenable policy. As a Senator, I strongly support passage of the

Armenian Genocide Resolution (H.Res.106 and S.Res.106), and as President I will recognize the Armenian Genocide."[22]

Armenian American efforts to gain recognition of the Armenian Genocide and to support the republic of Armenia have been so successful that in 2006 Zbigniew Brzezinski, the former national security adviser to President Jimmy Carter and then a professor at Johns Hopkins University's School of Advanced International Studies, named the Armenian American lobby, the Israeli American lobby, and the Cuban American lobby the three most effective ethnic or foreign-supported lobbying coalitions in the United States.[23] The Armenians now also ascend the steps of Capitol Hill with their heads held high.

How has the Armenian American community—which, according to a recent survey by the U.S. Census Bureau, contains fewer than half a million members—been able to, in the words of Gregg, "*hyper-mobilize* support both among its constituents and within Washington" in order to so effectively advocate its causes?[24] What has happened in the last decades that has made the Armenian lobby one of the most powerful foreign-policy lobbying coalitions in the United States?

The answer is in no small part linked to Armenian independence. For Armenians, as for Jews, national sovereignty has profoundly altered their people's international standing. American Jews who doubt the importance of Israel to the way of life that they now take for granted would do well to take careful note. People across the globe who care about restoring vitality and pride to nations that have for too long absorbed the brunt of history's cruelty should also take note. Armenia has had an enormous impact on the Armenians even of the United States, and Israel has fundamentally changed the existential condition of Jews around the globe. Could this new sense of possibility, a new lease on the future, be extended to other peoples if only they too had nation-states of their own?

There is a commonly heard argument in response to the above argument. As soon as people hear the claim that the state of Israel is central to the survival of diaspora Jewish life as we know it, some of them invariably respond this way: "Jews survived in the diaspora for two thousand years. How is it even conceivable that six and a half decades of Israeli independence have erased our ability to do the same—for longer, if we have to?" But with all due apologies to Alfred Lord Tennyson, it is not the case that it is "better to have loved and lost than never to have loved at all." There are times when gaining something and losing it *is* worse than never having had it at all. And that is true of the re-created sovereignty that the Jews have enjoyed for nearly two-thirds of a century.

The belief that many diaspora Jews, and particularly American Jews, now have, that two thousand years of survival without sovereignty has somehow equipped them to survive again should Israel be lost, simply misreads the way in which Jewish life is different today. Their confidence is misplaced, and it is very dangerous.

One can easily understand why American Jews would wish to declare their existential and emotional independence from the state of Israel. At first glance, it simply makes no sense to have a dependence of any sort on an embattled country the size of New Jersey across the ocean and wholly unlike the culture that American Jews take for granted. But the dependence is real. The fate of American Jews is intimately linked to the fate of Israelis, just as the fate of Israelis is linked to the fate of American Jews. This is the ultimate mutually interdependent relationship.

Thus, American Jews have an enormous personal stake in the fight against the delegitimization of Israel. This is true even of young American Jews, even of those liberally inclined Jews who (often legitimately) see much about the Jewish state that bothers them terribly. A successful campaign to delegitimize and possibly destroy Israel could undo much more than the Jewish state. It could radically alter American Judaism as we know it. No one would have to be killed, exiled, or dismissed from a job. All that would have to happen is that Jews would suffer the second enormous blow to their people in the space of a century—and with that, the Jews would become stateless like the Chechnyans, the Tibetans, or the Basques. That would profoundly alter American Jewry. It would arrest the revival of Jewish life now unfolding in parts of Europe. And Israeli Jewry would be no more. In short, the end of Israel would mean the end of the Jewish people as we know it.

The stakes could not be higher. Since what's really at stake is not just the Jewish state but the Jewish people as we know it, this makes a refocused discussion of Israel all the more important, for both the international community and for the Jews themselves. As long as conversations about the Jewish state are centered on the conflict, the borders, the refugees, and allegations of Israel's legitimacy or misdeeds, many Jews and supporters of Israel will tire of the conversation, at best, or wash their hands of any devotion to the Jewish state, at worst. A new conversation, reframed in terms of what Israel does for Jewish flourishing and how it models a profound conception of the life well lived to humanity at large, is long overdue.

The time has come for a paradigm shift in our conversations about Israel. We need to move beyond the conflict and Israel's enemies and focus instead on what Israel represents. Our discussions of the Jewish state should center on the importance of difference and the human need for dignity. We need to think of Israel in terms of the rich way of life that it makes possible, the ways in which a nation-state addresses the deep and abiding human need to inherit and bequeath culture. Thinking about Israel in this way could well convince the international community that it is time not to destroy Israel but to create more Israels, including one in the future Palestinian state. Israel is more than a conflict and even more than a "mere" country—it is a bold experiment with great significance not only for Israelis and the entire Jewish people but for freedom-loving human beings everywhere.

Conclusion

SURVIVAL IS NOT
A PURPOSE

Again you shall plant vineyards on the hills of Samaria;
For the day is coming when watchmen shall proclaim . . .
Come, let us go up to Zion . . .
Thus said the Lord: Restrain your voice from weeping, your
eyes from shedding tears;
For there is a reward for your labor, they shall return from the
enemy's land.
And there is hope for your future—your children shall return
to their country.

—Jeremiah 31:5–17

Hebrew is a strange word. Where does it come from? We take it for granted that the language that Eliezer Ben Yehuda re-created is called Hebrew, but we seldom ask ourselves why. The obvious answer, that it's biblical—for Abram was called the first Hebrew—only begs the question. Why was Abram called a Hebrew? What is the epithet supposed to mean?

The rabbis wondered about that, too. In the Midrash, a series of rabbinic explorations of the biblical text, the sages offered a proposal. Abram is called a Hebrew, they explain, for the following reason. The word *ivri* ("Hebrew") is of the same root as *ever*, which refers to a side that is opposite another side (the root of these words means to "pass" or "cross"). In this case it refers to the bank of a river: the Jews stood on one side, or bank, of the Euphrates, and the rest of the world stood on the other.[1] From the Jews' earliest days, the rabbis asserted, it has been their fate to play a countercultural role in human history. It has been their lot to assume positions that have not been popular, that have often been at odds with many a prevailing ethos.

Abraham stood utterly alone because he was a monotheist. Over time, however, his transformative insight was adopted by almost the entire Western world. Later still, there were other innovations. In a world in which child sacrifice was rampant, Judaism forbade it absolutely. In a world in which women were treated like chattel and could be discarded like yesterday's garbage when their husbands tired of them, Judaism's divorce laws required that a man provide for his former wife's financial welfare if the marriage was dissolved. In a world in which slavery was rampant and was even sanctioned by the Bible, the rabbis ended it by imposing so many protections for the slave that with time, the practice became financially counterproductive and disappeared from Jewish life.

These innovations did not always make financial or political sense for those who instituted them, and they also often brought with them the wrath of the world. But there is a sense, rooted deep within Judaism and now well established in Israel, that the Jews and their state are not in the business of expediency. They are in the business of standing for something. This is no less true today than it was in ancient times. Today, Israel is the most watched nation-state in the world, and the Jewish state finds itself standing for yet another unpopular principle: the belief that a shared sense of national purpose and uniqueness coupled with a deep commitment to tolerance are the two most important building blocks of a nation.

This commitment to the importance of the nation-state is not new, as we now know. It was initially introduced by the story of the Tower of Babel and later by the rest of the Hebrew Bible; indeed, the entire Hebrew Bible can be read as promoting the goal of a people struggling to achieve and perpetuate its independence on its own ancestral land.

To be sure, not everyone has accepted this notion. The New Testament has a much more universal ideal for human beings than the Hebrew Bible does. Imperial powers ancient and modern—the Assyrians and the Egyptians, the Greeks and the Romans, the early Catholic Church, the Ottoman Turks, and the modern French, British, Germans, and Russians—have all had their imperialist phases. Today, radical Islam and universalism are the world's newest imperialisms.

Throughout all these periods, the Jewish people struggled to maintain their independence. At times the Jews were successful. Ultimately, however, they lost their struggle to remain on their land, and for two thousand years they were dispersed across the globe. Yet the dream of returning to Zion remained paramount—not only because the Jews believed that the land was theirs but also because they believed that they bore a message about how human beings everywhere could flourish. The goal was never statehood for statehood's sake. It was statehood for the sake of a platform from which to model a different sort of national, ethnic, and religious life.

Israel is a country with a purpose and a message. For the Jews, survival alone has never been a purpose. As the Jewish philosopher Martin Buber put it, "Just as an individual who wishes only to preserve and assert himself leads an unjustified and meaningless existence, so a nation with no other aim deserves to pass away."[2] Israel's aim is to be the platform from which the Jewish people continues to make its countercultural claim. It is a claim about human differentness, the importance of diversity, and the vitality that is possible when a people lives with its culture and its traditions at the center of its public square.

Today, Israel is the most high-profile way in which the Jews live up to the responsibilities inherent in being the descendants of the Hebrews. In a world in which the alleged ideal of a European Union seems to suggest that borders are infinitely less important than they once were, Israel insists that borders still matter. In a world in which technology threatens to homogenize language, Israelis celebrate the rebirth of Hebrew.[3] In a world in which the Internet blends and erases cultures worldwide, statehood has allowed the Jews to share in the expansion of knowledge while cultivating their own culture, with its own messages and even its own angst.

In a world that is increasingly unwilling to fight for the freedom that the West too often takes for granted, Israel is the world's reminder of the message that appears on the Korean War Memorial in Washington, D.C.: "Freedom is not free." Torn between an expansionist Islamist world seeking to reshape the West in its own image and a West suffering from battle fatigue, Israel models the struggle to maintain freedom even in the face of incessant warfare. Europe and much of the international community would do well to take note.

Israel is far from a perfect country. At times, it is heartbreakingly flawed. But it is also profoundly threatened. There is no assurance that this noble balance—of Jewishness and democracy, of honoring the past while embracing the future, of seeking peace yet being willing to wage a continuous battle against evil—will ultimately withstand all the forces now arrayed against it. In fifty years, Israel may well be an even greater leader in technology, freedom, democracy, and general success than it is now. But it is also not out of the question that in fifty years, Israel will simply not exist. We still do not know, as Abraham Lincoln said about the United States at Gettysburg, "whether any nation so conceived and so dedicated can long endure."

For now, however, Israel does exist. The purpose of this book has been to articulate why Israel's survival matters not only to the Jews but also to freedom-loving human beings everywhere; the purpose of this volume has been to suggest a new way of articulating why people everywhere should care that Israel not only continues to exist but flourishes.

What *is* this "nation so conceived" really about? Michael Walzer has said that a nation is a "historic community, connected to a meaningful place, enacting and revising a way of life, aimed at political or cultural self-determination."[4] What does that look like? What does it mean for a people to reestablish itself on its ancestral land, with its own language, engaged in a modern dialogue with its ancient culture and way of life?

It looks like a society linked by a sense of shared destiny. It is that moment at the red light listening to a letter from Gilad Shalit's parents to their recently captured son; it is the realization that you are weeping, and so are the drivers on either side of you (see chapter 6). It is, thank goodness, that very same sense of shared destiny on the day he finally returned home. It is the utter silence of an entire country momentarily immobile during the sound of the air raid siren on Yom ha-Zikaron, the memorial day for fallen soldiers, mourning the losses of the past, dreading the losses still to come. It is the wordless pedestrians stopped in their tracks, drivers who have come to a halt on the highway, and even the radio stations that broadcast the siren, too.

A people's renewed flourishing is about an engagement with its ancient texts. At times the dialogue with those texts is obvious. At the end of basic training, IDF recruits stand in rows in a moving ceremony. Among the speeches is one in which an officer reads from the first chapter of the book of Joshua, including the verses that read "Be strong and resolute, for you shall apportion to this people the land that I swore to their fathers to assign to them. . . . Let not this Book of the Teaching cease from your lips, but recite it day and night, so that you may observe faithfully all that is written in it."[5] The same charge that Joshua called out to his troops as they entered the land thousands of years ago rings loud as the new recruits are formally given the weapon with which they will protect their re-created state.

This dialogue with ancient texts happens not only consciously but unconsciously as well. It takes place not only with soldiers but also with children playing on seesaws. All across Israel, little children play on playgrounds and sing a song that says, in part, the following:

> Seesaw, seesaw
> Fall and rise, rise and fall.
> What is up, and what is down? (*Mah le-ma'alah, mah le-matah*)
> Just me, me and you.[6]

What, on the surface, could be more innocent, playful, and wholesome? It's simple child's play, it would seem. But there's a battle going on here, an intense dialogue that is part and parcel of a people reconstituting itself in disputation with its ancient texts. The Mishnah (a first-century rabbinic text) says, "Whoever reflects upon four things would have been better off had he not been born: what is above, what is below (*mah le-ma'alah, mah le-matah*), what is before, and what is beyond."[7]

What is up and what is down? What is above and what is below? In the Mishnah, the reference is to the mysteries of life, the great theological questions with which every great civilization wrestles. Those are the matters we are better off not contemplating, according to the Mishnah. But Hayim Nahman Bialik, Zionism's poet laureate who wrote the little ditty above long after he'd rejected much of the traditional Jewish world, answers "What is up and what is down?" with "Just me, me and you."

You and I are the center of the world, he says to the children who do not even know that he wrote their song. You and I—chatting away in a language that had almost been forgotten, still living in the shadow of an ancient tradition that gave us life but for which we were also slaughtered—are what matters. In the face of the Mishnah's warning that we dare not contemplate the big questions, Bialik seems to say that his generation had already figured out what the big questions were. They had revived a language. They had reunited a people. A state was on the way. That was all that mattered.

You know that you are in a country where a national culture is flourishing when playful engagement with its ancient texts even makes its way into Supreme Court banter, as a lawyer attempts to introduce a final argument after the judge has already decided that the arguments have concluded. The attorney, a secular man, begins to speak, but the judge, equally secular, gently admonishes him, "*Ein maftirin achar ha-pesach afikoman*" (after the Passover meal, we do not add more dainties).[8] That too is cited in the Mishnah, but the players all knew the phrase from the Passover Haggadah, in which the line figures prominently. The judge could have said, "I'm sorry. Arguments are closed." But he didn't say that. He quoted a line from the Haggadah that made the same point, and in so doing, he reminded all the participants that what was unfolding in his Jerusalem courtroom could not have unfolded in a New York or Philadelphia courtroom.[9]

What was happening was more than the particular case being argued. Far more important than that individual case was the fact that a people was judging itself in its own sovereign capital and in its own reconstituted language. For the first time in centuries, when Jews turned to the authorities to adjudicate a matter, they were turning to Jews. That is a privilege not to be taken lightly.

When a culture is fully alive, its ancient texts inform not only conversations but also life-altering decisions. This was evident when even the harrowing decision about what price to pay for Gilad Shalit was being debated. On Israeli radio stations, whenever it seemed that there might be a deal in the offing, a passionate argument ensued. Some of those in favor of getting him back at virtually any price cited traditional Jewish sources on the commandment of *pidyon shevuyim*, the redemption of captives, which is considered a prime obligation of any Jewish community.[10]

But those who opposed a costly trade made reference to Rabbi Meir of Rothenburg, one of the leading Jewish scholars of the thirteenth century, who was captured trying to evade the edicts of Emperor Rudolf I of Hapsburg. The emperor imprisoned him and demanded an exorbitant ransom from the Jewish community for his release. The Maharam, as Rabbi Meir of Rothenburg is known today, was unwilling to be set free under these conditions. He feared that this precedent would lead other rulers to capture high-profile Jews, demand high sums for their release, and thus slowly but surely bankrupt and destroy the Jewish community, to which he had devoted his life. Despite widespread appeals that he relent, Rabbi Meir languished in prison for seven years until his death.

National flourishing takes many different forms. Michael Walzer reminds us that we witness such flourishing when a "historic community, connected to a meaningful place, enact[s its] way of life."[11] That is precisely what is so extraordinary about the morning pageant of the festival of Shavuot. In Jerusalem on that morning, people of many walks of life have stayed awake all night studying the Torah.

As dawn approaches, they begin to make their way by foot to the Old City of Jerusalem so that they can pray at the Western Wall. Half an hour before dawn, there are only a handful of people walking toward the Old City from a few different directions. Fifteen minutes later, the handful has quickly become hundreds. But within half an hour, as the sun is actually rising, there are thousands of people streaming in from every direction.

Just as they did for the pilgrimage festivals (Passover, Shavuot, and Sukkot) in biblical and talmudic times, Jews pour in toward the Temple Mount. Men and women, young and old, Ethiopians in their traditional robes and headdresses, Yemenites and Haredim in their traditional garbs, people dark-skinned and light, Orthodox men and women in traditional dress and secular people in shorts and T-shirts—as far as the eye can see, Jerusalem is teeming with life and with people, all headed back to the place that was once the focal point of the Jewish world. Jerusalem at that moment is the very embodiment of Barbara Tuchman's observation, mentioned in an earlier chapter, that only the Jews live in the same place, speak the same language, and practice the same religion now as they did three thousand years ago.[12]

When an agonizing question such as what price to pay to get Gilad Shalit out of captivity results in people calling in to the country's main radio stations, citing both the law of the redemption of captives but also the case of the Maharam, a people is in dialogue with its own internally conflicted tradition in a way that simply cannot happen when it is not the majority culture.

When the Israel Philharmonic Orchestra periodically discusses the possibility of playing a piece by Richard Wagner, the nineteenth-century German composer who is widely believed to have contributed to Aryan supremacist (and hence Nazi) ideology, debate breaks out in Israel. To what extent should the Jewish state and its national orchestra be so focused on memory? When should art and belief be distinguished? Should Israel join the family of nations that repudiate Wagner's thought but respect his musical genius? Or should the ongoing wishes of Shoah survivors that he not be played still be honored? That debate, public and anguished, historical and artistic, is also part of what a national ethnic revival looks like.

National flourishing is Jews taking in Jewish refugees from wherever they may come, but it is also welcoming Vietnamese boat people and Sudanese refugees, because, as countless Israelis remembered, their tradition had warned, "Do not oppress the stranger, because you were strangers in the land of Egypt."[13]

Jewish history guiding Jewish public policy is also part of national flourishing. It is the radio and the seesaw. It is a military ceremony and courtroom banter. It is a pilgrimage festival reconstituted with Jews from all walks of life. It is park benches in a small town in the Golan Heights on the backs of which are engraved the biblical verses referring to the Israelites' coming to that portion of the land; this is Israel's way of saying that for Israelis, *that* is Plymouth Rock. It is the moment when my son looked up from his electronic game in the back of the car on a family road trip when he was young, peered out the window, saw a sign to Gilgal, and asked if that was the same Gilgal he'd just learned about in Bible class. It was, we assured him—the Bible he was referring to was no mere book; it was *our* story, and he was living where it took place. That was why we'd moved to Israel.

In the summer of 2010, my wife and I attended the opening of the Jerusalem Film Festival, an outdoor event held in the Sultan's Pool just outside the walls of the Old City. The opening film that year was *La Rafle* (*The Roundup*), an account of French police who were Nazi accomplices and how they aided the Nazis in the roundup of France's Jews. It was, like most Shoah films, a painful movie to watch. But as I sat in the Sultan's Pool, that ancient water source, which had been modernized by Suleiman the Magnificent, the Ottoman sultan who built the current walls of the Old City, I looked to my right. There I saw the walls of the Old City, where King David had based his monarchy, the site where his son Solomon had built the Temple, and the site where the Romans had destroyed the second Temple and sent the Jews into exile. That exile, tragically, eventually led to *The Roundup*.

Then I looked to my left. There I saw the glittering new city of Jerusalem, lights aglow in the summer night. It was as though the lights of the new city and the modern buildings from which they glowed were meant to reassure us that the glories of the Old City did not have to end with *The Roundup*. There would be life and renewal. There could be an ingathering of Jews and a rebirth of their language.

There would be new Jewish army recruits listening to verses from Joshua, young Jewish children unwittingly quoting the Mishnah, and lovers in the Golan Heights sitting on park benches with ancient verses on them. Modern Jews could sit and watch the movie about the French roundup in what had once been the Valley of Gehenna, where the Canaanites offered their children as sacrifices to Molekh, a practice against which the Jewish prophets of old railed and won.

The Canaanites are gone, and no one quotes anything they said. The prophets are gone, too, but their words still ring loud and true. The prophets believed that the Israelites should stand for justice and should not step aside simply because what they advocated was unpopular. Seated that night in the Sultan's Pool, I had a sense that Amos, Hosea, or Isaiah would have been elated at the sight of modern Jews regathered, speaking their ancient language, reconstituted as a nation in their ancestral homeland. The opening of the film festival was conducted in Hebrew, even though all the actors being honored spoke only French. The Jews had chosen Eliezer Ben Yehuda over Ludwig Zamenhof, particularism over universalism, belonging to their ancient people rather than blending into an undifferentiated mass of humanity.

The prophets had promised a renewed Israel, and sitting in that valley, between the Old City and the new, with the awful specter of France in the 1940s on the screen in front of us, it would have been difficult to fail to sense the unfolding of the three different images: the Old City to our right, the Shoah on the screen in front of us, and a renewed Jerusalem to our left. It seemed at that moment that a medieval triptych recounting a historical narrative was unfolding before us. What the prophets had promised had come to be.

This national rebirth, and the richly woven tapestries of life that it makes possible, need not be the province of the Jews alone. That was the point of the Tower of Babel: this is a vision for all of humanity. In a perfected world, other peoples too could experience the national rebirth that sovereignty has made possible for the Jews: Chechnyans, Basques, and many more, including the Palestinians.

Like the Jews, the Palestinians are heirs to a rich and noble tradition. It may not have developed much in recent centuries, but it could develop more in the future. Imagine that the Palestinians have the courage to create a country in which Islam and the West meet, in which Muslim tradition and democratic liberal values are in dialogue in the public square, just as Israel has done for Judaism and the West. Imagine a world in which Palestine does for the Palestinians what Israel has done for the Jews.

Then imagine that Palestinian culture thrives so profoundly and the Palestinians achieve such great heights that they inspire other stateless peoples to seek *their* own independence. What might emerge then? A secure and thriving independent Tibet? A new lease on life, somehow, for Native Americans? Ethnicities and ancient peoples thriving across the globe?

What would emerge would be a richer, more nuanced, intellectually and morally inspiring world. What would happen is that human beings everywhere would be reminded of the glories of their cultures, of the profundities of their histories, of the importance of their traditions, and of the singularity of their languages. What would happen would be that Jews and Muslims, Israelis and Palestinians, would find that they were partners in changing the world as we know it, and the dream that began with the Tower of Babel story thousands of years ago would finally begin to be realized.

Only time will tell if this can happen. But for this dream to have even a chance, we must begin to speak about Israel in terms that recognize the Jewish state for what it is: a model of human defiance and human difference, an ode to the nobility of culture, a state in which its own heritage is in constant dialogue with Western culture. We would have to see Israel not as a country locked in incessant warfare but as a hope—as a model of what human life can still become.

There are signs that this can happen. Just as the Western world eventually adopted Abraham's insight about monotheism, even those societies in Europe that are often the most critical of Israel are beginning to acknowledge the profound truth that lies at the heart of Zionism's aspirations, even if they do not give Israel credit. The passion for transcending peoplehood and nations is beginning to fade; more and more, people acknowledge that their belief in universalism may have been a mistake.

Germany's Angela Merkel admitted that "the approach [of building] a multicultural [society] and to live side-by-side and to enjoy each other . . . has failed, utterly failed."[14] France's Nicolas Sarkozy said essentially the same thing about multiculturalism: "It's a failure. . . . The truth is that, in all our democracies, we've been too concerned about the identity of the new arrivals and not enough about the identity of the country receiving them."[15] Britain's David Cameron agreed that England had allowed its national identity to weaken, and he lamented the "state[-sponsored] multiculturalism" that had taken its place.[16] As one observer opined in the *New York Times*, "The challenge facing Europe today, therefore, is how to reject multiculturalism as a political policy while embracing the diversity that immigration brings. No country has yet succeeded in doing so."[17]

But that is not entirely true. No country has fully succeeded, of course, but one country is trying, and it is modeling something extraordinary to the rest of the world. If only the international community was less set on marginalizing Israel, it might come to see that Israel, once again, is a bellwether, addressing critical challenges long before Europe and the United States have to face them. Israel once fought terrorism before the rest of the world had to. Today, the Jewish state is battling for human differentness, hoping that the world might soon join the cause.

Now is the hour to see Israel in a renewed light, to view the Jewish state as proof of what can happen when peoples are restored to their ancestral lands as liberal, democratic nation-states. We are witness to an extraordinary phenomenon in today's Jewish state: a miracle of a people recovering its story, sanctifying its memory, reviving its language, and, most important, securing its freedom. Israel has become a proverbial lighthouse, a small and still threatened country that in the midst of all its other challenges shines a beacon of light into the darkness of the world we inhabit.

Israel begs humanity to embrace once again a vision of human differentness, a belief in the importance of cultural diversity. In its inimitable way, the Jewish state embodies the hope, not just for Jews but for human beings everywhere, that they too might someday weave richly colored tapestries of life, empowered by glorious freedoms of which they now can only dream.

Acknowledgments

In writing this book, I have been assisted and encouraged by a wide array of colleagues, students, and friends; it is a pleasure to have an opportunity to thank them.

The Shalem Center in Jerusalem is an extraordinarily rich intellectual environment. Many of my colleagues at Shalem, too numerous to name individually, have contributed to my thinking as it is reflected in this volume, and I am grateful to them all. Particular thanks are due to Dr. Daniel Polisar, the president of the Shalem Center, who insisted that I take a mini-sabbatical to make significant progress on this book and who could not have been more supportive of this project throughout. Dan did a thorough read of a very late version of this manuscript, made numerous wise suggestions and significant corrections. I'm grateful beyond words. Yair Shamir, the chairman of the board of the Shalem Foundation, has been very supportive of my writing during the years that we have worked together, while David Messer, a member of the Shalem Foundation's board of directors, exhibited extraordinary friendship as this project was nearing conclusion. I am deeply indebted to them both. Sharon Ben Hamo, as always, kept our office running with the utmost efficiency and protected my time with wisdom and sensitivity.

I would also like to express my gratitude to the Koret Foundation for their support of the work of the Shalem Center. I am honored by their creation of the Koret Distinguished Fellowship at Shalem.

Stephen Kippur, the president of the Trade Division at John Wiley & Sons until his retirement, invited me to write for Wiley. I remain grateful to him for the wonderful relationships that I have developed with John Wiley & Sons in the intervening years. This is the third book on which Eric Nelson, executive editor at Wiley, and I have collaborated. Eric is a profoundly gifted and thoughtful editor and someone from whom I have learned a great deal. Just when you think that a project is all but done, Eric has an ability to reimagine it in the most creative way. I am deeply grateful for all he has done to shape this book. Richard Pine, literary agent extraordinaire, has long since also become a friend; my continued thanks for all he has done on my behalf over the past two decades.

I have been very fortunate to have benefited from the research of a group of very talented students who worked as research assistants on this project; many of them were part of the Shalem Center's summer internship program.

In the summer of 2009, as this project was first taking shape, I was privileged to work with four students who undertook the challenge of working on a project that was still very amorphous and who did so with creativity, passion, and great intelligence. To Kerry Brodie (Princeton University), Ross Jacobs (Bowdoin College), Caroline Landau (Brown University), and Harry Reiss (Brown University), I extend great thanks.

Our interns in the summer of 2010 began to turn these ideas into outlines and chapters in formation. They moved the project forward significantly, sharpening the arguments, discarding material that no longer fit, and, in general, turning a set of ideas into the beginning of a book. To Elias Kraushaar (Cornell University), Ben Ratskoff (Northwestern University), and Brandi Ripp (Columbia College), many thanks.

A number of other people contributed research during this period, and I'm grateful to them all: Sarah Abrams, Aaron Applbaum, David Caron, Ari Rudolph, Guy Seemann, and Aaron Taxy. Tamar Newman was my research assistant during the 2010–2011 academic year and did extensive and valuable work—including research, writing, and editing—on this book as it took shape. Yakov Lozowick, state archivist at the Israel State Archives, offered thoughtful responses to a very early draft of the manuscript. To all, I am deeply grateful.

Particularly special thanks go to my Shalem summer interns of 2011, who worked at a feverish pace for exceedingly long and arduous days throughout the summer, taking a manuscript that was terribly rough and working with me to turn it into something dramatically different. Insightful readers, passionate debaters, careful editors, and extraordinarily capable researchers, these four people did more heavy lifting in the course of one summer than I would have imagined possible.

This finished product has each of their fingerprints all over it, and I will long be grateful to them for their devotion, energy, intelligence, and unique styles of humor during a very intensive summer. That they continued to send references, suggestions, and thoughts long after their internships were over and they'd returned to their respective campuses was simply a further indication of their commitment to this book, for which I am beyond grateful. Heartfelt thanks, coupled with profound admiration, to Abigail Klionsky (Princeton University), Adriel Koschitzky (University of Pennsylvania), Leah Sarna (Yale University), and Samuel Telzak (Yale University).

My thanks to Rabbi Lenore Bohm and the Leichtag Foundation for their generous underwriting of the 2011 Shalem summer student internship.

Zahava Stadler, a Shalem summer intern in 2008, did extensive editing of my book *Saving Israel: How the Jewish People Can Win a War That May Never End*. She then edited the book I cowrote with Dr. David Ellenson, *Pledges of Jewish Allegiance: Conversion, Law, and Policy-Making in Nineteenth- and Twentieth-Century Orthodox Responsa*. Since the completion of the current book coincided with her graduation from Princeton, I asked her to edit it as well, which she did with wisdom, a wonderfully critical eye and high standard for clarity, an unparalleled mastery of the subtleties of English grammar, and her characteristic attention to detail. I consider myself very fortunate that Zahava and I have now worked on three books together.

Several people offered very helpful advice or referred me to sources that proved exceedingly useful. My thanks to Professor Moshe Bar Asher, Scott Copeland, Claire Goldwater, Yossi Klein Halevi, Yoram Hazony, Dr. Yossi Lang, Rabbi Yitzchak Lifshitz, Sandra Lozowick, and Jacqueline Cooper Melmed. I was also fortunate to have opportunities to present some of this material in lectures and to receive valuable feedback at the following places in Jerusalem: the Pardes Institute during the fall of 2009, the Shalom Hartman Institute in the summer of 2010, and the Great Synagogue in January and October 2010.

As has now become our tradition, Zion Ozeri took the author photo for this volume. Zion, a former tank commander in the Israel Defense Forces and now a world-class photographer, cares deeply about the ideas in this book, many of which we have discussed at length over the past several years. I'm grateful for both his talent and his friendship.

My thanks, as well, to Erica Halivni, art director at the Shalem Center, for the design of the cover.

Some of the ideas presented here were first explored in writing in other forums. The material on the Tower of Babel and the Hebrew Bible's conception of history first appeared as "The Tower of Babel and the Birth of Nationhood," in *Azure* 40 (Spring 5770/2010): 19–36, and as "An Inquiry into the Shape and Meaning of Biblical History," in *Azure* 45 (Summer 5771/2011): 80–98.

I wrote about the impact of an Iranian nuclear weapon on Zionism's dream in "The Real Existential Threat: Iran's Bomb, Israel's Soul and the Future of the Jews," *Commentary*, October 2010, 11–15, and I explored the Zionist inclinations of young American Jews in "Are Young Rabbis Turning on Israel?", *Commentary*, June 2011, 18–24, and in "An Exchange on 'Are Young Rabbis Turning on Israel?'," *Commentary*, September 2011, 64–69. Several of my columns in the *Jerusalem Post* also raised some of the issues presented in this volume.

Translations from the Hebrew Bible are taken from *Tanakh: The Holy Scriptures, the New JPS Translation According to the Traditional Hebrew Text*, often with emendations on my part.

This volume is dedicated to my family's "in-laws"—that is, the parents of my daughter's husband—Professor Menahem Ben Sasson and Dr. Ada Ben Sasson, and to the children we now share. From the moment that my daughter, Talia, became engaged to their son, Avishay, Menahem and Ada have welcomed us into their lives and into their home in a fashion we could never have anticipated. Children of Israel's founders and leaders of Israel in their own right, they have embraced us with a warmth for which we remain deeply grateful, and we look forward to many causes for shared celebration in the years to come.

As this book goes to press, my wife, Elisheva, and I now have three adult children, all of whom we raised in Israel and each of whom is making her or his own way in this unusual and extraordinary country. Talia is about to graduate from law school, Aviel is an officer in the Israel Defense Forces, and Micha is completing a year of study at a yeshiva in the north before heading to the army. That Avishay, who just left the army after seven years of service, has now joined the ranks of our family is an enormous blessing to us all. None of them agrees with all of the ideas in this book, but each of them is an articulate and passionate Zionist; we have all debated many of the issues presented in these pages on dozens of occasions. Their wisdom and moral sensibilities have done much to enrich this project, and I love them each for that and for much more.

Finally, words cannot adequately convey my thanks to Elisheva. She has read and marked up more versions of this book than I imagine she cares to recall, but that contribution is merely a minuscule reflection of her larger impact on this book and on all of our lives. We live in Israel thanks to Elisheva's courage and her vision for our family; in ways more numerous than can be counted, it is she who has made our lives here as wondrous as they are. Our youngest child is now the age that she and I were when our paths first crossed one sunny California day. Although I knew right away that I'd just met someone unlike anyone I'd ever encountered, I could never have predicted the journey she would design for us, the abundant love she would both share and evoke, or the extraordinary mother she would one day become. I am blessed beyond measure.

Erev Yom Ha-Atzma'ut 5772
April 2012
Jerusalem

Notes

Introduction

1. Alfred Lord Tennyson, *Works of Alfred Lord Tennyson: Idylls of the King, The Lady Clare, Enoch Arden, In Memoriam, Becket, The Foresters: Robin Hood and Maid Marian, Queen Mary . . . Lyrical, Suppressed Poems and More* (Boston: MobileReference, 2007, Kindle edition, "Locksley Hall")
2. Babylonian Talmud (hereafter, B.T.), *Sanhedrin* 37a.
3. "How Were the Modern Nation-States of the Middle East Created?", PBS, http://www.pbs.org/wgbh/globalconnections/mideast/questions/nations/index.html.

1. The Israel Model

1. James W. Ceaser, *Liberal Democracy and Political Science* (Baltimore: Johns Hopkins University Press, 1990), 8; John Fonte, *Sovereignty or Submission: Will Americans Rule Themselves or Be Ruled by Others?* (New York: Encounter Books, 2011), 35, 41.
2. Israel's Declaration of Independence, http://www.mfa.gov.il/MFA/Peace%20Process/Guide%20to%20the%20Peace%20Process/Declaration%20of%20Establishment%20of%20State%20of%20Israel.

   Freedom of religion is enshrined in Israel's Basic Law (Israel does not have a constitution, but rather a set of basic laws that would form the backbone of a constitution should one ever be enacted), which states that human rights in Israel are based on "the principle that all persons are free; these rights shall be upheld in the spirit of the principles set forth in the Declaration of the Establishment of the State of Israel." Israeli Knesset, "Basic Law: Human Dignity and Liberty," section 1a (as amended in 1994), in *Sefer Ha-Chukkim* [Book of Statutes], No. 1454 of 27 Adar 5754 (March 10, 1994), 90. The Basic Law with its amendment can be seen on the Knesset website, http://www.knesset.gov .il/laws/special/eng/basic3_eng.htm).

Moreover, the Universal Declaration of Human Rights and the International Covenant on Civil and Political Rights, including their religious freedom provisions, have been cited in many Israeli Supreme Court rulings and, as a result, have been integrated into Israel's body of law. U.S. Department of State, Bureau of Democracy, Human Rights, and Labor, *International Religious Freedom Report 2009: Israel and the Occupied Territories* (Washington, DC: U.S. Government Printing Office, 2009), http://www.state.gov/g/drl/rls/irf/2009/127349.htm.

3. Israeli courts have blocked Arabs from living in some Jewish communities, just as they have stopped Jews from moving into some Arab communities—all in an attempt to allow those respective communities to preserve the sort of communal life that can be achieved with a reasonably uniform demographic.

4. As of this writing (August 2011), there is some discussion of a bill that could change that status. The authors of the proposed law, representing a wide swath of the Israeli political spectrum, wish to assert that Israel is first and foremost a *Jewish* state. They would therefore like to give privileged status to Hebrew over Arabic, English, and other languages.

5. The Arab Israeli population is exempt from conscription in the IDF, but the Druze and Bedouin communities serve voluntarily.

6. In one particularly disturbing case (January 2011), some rabbis actually sought to convince Israeli Jews not to rent or sell property to non-Jews. Their letter prompted responses of outrage from thousands of young Israelis, the prime minister, and many others. That a current of racism exists in Israeli society cannot be denied. Eli Ashkenazi, "Safed Rabbis Urge Jews to Refrain from Renting Apartments to Arabs," *Haaretz*, October 20, 2010, http://www.haaretz.com/print-edition/news/safed-rabbis-urge-jews-to-refrain-from-renting-apartments-to-arabs-1.320118.

7. I have addressed some of the policy challenges that a large Arab minority creates for Israel in *Saving Israel: How the Jewish People Can Win a War That May Never End* (Hoboken, NJ: John Wiley & Sons, 2009); see especially chapter 6, "Israeli Arabs in a Jewish State," 93–111. See also Nurit Yaffe, ed., "The Arab Population in Israel: 2008," in *Statisti-Lite* (Jerusalem: Central Bureau of Statistics, 2010), 5, http://www.cbs.gov.il/ www/statistical/arab_pop08e.pdf.

8. The Or Commission was established in 2003 to investigate the causes of the outbreak of the Second Intifada in 2000. "Official Summation of the Or Commission Report," *Haaretz*, September 2, 2003, reprinted by the Jewish Virtual Library, http://www.jewishvirtuallibrary.org/jsource/ Society_&_Culture/OrCommissionReport.html.

9. Amnon Rubinstein, "The Curious Case of Jewish Democracy," *Azure* 41 (Summer 2010): 38.

10. Ibid., 38–39; italics added.

11. The phrase *by the people* is commonly attributed to the U.S. Constitution, but that is an error. Its source is Lincoln's Gettysburg Address.

12. Shlomo Sand, *The Invention of the Jewish People*, trans. Yael Lotan (New York: Verso, 2010). For several critical reviews of Sand's book, see Jonathan Wittenberg, "The Invention of the Jewish People by Shlomo Sand," in *Guardian*, January 9, 2010, http://www.guardian .co.uk/books/2010/jan/09/invention-jewish-people-sand-review; Evan Goldstein, "Where Do Jews Come From?", *Wall Street Journal*, October 29, 2009, http://online.wsj.com/article/SB100014240527487037466045 74464023091024180.html; and Hillel Halkin, "An Indecent Proposal," *New Republic*, January 9, 2010, http://www.tnr.com/article/books-and-arts/indecent-proposal?page=0,0. Sand's thesis that Judaism was first a religion and only much later developed a notion of peoplehood or nationhood has been soundly refuted by Leora Batnitzky, *How Judaism Became a Religion: An Introduction to Modern Jewish Thought* (Princeton, NJ: Princeton University Press, 2011).

13. Ilan Pappe, *The Ethnic Cleansing of Palestine* (Chino Valley, AZ: Oneworld Press, 2007).

14. Barak Ravid, "L.A. Jews Mull Boycott of Israeli University over 'Apartheid' Op-Ed," *Haaretz*, August 22, 2009, http://www.haaretz .com/news/l-a-jews-mull-boycott-of-israel-university-over-apartheid-op-ed-1.282469.

15. Anthony Julius, *Trials of the Diaspora: A History of Anti-Semitism in England* (Oxford, UK: Oxford University Press, 2010), 559.

16. David Grossman, "Looking at Ourselves," speech given at Yitzhak Rabin's memorial ceremony, Tel Aviv, November 4, 2006, trans. Haim Watzman, *New York Review of Books*, January 11, 2007, http://www .nybooks.com/articles/archives/2007/jan/11/looking-at-ourselves.

17. Jonathan Lis, "Author David Grossman Snubs Olmert upon Receiving Prize," *Haaretz*, July 11, 2007, http://www.haaretz.com/news/ author-david-grossman-snubs-olmert-upon-receiving-prize-1.232729.

18. Three countries (Morocco, Lebanon, and Kuwait) were found to be partly free, and the rest (fourteen in all) were considered not free. Freedom House, *Freedom in the World*, 2010 survey, http://www.freedomhouse .org/template.cfm?page=15&year=2010.

19. Economist Intelligence Unit, "Index of Democracy 2008," *Economist*, http://graphics.eiu.com/PDF/Democracy%20Index%202008.pdf.

20. Joseph J. Ellis, *Founding Brothers: The Revolutionary Generation* (New York: Vintage Press, 2000), 15.

21. The murders of Jewish Agency political director Haim Arlozoroff in 1933, Peace Now activist Emil Grunzweig in 1983, and Prime Minister Yitzhak Rabin in 1995 were horrendous, but they are also dramatic exceptions to the rule.
22. Ellis, *Founding Brothers*, 39–40.

2. Where a Tradition Meets the World

1. The original source of the blessing is B.T. *Berakhot* 58a.
2. Ricardo Hausmann, Laura Tyson, and Saadia Zahidi, *The Global Gender Gap Report 2009*, World Economic Forum, 8–9, http://www.weforum .org/pdf/gendergap/report2009.pdf.
3. Ibid., 22.
4. This "award" originally appeared in James Kirchick, "Was Arafat Gay? An Old Rumor Gains New Force," *Out*, July 29, 2007, http://www.out .com/entertainment/2007/07/29/was-arafat-gay.
5. Gideon Alon, "Uzi Even Sworn in as First Openly Gay Member of Knesset," in *Haaretz*, November 3, 2002, http://www.haaretz .com/news/uzi-even-sworn-in-as-first-openly-gay-member-of-knesset-1.29513.
6. The U.N. Declaration on Sexual Orientation and Gender Identity has thus far been sponsored by 67 of the 192 member states of the United Nations. The content of the declaration was distributed on December 22, 2008, as an annex to the letter to the United Nations from the permanent representatives of Argentina, Brazil, Croatia, France, Gabon, Japan, the Netherlands, and Norway. It is agenda item 64 (b) of the sixty-third session of the General Assembly. See http://en.wikisource.org/wiki/ UN_declaration_on_sexual_orientation_and_gender_identity.
7. Patrick Worsnip, "U.N. Divided over Gay Rights Declaration," Reuters, December 18, 2008, http://www.reuters.com/article/ idUSTRE4BH7EW20081218.
8. Associated Press, "US Supports UN Statement Calling for Decriminalisation of Homosexuality," *Guardian*, March 18, 2009, http://www.guardian .co.uk/world/2009/mar/18/homosexuality-un-statement-obama.
9. Amnon Meranda, "Homosexual Activity Cause of Earthquake, Shas MK Says," *Ynetnews*, February 20, 2008, http://www.ynetnews.com/ articles/0,7340,L-3509263,00.html.
10. Laura Secor, "Iran's Leading Reformist Intellectual Tries to Reconcile Religious Duties and Human Rights," *Boston Globe*, March 14, 2004.
11. Ruth Eglash, "Reporters without Borders: Israel Capable of Best and Worst," *Jerusalem Post*, May 1, 2011, http://www.jpost.com/International/ Article.aspx?id=202275.

12. Reporters without Borders, "Press Freedom Index 2010," http://en.rsf .org/press-freedom-index-2010,1034.html.

13. Robert Mackey, "Blogger Jailed for Insulting Egypt's Military," *New York Times*, April 11, 2011, http://thelede.blogs.nytimes.com/2011/04/11/ blogger-jailed-for-insulting-egypts-military-is-pro-israel/?ref=moham medhusseintantawi.

14. Associated Press, "Palestinian Reporter Faces Trial for Insulting PA President Abbas on Facebook," *Haaretz*, January 22, 2011, http://www .haaretz.com/news/diplomacy-defense/palestinian-reporter-faces-trial-for-insulting-pa-president-abbas-on-facebook-1.338532.

15. Peter N. Stearns, ed., *The Encyclopedia of World History*, 6th ed. (Boston: Houghton Mifflin, 2001), 996; David Singer and Lawrence Grossman, eds., *American Jewish Year Book*, vols. 58 and 105 (New York: American Jewish Committee, 2007). Estimates of the populations vary, though only slightly, depending on the source. For an aggregation of several countries, see "The Displacement of Jews from Arab Countries: 1948–2005," Justice for Jews from Arab Countries, http://justiceforjews .com/pop_chart.pdf.

16. Stearns, *Encyclopedia of World History*, 996; Miriam Jordan, "Secret Mission Rescues Yemen's Jews," *Wall Street Journal*, October 31, 2009, http://online .wsj.com/article/SB125693376195819343.html; "The Displacement of Jews from Arab Countries," http://justiceforjews.com/pop_chart.pdf.

17. Arieh L. Avneri, *The Claim of Dispossession: Jewish Land Settlement and the Arabs, 1878–1948* (Edison, NJ: Transaction, 1982), 276; and "The Displacement of Jews from Arab Countries," http://justiceforjews.com/ pop_chart.pdf.

18. Avneri, *The Claim of Dispossession*, 276; and "The Displacement of Jews from Arab Countries," http://justiceforjews.com/pop_chart.pdf.

19. For the best discussion of this, see Benny Morris, *The Birth of the Palestinian Refugee Problem*, 1947–1949 (Cambridge, UK: Cambridge University Press, 1989). For a more radical view by the same author, see Benny Morris, "Survival of the Fittest," *Haaretz*, January 9, 2004, http://www.haaretz.com/survival-of-the-fittest-1.61345. This highly controversial interview is occasionally removed from the Web. A copy is on file with the author.

20. The Palestinians commonly say that no *Israelis* will be permitted to remain, for no *Jews* would clearly be seen as racist. The distinction, in effect, is meaningless. See, for example, Khaled Abu Toameh, "Abbas Vows: No Room for Israelis in Palestinian State," *Jerusalem Post*, December 25, 2010, http://www.jpost.com/MiddleEast/Article .aspx?id=200935/.

21. Nabi Salah, "Might Some Stay?", *Economist,* July 21, 2011, http://www
     .economist.com/node/18988684.

22. Hausmann et al., *Global Gender Gap Report 2009,* 22.

23. Sameena Nazir, "Challenging Inequality: Obstacles and Opportunities
     towards Women's Rights in the Middle East and North Africa," Freedom
     House, 2005, http://www.freedomhouse.org/template.cfm?page=163.

24. "Saudi Police 'Stopped' Fire Rescue," BBC, March 15, 2002, http://news
     .bbc.co.uk/2/hi/1874471.stm.

25. "Culture of Discrimination: A Fact Sheet on 'Honor' Killings," Amnesty
     International USA, 2007, http://www.amnestyusa.org/violence-against-
     women/stop-violence-against-women-svaw/honor-killings/page
     .do?id=1108230. In Israel, honor killings are illegal. They do happen
     periodically in the Arab community, but rarely. When they do occur, the
     killers are hunted down by the police.

26. Palestinian Central Bureau of Statistics, "Domestic Violence Survey,
     2005/2006," 149, http://www.pcbs.gov.ps/Portals/_PCBS/Downloads/
     book1340.pdf.

27. Scott Long, "They Want Us Exterminated," *Human Rights Watch
     Report*, August 17, 2009, http://www.hrw.org/en/reports/2009/08/17/
     they-want-us-exterminated-0.

28. Daniel Ottosson, "State-Sponsored Homophobia: A World Survey
     of Laws Prohibiting Same-Sex Activity between Consenting Adults,"
     *International Lesbian, Gay, Bisexual, Trans and Intersex Association (ILGA)
     Report*, May 2010, 24, http://old.ilga.org/Statehomophobia/ILGA_State_
     Sponsored_Homophobia_2010.pdf. Male homosexuality is outlawed in
     the Gaza Strip by Section 152, "Unnatural Offences," of the Criminal
     Code Ordinance of 1936.

29. Associated Press, "Nine Saudi Transvestites Jailed," Sodomy Laws, April
     16, 2000, http://www.sodomylaws.org/world/saudi_arabia/saudinews02
     .htm.

30. "Together, Apart," *Human Rights Watch Report*, section 2, Middle East
     and North Africa, June 11, 2009, http://www.hrw.org/en/node/83161/
     section/4.

31. Ottosson, "State-Sponsored Homophobia," 4.

32. "Iran Executes Two Gay Teens in Public Hanging," *UK Gay News*, July
     21, 2005, http://www.ukgaynews.org.uk/archive/2005july/2101.htm.

33. He made this statement at Columbia University in September 2007 in
     response to a question about the execution of two gay men in Iran.

34. Integrated Regional Information Networks (IRIN), "Egypt:
     Illiteracy Still Rife among Rural Women," U.N. Office for the
     Coordination of Humanitarian Affairs, http://www.irinnews.org/
     report.aspx?reportid=26179; Central Intelligence Agency, *The World*

Factbook, https://www.cia.gov/library/publications/the-world-factbook/fields/2103.html.

35. "Hebrew University Climbs to 57th Place on Global Ranking List," *Haaretz,* August 18, 2011, http://www.haaretz.com/print-edition/news/hebrew-university-climbs-to-57th-place-on-global-ranking-list-1.379203; "QS World University Rankings," Top Universities, 2009, http://www.topuniversities.com/university-rankings/world-university-rankings/home.

36. Fouad Ajami, "The Sorrows of Egypt," *Foreign Affairs* 74, no. 5 (September/October 1995), cited in Fareed Zakaria, *The Future of Freedom: Illiberal Democracy at Home and Abroad* (New York: W. W. Norton, 2007), 134–135.

37. Bernard Lewis, *The Crisis of Islam: Holy War and Unholy Terror* (New York: Random House, 2004), 115–116.

38. Zakaria, *The Future of Freedom*, 131; see also Bernard Lewis, *What Went Wrong? The Clash between Islam and Modernity in the Middle East* (New York: HarperPerennial, 2003), and Lewis, *The Crisis of Islam*.

39. Lewis, *What Went Wrong?*, 148.

3. Difference Matters

1. Tony Judt, "Israel: The Alternative," *New York Review of Books*, October 23, 2003, http://www.nybooks.com/articles/16671.

2. How and why Palestinians "fled" is a highly contended issue. What is clear is that many fled, some were pressured, and some were forced out. The finest book on the subject is Benny Morris, *The Birth of the Palestinian Refugee Problem, 1947–1949* (Cambridge, UK: Cambridge University Press, 1989).

3. Thomas Fuller, "European Poll Calls Israel a Big Threat to World Peace," *New York Times*, October 31, 2003, http://www.nytimes.com/2003/10/31/news/31ihtpoll_ed3_.html. For the original poll, see http://www.libertysecurity.org/IMG/pdf/fl151_iraq_full_report.pdf.

4. Richard Goldstone, "Reconsidering the Goldstone Report on Israel and War Crimes," *Washington Post,* April 2, 2011, http://www.washingtonpost.com/opinions/reconsidering-the-goldstone-report-on-israel-and-war-crimes/2011/04/01/AFg111JC_story.html; Amnesty International, "Israel's Campaign to Avoid Accountability for Gaza War Crimes," Center for Research on Globalization, April 5, 2011, http://www.globalresearch.ca/index.php?context=va&aid=24167.

5. "Review of Amnesty International in 2007: Attacking Democracy Instead of Oppression in Middle East," NGO Monitor, May 27, 2008, http://www.ngo-monitor.org/article/review_of_amnesty_international_in_attacking_democracy_instead_of_oppression_in_middle_east.

6. Robert Bernstein, "Right Watchdog, Lost in the Middle East," *New York Times*, October 19, 2009, http://www.nytimes.com/2009/10/20/opinion/20bernstein.html.

7. Judt, "Israel."

8. "Preamble," Treaty on European Union, February 7, 1992, http://eur-lex.europa.eu/en/treaties/dat/11992M/htm/11992M.html.

9. Tony Judt, *Postwar: A History of Europe since 1945* (New York: Penguin, 2005), 796.

10. Emery Reves, "An Open Letter to the American People," in *The Anatomy of Peace* (New York: Harper and Brothers, 1945), cover, http://archive1.globalsolutions.org/wfi/documents/OpenLetter.pdf.

11. John Fonte, *Sovereignty or Submission: Will Americans Rule Themselves or Be Ruled by Others?* (New York: Encounter Books, 2011), 15.

12. Immanuel Kant, "Perpetual Peace: A Philosophical Sketch," in *Kant's Political Writings,* ed. Hans Reiss and trans. H. B. Nisbet (Cambridge, UK: Cambridge University Press, 1970), 105.

13. Barbara Demick, "The Good Cook: A Battle against Famine in North Korea," *New Yorker*, November 2, 2009.

14. José Maria Aznar, "If Israel Goes Down, We All Go Down," *Times* (London), June 17, 2010, reprinted by the World Jewish Congress, http://www.worldjewishcongress.org/en/news/9401/opinion_jos_mar_a_aznar_if_israel_goes_down_we_all_go_down. Certain European spellings were altered here to conform to American spelling.

15. John Noble Wilford, "Linguists Identify Endangered Language Hot Spots," *New York Times*, September 19, 2007, http://www.nytimes.com/2007/09/19/world/asia/19iht-talk.1.7564677.html.

16. Neil Gross and Solon Simmons, "The Social and Political Views of American Professors," working paper, Harvard University Department of Sociology, September 24, 2007; and Alan Wolfe, "Academia (Kind of) Goes to War: Chomsky and His Children," *World Affairs* (Winter 2008): 38–47.

17. "Open Letter: More Pressure for Mideast Peace," *Guardian*, April 6, 2002.

18. Andy Beckett, "Andy Beckett Investigates the Academic Boycott of Israel," *Guardian*, December 12, 2002, http://www.guardian.co.uk/education/2002/dec/12/highereducation.uk.

19. Suzanne Goldberg, "Israeli Boycott Divides Academics," *Guardian*, July 8, 2002, http://www.guardian.co.uk/uk/2002/jul/08/highereducation.israel.

20. "Brits Ban Israeli Universities," *Ynetnews*, April 24, 2005, http://www.ynetnews.com/articles/0,7340,L-3076464,00.html; Abraham H. Foxman, "Academic Boycott: Bashing Israel," *New York Times*, April 22, 2005,

http://www.nytimes.com/2005/04/21/opinion/21iht-edfoxman.html. Additional incidents include the following.

The Ariel University Center of Samaria was disqualified by the Spanish Housing Ministry, sponsor of the Solar Decathlon, from competing in the decathlon's finals in Madrid in June 2010. The decathlon is an international competition among university architecture departments to design and build a self-sufficient house using solar power. Ariel University had reached the competition's finals along with twenty other universities. Sergio Vega, the project manager of the Solar Decathlon, wrote to the school, "The decision was made by the Spanish government based on the fact that the university is located in occupied territory in the West Bank. The Spanish government is committed to uphold the international agreement under the framework of the European Union and the United Nations regarding this geographical area."

Similarly, in March 2011, a literary conference titled "Writing Today in the Mediterranean" slated to be held in southern France by the University of Provence Aix-Marseille, was canceled because of the uproar generated by the French Jewish community in light of the organizers' boycott of Israeli academics. Esther Orner, an Israeli author who had planned to attend the conference, decided to wage a media war against its organizers when she was told that she could not participate in the event because she is an Israeli. On June 17, when the organizers met to finalize the details of the conference's timetable, they received a notice from certain authors who refused to participate if Israeli authors were allowed to attend. The organizers thus decided to cancel Orner's participation. As a result, Ann Roche, the organizer who had invited Orner in the first place, decided to resign. The letter from the organizers to Orner read, "We don't have anything against you, and we are against the boycott of intellectual and cultural figures, but we are against Israel's politics."

21. Eric Gould and Omer Moav, "The Israeli Brain Drain," Shalem Center, July 2006, https://www.shalemcenter.org.il/FileServer/df4b061c96a6fbceb95026260cb4de8a.pdf.

22. Anthony Julius, *Trials of the Diaspora: A History of Anti-Semitism in England* (Oxford, UK: Oxford University Press, 2010), 479.

23. Ibid., 482.

24. Howard Jacobson, *The Finkler Question* (New York: Bloomsbury, 2010), 143.

4. Universalism's Betrayal

1. Quoted in Ulrich Mattias, *Esperanto: The New Latin for the Church and for Ecumenism* (Antwerp: Vlaamse Esperantobond, 2002), 23.

2. My thanks to Dr. Yossi Lang, Israel's foremost expert on Eliezer Ben Yehuda, for confirming to me (September 26, 2010) that no one is aware of any contact of any sort between the two men.

3. Jehuda Reinharz and Yaakov Shavit, *Glorious, Accursed Europe* (Waltham, MA: Brandeis University Press, 2010), 25.

4. Ibid., 20.

5. For this list of events I am indebted to Amnon Rubinstein, "The Curious Case of Jewish Democracy," *Azure* 41 (Summer 2010): 44. For the First International Anti-Jewish Congress, see "Manifesto to the Governments and Peoples of the Christian Nations Threatened by Judaism," Dresden, Germany, 1882, http://germanhistorydocs.ghi-dc.org/.

6. Mark Lilla, "The End of Politics: Europe, the Nation-State, and the Jews," *New Republic,* June 17, 2003.

7. Ibid.

8. Pierre Manent, *Democracy without Nations? The Fate of Self-Government in Europe*, trans. Paul Seaton (Wilmington, DE: ISI Books, 2007), 7.

9. Sidney Tarrow, *The New Transnational Activism* (Cambridge, UK: Cambridge University Press, 2005), 70.

10. George Eliot, *Daniel Deronda* (New York: Modern Library, 2002), 476. *Daniel Deronda* was initially published by William Blackwood and Sons in eight parts from February to September 1876. It was republished in December 1878 with revisions primarily in those sections dealing with Jewish life and customs.

11. Shmuel Trigano, e-mail to author, September 13, 2010.

12. Jed Rubenfeld, "The Two World Orders," *Wilson Quarterly* (Autumn 2003): 35.

13. Amos Oz, *A Tale of Love and Darkness*, trans. Nicholas de Lange (New York: Harcourt, 2005), 5.

14. Anthony Julius, *Trials of the Diaspora: A History of Anti-Semitism in England* (Oxford, UK: Oxford University Press, 2010), 97.

15. Ibid., 98.

16. Shelby Steele, "Israel and the Surrender of the West," *Wall Street Journal*, June 21, 2010, http://online.wsj.com/article/SB10001424052748704198004575311011923686570.html.

17. Leon de Winter, "Anti-Semitism Is *Salonfähig* Again," *Wall Street Journal*, June 14, 2010, http://online.wsj.com/article/SB1000142405274870457530457529646351278591 0.html.

18. Ibid.

19. Ibid.

20. Christopher Caldwell, *Reflections on the Revolution in Europe: Immigration, Islam, and the West* (New York: Anchor Books, 2009), 83.

21. For this formulation I am indebted to Yoram Hazony and a lecture on the power of ideas that he presented at the Shalem Center in Jerusalem in the summer of 2008.

22. Rabbi Jonathan Sacks, *The Dignity of Difference: How to Avoid the Clash of Civilizations* (London: Continuum, 2002).

5. A Biblical Tug-of-War

1. Roger Cohen, "In Croatia, a Frail Pope John Paul II Urges a 'Culture of Peace,'" *New York Times*, September 11, 1994, http://www.nytimes.com/1994/09/11/world/in-croatia-a-frail-pope-john-paul-ii-urges-a-culture-of-peace.html.

2. Alan Cowell, "Pope Goes to Albania and Warns of 'Aggressive Nationalism,'" *New York Times*, April 26, 1993, http://www.nytimes.com/1993/04/26/world/pope-goes-to-albania-and-warns-of-aggressive-nationalism.html.

3. Genesis 11:1–9. Throughout this book, translations of the Hebrew Bible are based on *Tanakh: The Holy Scriptures* (Philadelphia, PA: Jewish Publication Society, 1985), often with emendations.

4. Genesis 9:19.

5. Genesis 10:25.

6. Genesis 10:5; italics added. The insertion, quoted in the Jewish Publication Society translation, is based on verses 20 and 31.

7. Leo Strauss, *Jewish Philosophy and the Crisis of Modernity: Essays and Lectures in Modern Jewish Thought*, ed. Kenneth Hart Green (Albany: State University of New York Press, 1997), 390.

8. Ludwig Wittgenstein, *Tractatus* (New York: Harcourt, Brace, 1922), 149, http://www.kfs.org/~jonathan/witt/t5en.html.

9. A similar view is advanced by the classical commentary of Hezekiah ben Manoach, usually referred to as the Chizkuni, in his notes on Genesis 11:4. He notes that the sin of this generation was not the building of the tower but rather an unwillingness to disperse. God had commanded humanity to "be fruitful and multiply and fill the earth," so their insistence on staying in one place thus violated the latter part of God's express command.

10. Genesis 11:9.

11. Ernest Gellner, *Nations and Nationalism* (Ithaca, NY: Cornell University Press, 1983); Carlton J. H. Hayes, *A Political and Social History of Europe* (New York: Macmillan, 1926); E. J. Hobsbawm, *Nations and Nationalism since 1780: Programme, Myth, Reality* (Cambridge, UK: Cambridge University Press, 1990).

12. Anthony Smith sees in the premodern ethnic community the antecedent of what later became the nation-state. Anthony D. Smith, *The Ethnic Origins of Nations* (Oxford, UK: Blackwell, 1986).

13. Genesis 12:1; italics added.

14. Genesis 17:6.

15. Exodus 12:40. In Genesis 15:13, God told Abram that his descendants would live and be afflicted in a land that was not their own for four hundred years. In the view of the Bible, this is clearly part of a divine plan.

16. Exodus 1:9.

17. Exodus 1:10. This view is endorsed by Arnold B. Ehrlich, *Mikra Ki-pheshuto: The Bible According to Its Literal Meaning* (New York: Ktav, 1969), 1:134–135. I first examined these literary parallels in Daniel Gordis, "The Tower of Babel and the Birth of Nationhood," *Azure* 40 (Spring 2010): 19–36. For a similar treatment, see Judy Klitsner, *Subversive Sequels in the Bible* (Jerusalem: Koren, 2011), 31–62.

18. Genesis 11:3.

19. Exodus 5:18. The word also appears in Exodus 1:14 and 5:16.

20. Ezra 1:1–3.

21. 2 Chronicles 36:22–23.

22. It is interesting and sad that some groups have used the Tower of Babel story to promote societies that suppressed rather than encouraged freedom. For example, "Theologians of the South African Dutch Reformed Church found their scriptural warrant not in the Curse of Ham that had served some of the slaveholding ancestors, but in the story of the destruction of the Tower of Babel. In their exegesis of this tale, the religious apologists for apartheid identified a God who regarded attempts to unify the human race as manifestations of sinful pride. As a remedy to the evils of universalism, he prescribed a strict division of humanity into separate linguistic and cultural groups, which were commanded, in effect, to keep their distance from each other and to 'develop along their own lines.' If we were to take these ideologues at their word, cultural relativism rather than hierarchical racism would have to be acknowledged as the essence of apartheid." George M. Frederickson, *Racism: A Short History* (Princeton, NJ: Princeton University Press, 2003), 135–136.

23. Harold Bloom, *The Shadow of a Great Rock* (New Haven, CT: Yale University Press, 2011). The original phrase is from Isaiah 32:2.

24. Revelation 7:9. Translation is from *The New Jerusalem Bible* (New York: Doubleday, 1966).

25. Matthew 22:21. The verse has been interpreted in many conflicting fashions. For instance, some scholars argue that Jesus was evading the question of whether his followers should pay taxes and thus the verse

was never intended to state a political or philosophical worldview. Its simple meaning, however, is that there are two realms: one is Caesar's and one is God's.

26. The best argument of this sort is found in Joshua Berman, *Created Equal: How the Bible Broke with Ancient Political Thought* (New York: Oxford University Press, 2008).

27. Eugene Shoenfeld, "Justice: An Elusive Concept in Christianity," *Review of Religious Research* 30, no. 3 (March 1989): 240. He writes, "Christianity, although differing from Roman religion, changed those features of its parent religion which would have detracted from its accommodation with Rome."

28. Galatians 3:28. Traditional Jews will find this verse interesting because they will immediately recognize the language from three morning blessings found in Jewish liturgy: thanking God for having made "us" Jews and not Gentiles, free people and not slaves, and men and not women. (In traditional Jewish circles, women recite a different third blessing, thanking God for having made them according to divine will, whereas in more liberal circles, the third blessing has been altered altogether.) I am very grateful to Professor Shaye J. D. Cohen of Harvard University for sharing his thoughts on the Galatians passage with me in the summer of 2010, prior to his publishing them. They can now be found in Amy-Jill Levine and Marc Zvi Brettler, eds., *The Jewish Annotated New Testament: New Revised Standard Version Bible Translation* (Oxford, UK: Oxford University Press, 2011), 339.

29. Roger Cohen, "Pope Urges Croats to Renew 'Unbreakable' Slavic Ties," *New York Times*, September 12, 1994, http://www.nytimes.com/1994/09/12/world/pope-urges-croats-to-renew-unbreakable-slavic-ties.html.

30. Text taken with slight emendations from "Declaration of Independence, July 4, 1776," Avalon Project, Yale Law School, http://avalon.law.yale.edu/18th_century/declare.asp.

31. Text taken with slight emendations from "Declaration of Israel's Independence 1948," Avalon Project, Yale Law School, http://avalon.law.yale.edu/20th_century/israel.asp.

32. Rabbi Jonathan Sacks, *The Dignity of Difference: How to Avoid the Clash of Civilizations* (London: Continuum, 2002), 49–50.

33. In fact, Sacks ultimately agreed to modify some of the language in a second edition of the book, although he refused to recall the copies that were already in bookstores. Jonathan Petre, "Chief Rabbi Revises Book after Attack by Critics," *Daily Telegraph* (London), February 15, 2003, http://www.telegraph.co.uk/news/uknews/1422145/Chief-Rabbi-revises-book-after-attack-by-critics.html.

34. "Law of Return 5710–1950," Jewish Virtual Library, http://www
    .jewishvirtuallibrary.org/jsource/Immigration/Text_of_Law_of_Return
    .html.

35. Alexander Yakobson and Amnon Rubinstein, *Israel and the Family of
    Nations: The Jewish Nation-State and Human Rights* (London: Routledge,
    2008), 139.

36. "Constitution of Ireland," Taoiseach (department of the Irish
    government), http://www.taoiseach.gov.ie/attached_files/Pdf%20files/
    Constitution%20of%20Ireland.pdf.

37. Text taken with slight emendations from "The Constitution,"
    Stortinget, http://www.stortinget.no/en/In-English/About-the-Storting/
    The-Constitution/The-Constitution/.

38. "Constitution of Denmark," Articles 4 and 6, Refworld, http://www
    .unhcr.org/refworld/country,,NATLEGBOD,,DNK,,3ae6b518c,0.html.

39. All quoted in Yakobson and Rubinstein, *Israel and the Family of Nations*,
    215.

40. Quoted in ibid., 219.

6. The Invention of the Invention of Nationalism

1. George Eliot, *Daniel Deronda* (New York: Modern Library, 2002), 15.

2. "Visit of Menachem Begin—Remarks of Carter and Begin at the
   Welcoming Ceremony," July 19, 1977, Jewish Virtual Library, http://
   www.jewishvirtuallibrary.org/jsource/US-Israel/Carter_Begin.html.

3. Ibid.

4. Quoted in Yehuda Avner, *The Prime Ministers* (Jerusalem: Toby Press,
   2010), 104–105.

5. Quoted in ibid., 105.

6. Elie Kedourie, *Nationalism* (Oxford, UK: Blackwell, 1993), 1.

7. Quoted in David Pryce-Jones, "The Chatham House Version, Yet
   Again," *Middle East Quarterly* 11, no. 2 (Spring 2004): 79–82, http://
   www.meforum.org/620/the-chatham-house-version-yet-again#.

8. Kenneth Minogue, "Obituary: Professor Elie Kedourie," *Independent*
   (London), July 3, 1992, http://www.independent.co.uk/news/people/
   obituary-professor-elie-kedourie-1530876.html.

9. Benedict Anderson, *Imagined Communities: Reflections on the Origin and
   Spread of Nationalism* (London: Verso, 2000), 6.

10. Steven Kemper, *The Presence of the Past: Chronicles, Politics, and Culture
    in Sinhala Life* (Ithaca, NY: Cornell University Press, 1991), 4.

11. Anderson, *Imagined Communities*, 7.

12. Martha Nussbaum, *For Love of Country?* (Boston: Beacon Press, 1996),
    10–11.

13. John Breuilly, "Introduction," in Ernest Gellner, *Nations and Nationalism: New Perspectives on the Past* (Ithaca, NY: Cornell University Press, 1983), xxv. The language here is Breuilly's summary of Gellner's views.

14. Thomas Bender, "No Borders: Beyond the Nation-State," *Chronicle of Higher Education*, April 7, 2006, http://chronicle.com/article/No-Borders-Beyond-the/34180.

15. Walter Scott, "The Lay of the Last Minstrel," Canto Sixth, Poets' Corner, http://www.theotherpages.org/poems/canto06.html.

16. Quoted in Edmund White, "Introduction," in George Eliot, *Daniel Deronda*, xx.

17. Nicholas Kulish, "Young Germans Dare to Celebrate Homeland," *International Herald Tribune* (Berlin), September 11–12, 2010.

18. John Stuart Mill, "On Representative Government," in *Utilitarianism: On Liberty and Considerations on Representative Government*, ed. H. B. Acton (London: Everyman, 1984), 391.

19. Johann Gottfried Herder, *Another Philosophy of History and Selected Political Writings*, trans. and ed. Ioannis D. Evrigenis and Daniel Pellerin (Indianapolis, IN: Hackett, 2004), 128.

20. Estimates of the percentage of non-Jews among these immigrants vary. For a discussion of the various positions, see Asher Cohen, *Non-Jewish Jews in Israel* [Hebrew] (Jerusalem: Shalom Hartman Institute and Keter, 2006), 34. Cohen, a political scientist who has studied the increasing non-Jewish population in Israel, suggests that since the 1990s, their percentage among immigrants from the former Soviet Union is, according to some estimates, about 40 percent while, according to others, it is 50 percent and more. Mark Tolts, a demographer at Hebrew University's Institute of Contemporary Jewry who specializes in the study of Soviet and post-Soviet Jewry, suggests a more moderate though still significant estimate.

21. Gellner, *Nations and Nationalism*, 7.

22. There is some debate about the origins of the Ethiopian Jewish community. Some scholars argue that a core of Jews who fled from Judea might have been joined by other peoples already living in Africa.

23. Isaiah Berlin, *Vico and Herder: Two Studies in the History of Ideas* (New York: Vintage, 1977), 159.

24. Michael J. Sandel, *Liberalism and the Limits of Justice* (Cambridge, UK: Cambridge University Press, 1998), 179. It is interesting that despite the views he has expressed here, he has also more than flirted with the notion of transcending nationalism. See Michael Sandel, "After the Nation-State: Reinventing Democracy," *New Perspectives Quarterly* (Fall 1992): 4–13.

25. Ruth Gavison, *The Law of Return at 60 Years: History, Ideology, Justification* (Jerusalem: Metzilah Center for Zionist, Jewish, Liberal and Humanist Thought, 2010).

26. "Bowe R. Bergdahl," *New York Times*, July 24, 2009, http://topics .nytimes.com/topics/reference/timestopics/people/b/bowe_r_bergdahl/ index.html.

27. Yitzchak Ben Horin, "A Second One in Captivity: A Soldier Is Held by the Taliban and His Family Is Silent" [in Hebrew], *YNet*, July 2, 2010, http://www.ynet.co.il/articles/0,7340,L-3913778,00.html.

28. Charles Taylor, *The Ethics of Authenticity* (Cambridge, MA: Harvard University Press, 1991), 40–41.

29. Avi Chai Foundation, "Portrait of Israeli Jewry: Beliefs, Observances and Values among Israeli Jews, 2000," Israel Democracy Institute, http://www.idi.org.il/sites/english/PublicationsCatalog/Documents/ PortraitofIsraeliJewry.pdf.

30. "The Chemistry of Love," *Time*, February 15, 1993, http://www.time .com/time/covers/0,16641,19930215,00.html.

7. Diversity Is the Key to Human Freedom

1. Pierre Manent, *Democracy without Nations? The Fate of Self-Government in Europe,* trans. Paul Seaton (Wilmington, DE: ISI Books, 2007), 7.

2. Thucydides, *History of the Peloponnesian War*, chapter 17, Mt. Holyoke College, http://www.mtholyoke.edu/acad/intrel/melian.htm.

3. John Stuart Mill, "The Contest in America," originally published in *Harper's*, April 1862, 683–684, http://www.gutenberg.org/dirs/etext04/ conam10h.htm.

4. Daniel N. Robinson, *Aristotle's Psychology* (New York: Columbia University Press, 1989), 111.

5. Rabbi Jonathan Sacks, *The Dignity of Difference: How to Avoid the Clash of Civilizations* (London: Continuum, 2002), 50.

6. Isaiah Berlin, *Liberty: Incorporating Four Essays on Liberty*, ed. Henry Hardy (Oxford, UK: Oxford University Press, 2002), 345.

7. Immanuel Kant, "Perpetual Peace: A Philosophical Sketch," in *Kant's Political Writings*, ed. Hans Reiss (Cambridge, UK: Cambridge University Press, 1970), 113.

8. John Locke, *The Second Treatise of Civil Government* (Amherst, MA: Prometheus Books, 1986), 117.

9. Quoted in Yoram Hazony, "Beyond Survival," *Azure* 13 (Summer 2002): 153.

10. Natan Sharansky, *Defending Identity: Its Indispensable Role in Protecting Democracy* (New York: PublicAffairs, 2008), 77.

11. Barry Schwartz, Yael Zerubavel, and Bernice M. Barnett, "The Recovery of Masada: A Study in Collective Memory," *Sociological Quarterly* 27, no. 2 (Summer 1986): 148.

12. Barbara D. Metcalf and Thomas R. Metcalf, *A Concise History of Modern India*, 2nd ed. (Cambridge, UK: Cambridge University Press, 2002), 48.

13. William Dalrymple, *The Last Mughal: Delhi, 1857* (New York: Alfred A. Knopf, 2006), 63–69.

14. Christopher Hibbert, *The Great Mutiny: India, 1957* (New York: Viking Press, 1978), 55.

15. Rob Cameron and David Vaughan, "Jaroslava Moserova—Remembering Jan Palach," Radio Prague, January 21, 2003, http://www.radio.cz/en/section/witness/jaroslava-moserova-remembering-jan-palach.

16. Sacks, *Dignity of Difference*, 58.

17. Michael Walzer, *Thick and Thin* (Notre Dame, IN: University of Notre Dame Press, 2006), 8.

18. Sharansky, *Defending Identity*, 15.

19. Ibid., 26–27.

20. Ibid., 27.

21. David Horowitz, "Maybe This Is the Moment to Put Our Trust in Freedom," *Jerusalem Post,* February 11, 2011, http://www.jpost.com/Opinion/Editorials/Article.aspx?id=207745.

8. The Only Thing We Should Not Tolerate Is Intolerance

1. Henry Miller, *Big Sur and the Oranges of Hieronymus Bosch* (New York: New Directions, 1957), 25.

2. Quoted in Daniel J. Boorstin, *The Image: A Guide to Pseudo Events in America* (New York: Atheneum: [1961] 1985), 78.

3. Wyatt Mason, "David Mitchell, The Experimentalist," *New York Times Magazine*, June 27, 2010.

4. Deuteronomy 2:3–5, 2:9, 2:19.

5. Michael W. Doyle, "Kant, Liberal Legacies, and Foreign Affairs," *Philosophy and Public Affairs* 12, no. 3 (Summer 1983): 205–235; Michael W. Doyle, "Kant, Liberal Legacies, and Foreign Affairs, Part 2," *Philosophy and Public Affairs* 12, no. 4 (Autumn 1983): 323–353.

6. Michael Walzer, "The Democratic Peace Theory," *Jewish Review of Books* 5 (Spring 2011): 49.

7. For a more extensive discussion of the nation-state as a means of freeing humanity from empire, see Yoram Hazony, "Empire and Anarchy," *Azure* 12 (Winter 2002): 27–70. Hazony makes this point in exceedingly compelling language: "Surely, it is far simpler to strive for the establishment of one world empire; or to permit an infinite number

of independent polities within anarchy, as many as there are human collectives capable of expressing the common will of their members. But I believe that one must choose: Whether it is simplicity that one desires in the political order, or freedom. If it be the former, then one must, indeed, place one's weight on the side of empire and anarchy, whose immense attractiveness and power derive from the irresistible beauty of the absolute. But if it be freedom that one seeks, then there is no choice but to learn the much more difficult craft that a complexity such as that suggested by the rabbis represents. I think that when the matter is weighed carefully, one must conclude that no less than the freedom of humanity depends on our ability to maintain the ideal of national liberty and sovereignty, and to strive for its judicious application as the basis of the political order" (48–49).

8. See the extended discussion of this issue in Daniel Gordis, *Saving Israel: How the Jewish People Can Win a War That May Never End* (Hoboken, NJ: John Wiley & Sons, 2009), especially chapter 6 and pp. 106–108.

9. There is an extensive literature on this. See, for example, Bennett Zimmerman, Roberta Seid, and Michael L. Wise, "Voodoo Demographics: The Palestinians' Missing Millions," *Azure* 25 (Summer 2006): 61–78; Joel Golovensky, "Immutable 'Conceptzia' Trumps Facts," *Jerusalem Post*, July 3, 2011, http://www.jpost.com/Opinion/Op-EdContributors/Article.aspx?id=227754.

10. Herb Keinon, "Cabinet Passes Loyalty Oath Requirement 22–8," *Jerusalem Post*, October 10, 2010, http://www.jpost.com/Headlines/Article.aspx?id=190850; Rupert Wingfield-Hays, "Israeli Orthodox Rabbi Stirs Up Racism Debate," BBC, November 30, 2010, http://www.bbc.co.uk/news/world-middle-east-11865711; Jonah Mandel, "Chief Rabbinate to Probe IDF, Civilian Conversion," *Jerusalem Post*, October 22, 2010, http://www.jpost.com/Israel/Article.aspx?id=192426.

11. At this writing, the Arab Spring's revolutions have yet to touch Jordan. If the Hashemite monarchy were to fall, and Palestinians were to take over Jordan, this objection would not be as relevant. But at present, there is no indication that scenario is about to happen.

12. Native Americans have even gone to the United Nations to make their case for admission to the international body as sovereign states, though unsuccessfully. Doug George-Kanentiio, "Iroquois at the UN," *Akwesasne Notes*, Fall 1995, http://www.ratical.org/many_worlds/6Nations/IroquoisAtUN.html.

13. Choe Sang-Hun, "Net Addresses to Make Use of Non-Latin Scripts," *New York Times*, October 30, 2009, http://www.nytimes.com/2009/10/31/technology/31net.html.

14. Manu Joseph, "Goddess English of Uttar Pradesh," *New York Times*, May 14, 2010, http://www.nytimes.com/2010/05/16/opinion/16joseph .html.

9. A Country with the Soul of a Church

1. John Jay, "Federalist #2," in *The Federalist Papers*, ed. Clinton Rossiter (New York: New American Library, 1961), 38, http://www.constitution .org/fed/federa02.htm.

2. Mrs. Brown, I learned many years later, was Margaret R. Brown, a Presbyterian who taught in several Jewish schools, marched with Martin Luther King Jr., was active in the National Organization for Women, and was active in many other social causes. That I remember her to this day is a testament to the power of her teaching. If only we seventh graders had had the maturity to better appreciate the remarkable character of the woman who was then teaching us social studies.

3. Quoted in Arthur M. Schlesinger Jr., *The Disuniting of America: Reflections on a Multicultural Society* (New York: W. W. Norton, 1992), 35.

4. Quoted in U.S. Department of Labor, Bureau of Naturalization, "Our Nation," *Federal Textbook on Citizenship Training* (Washington, DC: U.S. Government Printing Office, 1931), 236.

5. Stephen Meyer III, *The Five Dollar Day: Labor Management and Social Control in the Ford Motor Company, 1908–1921* (Albany, NY: State University of New York Press, 1981), 160–161. I wrote about this practice in a different vein in Daniel Gordis, *Does the World Need the Jews?* (New York: Scribner, 1997), 172–173. I'm grateful to Jacqueline Cooper Melmed for bringing this source to my attention many years ago.

6. In addition to the other sources mentioned in this chapter, see Ilan Stavans, ed., *Becoming Americans: Four Centuries of Immigrant Writing* (New York: Library of America, 2009).

7. Martha C. Nussbaum, *Poetic Justice: The Literary Imagination and Public Life* (Boston: Beacon Press, 1995), xiii.

8. Martha C. Nussbaum, *Love's Knowledge: Essays on Philosophy and Literature* (New York: Oxford University Press, 1990), 5.

9. Michiko Kakutani, "Fitting in Perfectly on the Outside, but Lost Within," *New York Times*, August 31, 1999, http://www.nytimes.com/1999/08/31/ books/books-of-the-times-fitting-in-perfectly-on-the-outside-but-lost-within.html.

10. Jhumpa Lahiri, *Interpreter of Maladies* (New York: Houghton Mifflin, 1999), 24.

11. Ibid., 26.

12. Ibid.

13. Ibid., 27.
14. Ibid., 31.
15. Ibid.
16. Ibid., 12.
17. Ibid., 197.
18. Michiko Kakutani, "Liking America, but Longing for India," *New York Times,* August 6, 1999, http://www.nytimes.com/1999/08/06/books/books-of-the-times-liking-america-but-longing-for-india.html; "India Calling," *Newsweek,* July 18, 1999, http://www.thedailybeast.com/newsweek/1999/07/18/india-calling.html.
19. "Migration, Assimilation, and Inebriation," *Bookforum,* April/May 2008, http://bookforum.com/inprint/015_01/2250.
20. Caleb Crain, "Subcontinental Drift," *New York Times,* July 11, 1999, http://www.nytimes.com/books/99/07/11/reviews/990711.11craint.html.
21. Nicole Krauss, *The History of Love* (New York: W. W. Norton, 2006).
22. Junot Diaz, *The Brief Wondrous Life of Oscar Wao* (New York: Riverhead Books, 2007), 270, 272.
23. Ibid., 276, 319.
24. Ibid., 318; italics added.
25. "American Exceptionalism," *Washington Times*, July 1, 2009, http://www.washingtontimes.com/news/2009/jul/1/american-exceptionalism/.
26. Barack Obama, *Dreams from My Father* (New York: Three Rivers Press, 2004), 309.
27. Genesis 10:31.
28. "Constitution Based in Christian Principles, McCain Says," *New York Times*, September 29, 2007, http://www.nytimes.com/2007/09/29/us/politics/29cnd-mccain.html.
29. Justice Antonin Scalia, *McCreary County, Kentucky, et al., Petitioners v. American Civil Liberties Union of Kentucky et al.* on writ of certiorari to the U.S. Court of Appeals for the sixth circuit, June 27, 2005; Scalia cites the following cases in his opinion: *Zorach* v. *Clauson,* 343 U.S. 306, 313 (1952), repeated with approval in *Lynch* v. *Donnelly*, 465 U.S. 668, 675 (1984); *Marsh*, 463 U.S., at 792; *Abington Township, supra*, at 213.
30. Samuel Huntington, *Who Are We?: The Challenges to America's National Identity* (New York: Simon and Schuster, 2005), 59.
31. Lahiri, *Interpreter of Maladies*, 137, 141.
32. Ibid., 146.
33. Ibid., 138, 146.
34. This phrase was coined by G. K. Chesterton. Sidney E. Mead, "The 'Nation with the Soul of a Church,'" *Church History* 36, no. 3 (September 1967): 262, http://www.jstor.org/pss/3162573.

35. Huntington, *Who Are We?*, 69.

36. Genesis 10:31.

37. Huntington, *Who Are We?*, 63.

38. Michael Walzer, *What It Means to Be an American: Essays on the American Experience* (New York: Marsilio, 1996), 58–59.

39. Ibid., 27.

40. Gordon S. Wood, "How the Complete Meaning of July Fourth Is Slipping Away," *New Republic*, July 4, 2011, http://www.tnr.com/article/politics/91247/july-fourth-declaration-independence-day.

41. Huntington, *Who Are We?*, 51.

42. Barbara Tuchman, *Practicing History* (New York: Ballantine Books, 1981), 134.

43. A fascinating account of the founding generation of the United States is Joseph J. Ellis, *Founding Brothers* (New York: Vintage Books, 2000).

10. A State unto the Diaspora

1. Peter Beinart, "The Failure of the American Jewish Establishment," *New York Review of Books*, May 12, 2010, http://www.nybooks.com/articles/archives/2010/jun/10/failure-american-jewish-establishment/.

2. Steven Cohen and Ari Kelman, *Beyond Distancing: Young American Jews and Their Alienation from Israel*, Jewish Identity Project of Reboot, Berman Jewish Policy Archive, 2007, http://www.bjpa.org/publications/details.cfm?PublicationID=326.

3. "American Views of Israel: The Great Divide and How to Overcome It" (unpublished manuscript, March 28, 2011), a research project jointly funded by the Conference of Presidents of Major American Institutions and Brand Israel Group, by S S + K and insight. Presentation is dated March 28, 2011; as of this writing, it has not been published. I am grateful to Fern Oppenheimer for having shared the results of this study with me.

4. See, for example, Daniel Gordis, "Of Sermons and Strategies," *Jerusalem Post*, April 1, 2011, http://www.jpost.com/Opinion/Columnists/Article.aspx?id=214664; Daniel Gordis, "The Stories We're Obliged to Tell," *Jerusalem Post*, April 15, 2011, http://www.jpost.com/Magazine/Opinion/Article.aspx?id=216542; Daniel Gordis, "Are Young Rabbis Turning on Israel?", *Commentary*, June 2011, http://www.commentarymagazine.com/article/are-young-rabbis-turning-on-israel/; Daniel Gordis, "An Exchange on 'Are Young Rabbis Turning on Israel,'" *Commentary*, September 2011.

5. Beinart, "The Failure of the American Jewish Establishment."

6. Jacob L. Wright, "A Nation Conceived in Defeat," *Azure* 42 (Autumn 2010): 85.

7. Ibid., 90, 91.

8. This idea has been written about most eloquently by Wright, with whom I had occasion to discuss it when he was a fellow at the Shalem Center in Jerusalem. I'm very grateful to him for sharing with me his thoughts and the drafts of articles and books he was working on. For examples of his exploration of this idea, see ibid.

9. Jeremiah 31:34–35. See also Exodus 32:13, Leviticus 26:44, Isaiah 54:10, Jeremiah 31:37, and Jeremiah 46:27.

10. Thomas Hobbes, *Leviathan* (Mineola, NY: Dover Publications, 2005), 70.

11. David Z. Hoffmann, *Melamed Le-Ho'il* [Instruction for Benefit (based on Isaiah 48:17)] (New York: Noble, 1954), 1:42, 1:43. The two responsa are very similar, but 1:42 is somewhat more elaborate. For a discussion of a similar issue faced by the French Jewish community, see Leo Landman, *Jewish Law in the Diaspora: Confrontation and Accommodation* (Philadelphia: Dropsie College for Hebrew and Cognate Learning, 1968), 135–136.

12. B.T. *Baba Batra* 12b.

13. Numbers 13:33.

14. For an interesting glimpse into the internal Jewish division that resulted, see Israel Kershner, "Belatedly Recognizing Heroes of the Holocaust," *New York Times*, August 6, 2011, http://www.nytimes.com/2011/08/07/world/middleeast/07israel.html; David S. Wyman and Rafael Medoff, *A Race against Death: Peter Bergson, America, and the Holocaust* (New York: New Press, 2002).

15. David Ben-Gurion, *Chazon ve-Derekh* [Vision and Path] (Tel Aviv: Workers Party of the Land of Israel, 1953), 300–301. The translation from the Hebrew is mine.

16. In April 2011, anticircumcision activists in San Francisco proposed a bill that would make circumcision in that city a crime punishable by fines of up to one thousand dollars and a year in jail when done to boys under the age of eighteen. The bill, which gained enough signatures to appear on San Francisco's November ballot, did not include exemptions for religious circumcisions. In July, San Francisco Superior Court Judge Loretta Giorgi ruled that the bill would not appear on the November ballot because it violated constitutional rights as well as a California law that makes legislation on medical procedures the jurisdiction of the state rather than of individual cities. Gabrielle Saveri, "Circumcision Ban in San Francisco Considered," Reuters, April 27, 2011, http://www.msnbc.msn.com/id/42784426/ns/health-kids_and_parenting/; Ryan Jaslow, "Judge Slices Circumcision Ban from San Francisco Ballot," CBS News,

July 29, 2011, http://www.cbsnews.com/8301-504763_162-20085484-10391704.html.

17. On May 31, 2010, the Gaza-bound Turkish flotilla, which carried pro-Palestinian activists who claimed to be bringing humanitarian aid to Gazan residents, was raided by Israeli commandos. The Israeli naval forces said that the raid was an act of defense because some of the flotilla's passengers jumped ship armed with weapons. The raid left nine Turkish activists dead. Although some American Jews opposed the raid, Israel's actions inspired rallies across the United States supporting Israel's response. Uriel Heilman, "Flotilla Fallout Becomes Rallying Cry for U.S. Jews," Jewish Telegraphic Agency, June 8, 2010, http://www.jta.org/news/article/2010/06/08/2739513/flotilla-fallout-becomes-rallying-cry-for-us-jews; Jamaica Kincaid, "The Gaza Flotilla, As Seen on TV," Haaretz, June 2, 2010, http://www.haaretz.com/haaretz-authors-edition/the-gaza-flotilla-as-seen-on-tv-1.293781.

18. Alana Newhouse, "The Diaspora Need Not Apply," New York Times, July 15, 2010, http://www.nytimes.com/2010/07/16/opinion/16newhouse.html?_r=1&scp=1&sq=rotem&st=cse.

19. "Police Arrest Women of the Wall Leader for Praying with Torah Scroll," Haaretz, July 12, 2011, http://www.haaretz.com/news/national/police-arrest-women-of-the-wall-leader-for-praying-with-torah-scroll-1.301457.

20. Heather S. Gregg, "Divided They Conquer: The Success of Armenian Ethnic Lobbies in the United States," paper presented at the annual meeting of the American Political Science Association, Boston, August 28, 2002, http://web.mit.edu/cis/www/migration/pubs/rrwp/13_divided.pdf.

21. California, Colorado, Maryland, Massachusetts, New Jersey, and New York all recognized the Armenian Genocide before 1990. Alabama, Indiana, Iowa, Mississippi, South Dakota, West Virginia, and Wyoming have yet to formally recognize the mass murder as a genocide. "International Affirmation of the Armenian Genocide," Armenian National Institute, http://www.armenian-genocide.org/current_category.11/affirmation_list.html.

22. "Barack Obama on the Importance of US-Armenia Relations," Armenians for Obama, January 19, 2008, http://www.armeniansforobama.com/armenian_issues.php.

23. Zbigniew Brzezinski, "A Dangerous Exemption: Why Should the Israel Lobby Be Immune from Criticism?", Foreign Policy, July/August 2006.

24. U.S. Department of Labor, Bureau of the Census, "American Factfinder," http://factfinder.census.gov/servlet/DTTable?_bm=y&-ds_name=ACS_2009_1YR_G00_&-mt_name=ACS_2009_1YR_

G2000_B04003&-CONTEXT=dt&-redoLog=true&-current selections=ACS_2007_1YR_G2000_B04001&-geo_id=01000US&-format=&-_lang=en; Gregg, "Divided They Conquer."

Conclusion

1. *Genesis Rabbah* 42:8.
2. Martin Buber, *Israel and the World: Essays in a Time of Crisis* (New York: Schocken Books, 1963), 221.
3. This should not be taken to suggest that Hebrew is flourishing without facing many of the same challenges that other languages around the world currently have to address. The internationalization of English, the ubiquitous nature of the Internet, and Israelis' desire to be as cosmopolitan and international as possible have all led to the embrace of English and a weakening of the devotion to Hebrew. That the early founders of the state were cognizant that this would be almost inevitable is evident, for example, in a fascinating poster in a small museum at the Tachanah (the refurbished old train station) in Tel Aviv. There, in an exhibit of the history of the movie theater that used to be there, one can see a poster advertising the arrival of the first "talking movie," along with a warning that people should enjoy the movie but resist the infiltration of foreign languages into the newly forming culture and society of Israel.
4. Michael Walzer, *Nation and Universe*, Tanner Lectures on Human Values, University of Utah, May 1989, 554, http://www.tannerlectures.utah.edu/lectures/documents/walzer90.pdf.
5. Joshua 1:6, 1:8.
6. Hayim Nahman Bialik, "Seesaw, Seesaw," in *My 100 Songs: Best Loved Israeli Nursery Rhymes,* ed. Daniella Gardosh and Talmah Alyagon (Jerusalem: Kinneret, n.d.), 10. The translation is mine.
7. Mishnah (hereafter, M.), *Hagigah* 2:1. Translation from Jacob Neusner, *The Mishnah: A New Translation* (New Haven, CT: Yale University Press, 1988), 330.
8. M. *Pesachim* 10:8. Translation from Neusner, *The Mishnah*, 251, with slight emendation.
9. My thanks to Leah Sarna, who witnessed this exchange, for sharing it with me.
10. This is a complex subject in Jewish law. One of the primary talmudic sources is B.T. *Hullin* 7a.
11. Walzer, *Nation and Universe*, 554.
12. Barbara Tuchman, *Practicing History* (New York: Ballantine Books, 1981), 134.

13. Exodus 22:20. See also Exodus 23:09, Leviticus 19:34, and Deuteronomy 10:19.

14. "Merkel Says German Multicultural Society Has Failed," BBC, October 17, 2010, http://www.bbc.co.uk/news/world-europe-11559451.

15. Tom Heneghan, "Sarkozy Joins Allies Burying Multiculturalism," Reuters, February 11, 2011, http://www.reuters.com/article/2011/02/11/us-france-sarkozy-multiculturalism-idUSTRE71A4UP20110211.

16. "State Multiculturalism Has Failed, Says David Cameron," BBC, February 5, 2011, http://www.bbc.co.uk/news/uk-politics-12371994.

17. Kenan Malik, "Assimilation's Failure, Terrorism's Rise," *New York Times*, July 6, 2011, http://www.nytimes.com/2011/07/07/opinion/07malik.html.

Index

Abbas, Mahmoud, 31, 32
Abraham, 77–78, 183–184
Afghanistan-U.S. War, 108
Africa, Meir and, 93
Ahmadinejad, Mahmoud, 34
Ajami, Fouad, 35
Albania, nationalism and, 73–74
Algeria
    gay rights in, 33
    Jewish population in, 31
    women's rights in, 32
aliyah, 80
Altneuland (Herzl), 93–94
American-Israel Public Affairs
    Campaign (AIPAC), 173, 176
Amnesty International, 33, 45
Anatomy of Peace, The (Reves),
    47–48
Anderson, Benedict, 95–97
Ankri, Etti, 111
anti-Semitism
    anti-Zionism as, 88–90
    Israel boycott and, 54

universalism and, 59–60, 66–68
    world opinion of Israel and, 44
Arab countries
    education in, 34–36
    Jewish population in, 31–32, 101
    U.N. Declaration on Sexual
        Orientation and Gender
        Identity and, 28
    women's rights in, 32–33
    See also individual names of
        Arab countries
Arab League, 52
Arab Spring
    education in Arab countries
        and, 36
    freedom of expression and, 30
    human freedom and, 123–124
    nation-state concept and, 5
    unknown outcome of, 12
Arad, Ron, 107
Arafat, Suha, 66
Arafat, Yassir, 22
Argentina, nationalism and, 89

229